PIONEERS
OF CHRISTIAN THOUGHT

FREDERICK D. KERSHNER

PIONEERS

OF

CHRISTIAN

THOUGHT

Essay Index Reprint Series

BOOKS FOR LIBRARIES PRESS

FREEPORT, NEW YORK

LIBRARY OF CONGRESS CATALOG CARD NUMBER:
68-57327

PRINTED IN THE UNITED STATES OF AMERICA

To

E. M. K.

Ζώη μôυ, σâς 'αγαπῶ

CONTENTS

CHAPTER   PAGE

I PHILO   19

The life of Philo—Influence upon Christian thought—
The city of Alexandria—The Ptolemies—The Alexan-
drian library—The Pharos—Commercial supremacy—
Syncretic tendencies—The triple population of Alexandria,
Greeks, Egyptians and Jews—Characteristics of each
group—The Alexandrian temple to Yahweh—Peculiar
quality of Alexandrian culture—Cleopatra as the typical
Alexandrian—Story of her life, as given by Plutarch—
Shakespeare's interpretation—The philosophy of Plotinus
—The literary and theological work of Philo—His fundamental purpose, a synthesis of Greek and Hebrew culture—Pantheism in ancient thought—Jewish aloofness
from this view of the world—The essential distinction
between Greek and Latin theology—The doctrine of the
Logos among the Greeks—Philo identifies it with the Old
Testament Wisdom—The interpretation of the Fourth
Gospel—Nature of the Logos conception—Verbal inspiration in Philo—The idea among the Greeks—The allegorical method of interpretation—Advantages and disad-
vantages of the method—Relation to verbal inspiration—
The modern interpretation—Summary of Philo's thought:
(1) the divine immanence, (2) the doctrine of the Logos,
(3) verbal inspiration of the Scriptures, (4) the allegorical method of interpretation.

II PAUL OF TARSUS   43

Scanty details of Paul's life—The story of Paul and
Thecla—Influences involved in his spiritual background:
(1) Hebrew ancestry and training, (2) Greek cultural
environment, (3) Roman citizenship, (4) conversion to
Christianity—The Pauline teaching upon certain disputed
questions: (1) the rights of women, (2) celibacy and
asceticism, (3) premillenarianism, (4) political theory—
The romance of Paul and Thecla—The chief doctrines of
Paul: (1) God; transcendent and personal, predestination
taken over from Phariseeism, (2) Christ; Messiah and
Lord, in what sense Deity, views of Peter and Paul, the
God of the Gentiles, Jesus versus Jehovah, meaning of
Paul's conception of the Lordship of Jesus; (3) man; importance of Paul in anthropology, theories of the origin
of the soul, the Pauline doctrine of sin, the personal problem, universal depravity, (4) Immortality; the first
epistle to the Corinthians, Paul's definition, conditional
or unconditional?, the Pauline influence.

CHAPTER   PAGE

III MARCION   67

The expansion of Christianity—Meager records of the
first century—Attitude of the Roman emperors—The literature of persecution—The book of Revelation—Gnosticism—Destruction of Gnostic books—Testimony of the
early Fathers—The ethical motive of Gnosticism—Its
chief ethical problems—The life of Marcion—Criticism
by Tertullian, Irenæus, and Hippolytus—Marcion's contributions to theology: (1) the New Testament canon,
(2) the Old Roman Symbol, (3) modern critical interpretation—Marcion and the development of theological
creeds—McGiffert's testimony—Opposition to the allegorical method of interpreting the Scriptures—The problem
of predictive prophecy—Faults of Marcion—Lack of
scholarship—Gnostic vagaries—Asceticism—Good qualities, especially his ethical idealism—If Marcion's views
had prevailed?

IV ORIGEN   90

Place of Origen in theology—The church at Alexandria
—The school of Pantænus—Clement of Alexandria—
Selections from Clement's works—Social customs of the
age—Theology of Clement: (1) immanence, (2) Greek
culture, (3) educational evangelism, (4) humanism, (5)
eclecticism—Clement demoted from sainthood—Origen—
The great eunuchs of history—Early life—Extent of his
works—Controversy with Celsus—Founder of systematic
theology—His doctrine of immanence—His Christology—
The freedom of the will—His allegorical method of interpretation: (1) historical, (2) ethical, (3) mystical—His
eschatology—No eternal hell—Doctrine of restitution—
Later development of Alexandrianism—Plotinus—Cyril of
Alexandria—Morbid asceticism—The story of Hypatia.

V ATHANASIUS   113

The place of Athanasius in theology—The six A's—
Greek and Christian views of God—The great trinities
of religion—The life of Arius—Attitude of Constantine—
The Council of Nicæa—History of the proceedings—The
three parties in the council—The real meaning of the
creed—The mystery explanation of the Trinity—Effect
of this explanation—Heresies—Sabellianism—Modern interpretations of the idea—The unity which the creed
secured—The Nicene-Constantinopolitan formula—Heresies of Macedonius and others—The Cappadocian school
—The two Gregories and Basil—The ransom to the devil
—Second Council of Constantinople—Athanasius as the
synonymn of orthodoxy.

CONTENTS—*Continued*

CHAPTER   PAGE

VI THEODORE   135

The most modern of the ancient theologians—The city
of Antioch, characteristics—Aristotle—Antioch as a center
of heresy—The problem of the person of Christ—The
doctrine of Theodore—Nestorianism (two natures)—
Monophysitism (one soul)—The Monothelites (one will)
—The Apollonarians (divine pneuma)—The final orthodox solution—Emphasis of Theodore upon the human
element in religion—The freedom of the will—Immortality of the soul—Denial of eternal perdition—The higher
criticism of Theodore—Denounced as a heretic—Greek
theology after Theodore—Theodoret—John Chrysostom—
Dionysius the Areopagite—John Damascene—The Iconoclasts—The Second Council of Nicæa—The Mother
Goddess—The Filioque clause—The Moslem avalanche.

VII AUGUSTINE   155

The greatest name in theology—Life of Augustine—
Ancestry—Father and mother—Early career—Youth at
Madaura—Life at Carthage—Religious experience—
Amours—Manicheanism—Experience in Italy—Contact
with Saint Ambrose—Neo-Platonism—Conversion—Death
of Saint Monica—Return to Africa—Doctrinal discussions
—Bishop of Hippo—Controversies: (1) Manicheans, (2)
Donatists, (3) Pelagians,—Controversy with Jerome—
Biography of the latter—Close of Augustine's life—
Theology of Augustine: (1) the greatness of God, (2)
the littleness of man, (3) predestination, (4) total de-
pravity, (5) supremacy of the church—Influence of
Augustine—His morbid temper—Anti-social attitudes—
Peculiar ethical conceptions—His teaching concerning hell
—Baneful influence of his theology.

VIII ANSELM   183

The Dark Ages—Influence of the popes—Gregory the
Great—Radbert and transubstantiation—Ratram—The
medieval substance—Emphasis upon miracle—Scotus
Erigena—Heresy discovered too late—Life of Anselm—
Works: (1) the *Prologium,* (2) the *Monologium,* (3) the
Cur Deus Homo—The ontological argument—Kant's
refutation—The cosmological and teleological arguments
—The satisfaction theory—The treasury of merit—Utility
of the doctrine—Legalism of Anselm—Realism and nomi-
nalism—Plato and Aristotle—Anselm's view of the Holy
Spirit—The schoolmen—Place of Anselm in modern
thought.

CONTENTS—*Continued*

CHAPTER   PAGE

IX ABELARD   202

Place in theology—Abelard as a teacher—The scholarly
ideal—The great romances of the world—Abelard's life—
Early teachers—Controversy with Champeaux—Romance
of Heloise—Tragedy of Abelard's life—Abelard and Bernard—The love-letters of Abelard and Heloise—End of
the romance—Abelard's theology: (1) rationalism, (2)
moral theory of the atonement, (3) critical tendencies—
Hostility to Augustine—The theology of Bernard: (1)
conservatism, (2) mysticism, (3) moral fervor—Final
place of Abelard.

X AQUINAS   221

Importance in theology—Standard of Roman Catholic
theology—Sketch of his life—Albertus Magnus—The
Summa—Aristotle—The ideal of synthesis—Reason and
revelation—The pyramid—Proofs of the existence of God
—Church authority—Attack on freedom—The *Summa*
and the Middle Ages—Dante as an interpreter of Saint
Thomas—Life of Dante—His eschatology: (1) the "Inferno," (2) the "Purgatorio," (3) the "Paradisio"—Saint
Thomas and art—The Spanish chapel—The church
militant and triumphant—The educational curriculum of
the Middle Ages—The Dominicans and the Franciscans
—Bonaventura—Duns Scotus—Emphasis on the will—
William of Occam—The Renaissance—Savonarola—
Gabriel Biel—The last of the schoolmen—Final position
of Saint Thomas.

XI ERASMUS   242

Biography of Erasmus—His place as a scholar—The
Renaissance period—The Netherlands—Life of Erasmus
—His relations with the popes—His association with
Luther and the reformers—Vitality of his correspondence
—His theology: (1) appeal to reason, (2) restoration of
New Testament Christianity, (3) Christian union, (4)
freedom of the will,—His irenic temper—Was he a
coward or a trimmer?—Catholic and Protestant views—
Criticism of parties—Erasmus ahead of his age—The con-
ception of humanism—The Socinians—The Anabaptists—
Relationship of both groups to Erasmus—Influence of the
latter upon the world.

XII LUTHER   261

Different views of Luther—Catholic and Protestant—
Biography—Early home life—Early religious views—
Education—He enters the monastery—His conversion—
Controversy with Tetzel—The Diet of Worms—Wart-
burg and the devil—Marriage—Later life—Cardinal

CONTENTS—*Continued*

CHAPTER   PAGE

principles of the Reformation: (1) the authority of the
Scriptures, (2) justification by faith, (3) the right of
private judgment,—Luther and democracy—His conservatism—Attitude toward the Anabaptists—Views upon
the sacraments—Effect of his teaching—Final influence.

XIII CALVIN   283

Cotton Mather's letter—Place of Calvin in theology—
Characteristics—Distinction from Luther—Zwingli, the
founder of Reformed theology—The Marburg conference
—The birth of denominationalism—Controversy with
Luther—Latter more ascetic and more mystical—Early
life of Calvin—Conversion—Banishment from Paris—
The *Institutes*—Calvin at Geneva—The story of Servetus
—Calvin's responsibility for his condemnation—Calvin's
home-life—His theological position—Augustinianism—The
divine sovereignty—Predestination—Church polity—Calvinism and capitalism—Later influence of Calvin's teaching—Jonathan Edwards—Modern interpretations of Calvinism.

XIV ARMINIUS   301

The Netherlands—*The Remonstrance*—The Synod of
Dort—The five points of Calvinism—Life of Arminius—
Free will in the modern age—The life of Grotius—Influence on theology—Founder of international law—The
legal theory of the atonement—Originator of Christian
evidences—Advocate of Christian union—Life of John
Wesley—His conversion—His organizing genius—Simplicity of his theology—His conservatism—Effect of Arminianism on Protestantism—The federal theology—Cocceius
—The two covenants—Modern position—Popularity of
Arminianism.

XV SCHLEIERMACHER   319

Place in theology—Obscurity—Mysticism—Life—Early
background—School-days among the Moravians—Life in
Berlin—Friendship with Schlegel—Love-affairs—translation of Plato—Works—Marriage—Professor in Berlin—
Publication of *The Christian Faith*—His wide-spread
popularity—Close of his life—Theology—Definition of
religion as feeling—The God-consciousness—Redemptive
Christology—The problem of evil—The immanence of the
Deity—Influence of Spinoza—Sharp distinction from
Augustine—Weak points in Schleiermacher's system: (1)
treatment of personality, (2) interpretation of evil, (3)
the freedom of the will, (4) the future life—Unity of
his system—Its significance for Protestantism—His final
place in theology.

CONTENTS—*Concluded*

CHAPTER   PAGE

XVI RITSCHL   336

Last of the great theologians—Karl Barth and the
psychology of defeat—Harnack—Kaftan—Hermann—Life
of Ritschl—Education—Professor at Bonn and Göttingen
—Popularity—Influence abroad—Rational element in
Ritschl—Opposition to mysticism and metaphysics—Relations to (1) Kant, (2) Hegel, (3) Lotze—Eclecticism of
Ritschl—The central feature of Ritschlianism—The
ellipse: (1) individual salvation, (2) the Kingdom of
God—Garvie's analysis of Ritschlianism: (1) religious
pragmatism, (2) philosophical agnosticism, (3) historical
positivism, (4) moral collectivism—The power of epithets
—Appeal of Ritschl to the modern mind—Opposition to
dogma—Opposition to mysticism—Judgments of value—
Loyalty to the historical Jesus—Emphasis upon the social
message—The future of Ritschl.

BIBLIOGRAPHY   351

INDEX   359

INTRODUCTION

THEOLOGY is often looked upon as the incarnation of all that is tedious and uninteresting. No doubt, it is dry enough in certain respects, and yet there are others in which it is aglow with romance. For one thing, the theologians, unlike the philosophers, have possessed points of contact with practical life which have been of the utmost consequence in shaping their personalities. The psychologists have been busy finding the bond of relationship between religion and passion. Perhaps they have exaggerated the situation, but it must be confessed that history lends no little support to their contentions. The mere fact that sex was once worshiped in religion and afterward made taboo is an interesting illustration of the thesis in question. Small wonder it is that nearly all of the theologians were touched in some way or another by the spirit of romance. Moreover, the story of theology itself is dramatic and fascinating. It contains the record of one aspect of progress in the life of the spirit. Tragic it is at times, and comic also in more places than one. The story is still incomplete because human progress is ever continuous and unfinished. Like philosophy, theology has to do with the infinite, and therefore has no last word for us.

No attempt has been made in this work to acknowledge indebtedness to source material or authorities. The standard histories of doctrine, especially Hagenbach, Shedd and Fisher, Harnack's *History of Dogma,* Workman's *Christian Thought to the Reformation,* McGiffert's *Protestant Thought before Kant,* as well as his other works in

INTRODUCTION

this field, Moore's *Christian Thought since Kant,* Allen's *Continuity of Christian Thought,* Newman's *Arians of the Fourth Century,* Froude's *Life and Letters of Erasmus,* Eddy & Page's *Makers of Freedom* (on John Wesley), Selbie on Schleiermacher, and many others which we can not pause to name have all furnished information and inspiration. In addition we have to mention the standard texts on church history and many others of general interest which we must pass with no attempt to catalogue. Above all, we must express our obligations to the works of the theologians themselves. The true story of theology is in their pages, and nowhere else. If this book can inspire a deeper interest in their productions it will not have been written in vain.

It remains for the author to express his indebtedness to his friend and colleague, Mr. A. T. DeGroot, of the Butler University faculty, for valuable assistance rendered in the preparation of the manuscript.

F. D. K.

PIONEERS
OF CHRISTIAN THOUGHT

PIONEERS OF CHRISTIAN THOUGHT

CHAPTER I

PHILO

THE founder of Christian theology was a Jew. This fact is not surprising in view of the more important consideration that the founder of Christianity itself was an adherent of the same religious faith. All of the exponents of the new movement which was to play such a prominent part in the history of the world were descendants of Abraham. Paul boasted of the fact, and the other Apostles were not averse to admitting it.

Philo Judæus, as he is generally styled, was a native of Alexandria in Egypt who was born somewhere toward the close of the first century B.C., and died somewhere near the middle of the first century A.D. Mr. H. A. A. Kennedy assigns tentative dates of 20 B.C. for his birth, and 41 A.D. for his death, but there is no certainty that these figures are correct. Assuming that they represent the truth, at least approximately, Philo was in all probability a contemporary of both Jesus and Paul. It is true that in the voluminous writings of the Jewish philosopher there is not the slightest reference to Christianity in any form, nor have we any certain evidence that the early Christians knew much about Philo. There are a few of the New Testament books, as for example the Gospel of John and the Epistle to the Hebrews, which appear to have been influenced by the Alexandrian philosopher. Mr. Kennedy will have it also that Paul was in certain respects a disciple of Philo. The difficulty about accepting these deductions consists chiefly in the fact that much of the thought of Philo was common to the philosophical currents of his day, and it is not necessary to assume that everything which resembles his speculative point of view was borrowed from him. As far as external evidence is concerned, there are no points of contact between the early Christian Apostles and the Jewish Platonist of Alexandria. The conclusions drawn from internal evidence must always be accepted with caution. Nevertheless, we believe the case to be reasonably sure that one of the two great currents of Christian theology must be traced back in its origin to Philo.

I

The city of Alexandria, where Philo was born and where he lived, as far as we know, all of his career, had been founded three centuries before the Christian era by Alexander the Great. Mr. H. G. Wells has written a few things about Alexander in his *Outline of History* which, in our judgment, needed to be said, but even Mr. Wells must admit that the Macedonian conqueror displayed rare foresight when he founded Alexandria. Egypt had possessed a civilization which stretched back for five millennia, but none of the mighty Pharaohs of the past had wisdom enough to select the one outstanding site in all the land for the capital of his empire. Alexander swept down like a whirlwind and apparently without consideration or hesitation picked the location for a city which in a few years became the rival of Athens in intellectual leadership and of Tyre or Carthage in the field of commerce. At the beginning of the Christian era Alexandria, next to Rome, was the leading city of the world. From the standpoint of

scholarship and intellectual interests, the capital of Egypt
was far superior to the metropolis built upon the seven
hills. Only the fact that the Empire centered at Rome
gave the imperial city the preeminence which it possessed
with the pagan world at large.

Much of the growth and progress of Alexandria was
due to the wise administration of the Macedonian rulers of
Egypt known as the Ptolemies. Those monarchs constituted, on the whole, an extraordinarily cultured and intelligent line of kings. They fostered science, literature,
commerce and all of the arts of peace. Although the first
Ptolemy, the founder of the dynasty, was one of the leading
generals in the army of Alexander the Great, his successors
for the most part were apostles of peace rather than men
of war. Perhaps the greatest and best known of them all
was Ptolemy Philadelphus, under whose singularly wise
and beneficent rule the translation of the Hebrew Scriptures
into Greek, usually known as the Septuagint, was made.
This work was only one out of a vast multitude of similar
undertakings, for the King of Egypt was so anxious to
gather the literary treasures of all the ancient nations into
his capital that he sent everywhere to secure copies of rare
manuscripts, and when they were preserved in foreign
tongues he had them translated into Greek in order that
they might be available for the use of his people. The
greatest university which humanity possessed before the
modern era was gradually developed at Alexandria. Its
nucleus was the Alexandrian library which contained many
hundreds of thousands of books and represented the foremost collection of its kind known to the ancient world.
Here were assembled the complete works of all the sages,
poets, critics, scientists and philosophers who had flourished
in all the nations of antiquity. The productions of many
authors whose names even are unknown to us were there,

and others whose contributions we possess in fragmentary form were represented in their most complete and adequate expression in this great collection. All the works of Plato and Aristotle and Herodotus and Sappho and countless others were there instead of the garbled editions which we possess to-day. When Omar, the Arabian zealot, used the volumes of the Alexandrian library as fuel for the public baths of the city he wrought the greatest single act of depredation that the cause of education has suffered throughout the course of human history. It matters little that he was pious and sincere in what he did. He was a devout Mussulman and looked upon the great accumulation of heathen lore contained in the library as simply a temptation which might lead people away from the true faith and plunge them into hell. If these books, he said, contain things which are not to be found in the Koran they are subversive and dangerous; if they contain the same things that are to be found in the Koran they are unnecessary and useless: therefore, the best thing to do with them is to have them burned. And burned they were, sufficing, so tradition says, the demand for fuel for the public baths for a period of two months.

Alexandria was famous not only by reason of its library but also because of the splendor of its public buildings which were not surpassed by those of any other capital in the world. Chief among them was doubtless the Pharos, or watch-tower, built by Ptolemy Philadelphus, and by common consent numbered as one of the seven wonders of the world. No other lighthouse in all the course of human history ever even approximated this shining miracle of marble which rose four hundred feet above the level of the sea and which combined the two outstanding motives of beauty and utility to an extent, in all probability, possessed by no other building ever erected by the hand of man. The Pharos, although the outstanding architectural triumph of the city, was only one of a vast multitude of splendid structures which served the needs or ministered to the esthetic satisfactions of the Alexandrian populace. Temples to all the gods were there, including one even to the Hebrew Jehovah. Museums, palaces, gardens filled with statues, theaters, baths, and all of the other characteristics of the Greek city civilization combined with the mystic splendor of ancient Egypt to produce a culture which has never since been paralleled in any other nation. Alexandria differed from Athens in the fact that it represented a syncretic civilization that was not only Greek and Egyptian but which assimilated the most valuable and characteristic features of all other peoples and nations. Moreover, Alexandria, while preeminently intellectual in its outlook, was likewise one of the great commercial centers of its day. Unless London be an exception, it is the only city in the course of human history which has managed to assimilate commerce and philosophy, education and business, culture and trade, on such a large scale and in such perfect and harmonious proportions.

II

The people of Alexandria were for the most part the representatives of three distinct racial groups. The first, embodying the ruling and most highly cultured class, was composed of the Greek followers of the Ptolemies, and others of the same nation who had been induced for various reasons to settle in Egypt. The Greek element in the population of Alexandria probably numbered less than a third of the total. Notwithstanding this fact it was by all odds the most significant and the most influential racial group in the city. Over against the Greek element in the population must be placed another group, probably constituting rather more than a third, and consisting of native Egyptians or other representatives of racial admixture, predominantly African tribes of the South. These people were almost the exact antithesis of their masters. They were hot-blooded, impetuous and superstitious, and lacked the cultural training which was so easily assimilated by the Greeks. They represented the larger part of the slave and servant class, although some of them were people of distinction. When Christianity first made headway in Alexandria the majority of its converts doubtless belonged to this section of the population. At any rate, as late as the days of Cyril of Alexandria, more than four centuries after Christ, the great majority of the adherents of the fiery Bishop were of African descent. It was this section which constituted the mob that tore Hypatia to pieces and which Charles Kingsley has so vividly pictured in his well-known romance which bears her name.

The third section of the Alexandrian population, probably more numerous than the Greeks and less numerous than the Egyptians, was made up of the Jews. The Ptolemies early discovered the value of the Hebrews as citizens and encouraged them to emigrate to Alexandria. The Syrian rulers who had control of Palestine were far less tactful, with the result that multitudes of the most intelligent and capable of the descendants of Abraham found their way again to the land of Egypt. While they were given, probably in accordance with their own desire, a separate section of the city in which to live, this arrangement did not constitute anything approaching the ghettos of modern Europe. The Alexandrian Jews enjoyed equal rights and privileges before the law with the other inhabitants of the city, and possessed the same educational and cultural opportunities. The great library and university were open to them on equal terms with all

others, and they were not slow to profit by such advantages.
As we have already indicated, the Jewish Scriptures were
translated into Greek at a very early period, certainly during the first century of the city's existence, and from this
time on Hebrew scholars were much in evidence in the
cultured circles of Alexandria. We have referred to the
temple to Jehovah which the pious Israelites erected with
the full permission and approval of the Egyptian rulers and
which served to keep alive the old-time faith in the overlordship of Jehovah. It was remarkable because it was the
only building of its kind constructed outside of Jerusalem.

The admixture and clash of so many races and civilizations resulted in the production of a new and strange type
of culture. The Alexandrians came to possess certain
distinct personal characteristics which were not to be duplicated in any other part of the world. Their philosophers
rivaled the ripest achievements of the Periclean age of
Athens with the addition of a subtle mystical charm which
even Plato never possessed. Their scientists struck out
along bold and original lines, continuing the traditions of
Aristotle and Pythagoras. In the fields of geography,
astronomy and general mathematics the Alexandrian masters reigned supreme down to the days of Galileo and
Copernicus. In the realms of pictorial and rhythmic art
they appear to have exerted less influence. It is possible
that Alexandria produced great poets, musicians, painters
and sculptors whose names are unknown simply because all
of their works have been destroyed by the hand of time.
This, however, is, and must probably always remain, a
matter of conjecture. All that we know is that Alexandrian
culture developed to an outstanding degree in the fields of
science, philosophy and theology. In these realms at least
the capital of Egypt for many centuries stood at the pin-
nacle of human civilization.

Perhaps the most typical representative of the strange elusive culture of Alexandria may be found in the personality of a woman. William Shakespeare, like many another author, has recognized in the character of Cleopatra the most baffling and subtle figure in the history of the ancient world. The daughter of the last of the Ptolemies, she was born about 69 B.C. and her tragic career came to an end thirty-nine years later, perhaps not more than a decade before the birth of Philo. In her short life she had been the consort of two emperors of the world, and she had come within a hair's breadth of subjecting a third to her sway. Over Julius Cæsar, and still more completely over Mark Antony, she wielded an influence which modern psychologists and historians seek in vain to explain. From Shakespeare to Ferrero the critics have been busy with her, but by their own confession they have not solved the mystery of her personality. She was the last of the Ptolemies, and embodied to an extraordinary degree the finest traits of her Greek ancestors. By the testimony of contemporary biographers she was not extraordinarily beautiful, but she had at her command a wealth of intellectual resources which enabled her to captivate completely ambitious and experienced adventurers like Julius Cæsar and Mark Antony. Had she not been at her worst when Octavius saw her she would doubtless have wielded the same power over him. The secret of her charm consisted in the rare combination of intellectual interest and subtlety which she inherited from her Greek forebears, with the mystical coloring of the oldest of the Oriental civilizations. It is this same combination which runs throughout the story of Alexandrian theology, and indeed of Alexandrian speculation of every type. Neo-Platonism, the one great philosophical system of the ancient world which was not formulated by a native of Greece, was developed at Alexandria. In

the dreamy thought of Plotinus, its chief interpreter,
we have that peculiar admixture of rationalism and mysticism, of Greek speculation and Oriental magic, of the
philosophy of Plato and the lore of the Pharaohs which still
excites the admiration of our modern age. Cleopatra was
Alexandrian to the core. She was born in the city and after
roaming over the civilized world she came back to Alexandria to die. It is characteristic of her that when she was
about to commit suicide upon the arrival of Octavius she
desisted from her purpose because Cæsar threatened to put
her children to death unless she prolonged her own life.
She waited long enough to attempt to secure the safety of
her family and then, in spite of the fact that she was a
prisoner and that the Roman conqueror used every means to
keep her alive for his triumph, she accomplished her
original purpose with ease. It was the irony of fate that
those to whom she had committed her children betrayed
her trust. Cæsarion, her oldest son and also the son of
Julius Cæsar, was put to death by Octavius after the
philosopher Areius had advised him that too many Cæsars
were not well. Some of her other children lived and became
the progenitors of the noblest families in Rome. The story
of her death is given in a well-known passage in Plutarch:

And a country fellow brought her a little basket, which
the guards intercepting and asking what it was, the fellow
put the leaves which lay uppermost aside, and showed them
it was full of figs; and on their admiring the largeness and
beauty of the figs, he laughed, and invited them to take
some, which they refused, and, suspecting nothing, bade
him carry them in. After her repast, Cleopatra sent to
Cæsar a letter which she had written and sealed; and, putting everybody out of the monument but her two women,
she shut the doors. Cæsar, opening her letter, and finding
pathetic prayers and entreaties that she might be buried in
the same tomb with Antony, soon guessed what was doing.

At first he was going himself in all haste, but, changing his mind, he sent others to see. The thing had been quickly done. The messengers came at full speed, and found the guards apprehensive of nothing; but on opening the doors they saw her stone-dead, lying upon a bed of gold, set out in all her royal ornaments. Iras, one of her women, lay dying at her feet, and Charmion, just ready to fall, scarce able to hold up her head, was adjusting her mistress's diadem. And when one that came in said angrily, "Was this well done of your lady, Charmion?" "Extremely well," she answered, "and as became the descendant of so many kings"; and as she said this, she fell down dead by the bedside.

Some relate that an asp was brought in amongst those figs and covered with leaves, and that Cleopatra had arranged that it might settle on her before she knew, but, when she took away some of the figs and saw it, she said, "So here it is," and held out her bare arm to be bitten. Others say that it was kept in a vase, and that she vexed and pricked it with a golden spindle till it seized her arm. But what really took place is known to no one. Since it was also said that she carried poison in a hollow bodkin, about which she wound her hair; yet there was not so much as a spot found, or any symptom of poison upon her body, nor was the asp seen within the monument; only something like the trail of it was said to have been noticed on the sand by the sea, on the part towards which the building faced and where the windows were. Some relate that two faint puncture-marks were found on Cleopatra's arm, and to this account Cæsar seems to have given credit; for in his triumph there was carried a figure of Cleopatra, with an asp clinging to her. Such are the various accounts.

III

Ten years after Cleopatra died Philo was born. The little Jewish lad who ran about the streets of Alexandria must have heard the gossip which Plutarch retails in such abundance many times from the lips of mother or nurse. Like his countrymen in Palestine, he and his associates were doomed to experience the loss of national freedom. Egypt was no longer under her culture-loving and tolerant Greek rulers, but had been swallowed up in the universal empire of Rome. Philo must have thought a great deal about these things, although he says next to nothing concerning them in his writings. Perhaps he reflected that it was more wholesome under the circumstances not to say anything about them. Like many other great souls in the course of human history he forgot the tempests of the present by burying himself in the glory of the past. He was an ardent student, and the great library of Alexandria was open before him. The Romans did not disturb the library, and according to their custom, so long as those who used it were orderly and submissive to the imperial power, they were permitted to read and study as much as they pleased. Philo must have used the library often and well. His works are filled with classical allusions, and with indications of his familiarity with the literature of the ancient world. He had the scholar's instinct and in Alexandria he had the scholar's opportunity. It was this combination which made him the founder of modern theology.

Like his great contemporary, Paul of Tarsus, Philo has left practically no information concerning his family or his personal history. He is peculiarly objective and impersonal in his work. We do not know anything of significance about even the most important details of his biography. We know, of course, that he was a devout Jew, and that he cherished his line of descent from the fathers of his people. Much of his work consists of various commentaries upon the Old Testament. In these productions, he always manifests the most thoroughgoing reverence for the ancient traditions of his race. While he sought to interpret the Jewish Scriptures in such a way as to commend them to the Greek mind he never once faltered in his faith

in the God of his fathers. Philo was sincerely religious.
There was nothing skeptical or frivolous about him. He
had a definite and serious purpose in mind throughout his
career. That purpose was the reconciliation of Jewish
religious faith and earnestness with the culture and intellectual interest which were so characteristic of Greek civilization. Syntheses of this kind were always to be found in
Alexandria. Philo tried to combine Greek and Jewish
thought in one harmonious system. Clement and Origen
sought to do the same thing with the difference that they
substituted the Christian tradition for the Jewish. Plotinus,
almost at the same time, produced his world-famous
synthesis of Greek philosophy with Oriental mysticism.
The Alexandrians were always attempting to harmonize
and adjust different points of view. They loved to formulate great and elaborate systems of speculation into which
they were forever trying to fit all the facts of the universe.
Origen, the first of the great systematic theologians, came
from Alexandria. Order and harmony, classification and
synthesis, devotion to scientific reasoning and scarcely less
complete allegiance to artistic imagination, constitute the
most striking characteristics of this, the latest and in many
respects the most fascinating of the cultures of the ancient
world.

IV

The first important contribution made by Philo Judæus
to theology was his emphasis upon the divine immanence.
The traditional Jewish thought had always stressed the
transcendence of God; that is, his complete separation from
the world. The Old Testament narratives picture Jehovah
as separate and distinct from His universe. In Genesis He
is depicted as a Being who walks and talks with Adam in
the Garden of Eden, and the story of the divine relations

with Moses, as given in the book of Exodus and other
writings of the Pentateuch, displays much the same characteristics. The Old Testament is singularly free from anything approaching pantheism, or an identification of God
with the universe. Occasionally a passage may be found
in the Psalms or in some of the prophetical books which
hints at the idea of immanence, but on the whole such references are rare.

It is precisely upon this question that the Hebrews
differed most radically from both the Greeks and the Hindus. The early thought of Hellas, it is true, was not inclined toward abstract pantheism, but there was always a
certain poetical coloring about the Greek mythology which
tended to identify God with nature and to make Him one
with His universe. This attitude is given philosophical
expression in certain of the best known dialogues of Plato,
although it can not be said that it represents the final conclusions of the great Athenian thinker. The Stoics especially, following the earlier lead of Pythagoras, were inclined toward a pantheistic view of the Deity. To them
God was the Soul of the world, and acquiescence in the
divine ordering of things became a fundamental tenet of
their philosophy. As one of their best known exponents
puts it, they felt that nothing could happen to them which
was not after all in harmony with the best interests of the
universe. The Stoics derived their pantheistic views from
both Pythagoras and Plato, and contributed not a little to
the formulation of the later Neo-Platonic philosophy.

It is, of course, in India that we find the most complete
development of pantheistic conceptions recorded in the
thinking of the ancient world. The earlier Hindu Scriptures contain a polytheistic view of religion, but in the course
of centuries the gods are all merged in One, and this One,
Brahman, or Brahma, is identified with the sum total of

reality. The Upanishads, as the later Hindu sacred writings are styled, contain the most complete and thoroughgoing exposition of pantheism to be found in the literature of the world. It is sometimes said that Jesus and Buddha drew their teachings from a common source, but those who made this statement forget that the background of Buddhism is complete philosophical pantheism while the background of Jesus represents precisely the opposite point of view.

Philo, as we have already stated, was Jewish to the core in his thinking. Nevertheless, in his constant association with Greek culture and with the philosophy of Plato and the Stoics, established through his studies in the Alexandrian library, he slowly came to modify his original point of view. He never, it is true, became a pantheist, but he did reach conclusions concerning the close relationship of God with the world which were quite beyond the viewpoint of early Judaism. He developed what later came to be the characteristic doctrine of the Greek-Christian theology, that is, a thoroughgoing belief that God dwells in His universe and is not to be thought of as afar off from it. This doctrine, which is technically known as immanistic theism, is the chief point which separates the Greek from the Latin theology. The Latins, much like the ancient Jews, emphasized the transcendence of God; that is, His separation from the world. The Greeks, beginning with Philo, stressed His immanence, that is, His presence in the world. Both Latin and Greek thinking, it is only fair to say, were not entirely exclusive of each other. The Greeks did not hold that God is so completely to be identified with the universe that He is not in any respect transcendent. Had they taken this extreme position they would have become pantheists instead of theists. On the other hand, the Latins never asserted that God is so completely separated from the world as to have no personal connection with it. Had they held to such a view they, in their turn, would have become deists instead of remaining advocates of theism. Both Latins and Greeks were of course devout believers in Providence; that is to say, in a Deity who possesses both transcendence and immanence. The Greeks emphasized immanence at the expense of transcendence while the Latins reversed the process.

We shall have occasion to deal with the development of the doctrine of immanence many times in the course of the history of theology. Philo must not be understood as in any sense its most thoroughgoing or complete advocate. He was simply the most outstanding forerunner and founder of the later systems that came to be. He paved the way for bridging the chasm between Hebrew tradition and the Greek speculative philosophy. It is this characteristic which makes him worthy of being styled the founder of Greek-Christian theology. Those who came after him went much farther, it is true, but they followed in his footsteps. Especially is this the case in the all important matter of the doctrine of divine immanence.

V

A second characteristic feature of Philo's contribution to theology was his formulation of the doctrine of the Logos. The term referred to is one to conjure with in the field of theology, but it is singularly devoid of meaning to the modern mind. Some irreverent wag is said to have parodied the opening verse of the Prologue to the Fourth Gospel after the following fashion:

In the beginning was the fog, and the fog was with God, and the fog was God.

Doubtless this is not an altogether inaccurate rendering of the meaning of the passage to the mind of the average layman. The fact is that the idea of the Logos is not easy to understand or to express. When the translators of the New Testament brought over the term literally from the Greek into the English they did not help matters very much. "Word," as it is used in our New Testament renderings, is not more illuminating to the average mind than would be the Greek original. Nevertheless, there is a really profound idea back of the Logos jargon, as some one has styled it, and it is an idea which ought not to be unintelligible to the average man or woman of the modern age. Let us attempt to get at the meaning by using the simplest possible method of approach.

It becomes easier to grasp the thought involved in the theology of the Logos when we understand how and why Philo came to formulate the doctrine. Of course, the starting-point of his teaching was not original with him. Both the word itself and the idea which lies back of it had been rather common property among the Greeks. Philo's contribution consists in his application of the idea to Jewish religious beliefs. The reason for his action arose from his gradual realization of the immanence of God in the world. He understood, and the Greeks before him had experienced the same difficulty, how impossible it is to link up the perfection of Deity with the crass and crude material of our workaday world. We must think of God as infinitely wise, pure and holy. How, then, can such perfection establish a point of contact with our frail and imperfect humanity, or with the unfinished and chaotic appearance of the material world? Obviously there must be some sort of bridge between the perfect and the imperfect, between the infinite and the finite, between God and the world. The Greeks styled this bridge the Logos because language is essentially

a bridge between human minds and the all essential go-
between which has universalized ideas and thereby constructed civilization. They had, it is true, various specific
interpretations of the Logos. The Stoics talked of the
Spermatikos Logos, or the Creative Will of the Deity, without, however, indicating very clearly what they meant by
the expression. Philo seized the term and identified it with
the Wisdom of the Old Testament, by which, according to
the book of Proverbs, the world came into existence. He,
of course, never identified the Logos with Jesus Christ.
Doubtless such an idea did not occur to him as he does not
seem to have known anything about Jesus. Nevertheless,
it was quite easy for Christian interpreters like the author
of the Fourth Gospel to amend Philo's views by substituting
Jesus for the Old Testament Wisdom as the true expression
of the divine Word through whom all things were made and
who later became the Light "which lighteth every man coming into the world."

Thus it was that out of his belief in the divine immanence and his attempt to explain the actual working of that
immanence in the creation and governing of the world Philo
formulated his identification of the Greek Logos with the
Old Testament Wisdom which became the starting-point of
the most fundamental of the later orthodox Christian
dogmas, the doctrine of the Trinity. As the Prologue to
John's Gospel puts it, the Logos was God, and in that assertion we have the germ of the later formulations of
Athanasius and his companions. Not that the Trinitarian
idea in itself is in the Prologue any more than it is in the
teachings of Philo, but the starting-point is there. The
Logos doctrine was destined to undergo a long and tedious
evolution from Philo to Nicæa, but the line of descent is
clear. The idea, it need scarcely be said, is Greek from beginning to end. It never bothered the heads of the Latins,

who swallowed the Greek formulations wholesale without making any special attempt to understand them. Moreover, it has never possessed any peculiar significance for the Oriental mind. Chinese, Hindus and Arabs alike do not seem to feel the need of it. To the Greeks, however, it was fundamental. It is in this particular cleavage between the Oriental and the Occidental ways of thinking that we find what is perhaps the chief obstacle to the world-wide extension of Christianity.

VI

In addition to his teaching concerning the divine immanence and his formulation of the Logos doctrine in order to explain the presence of God in the world, Philo stressed the third feature which was destined to play a great part in the later history of theology. The item to which we refer is his complete acceptance of the verbal inspiration of the Scriptures. This doctrine was an inheritance with him from his orthodox Jewish forebears, but in no other philosopher of his people is it so thoroughly formulated and defended. Philo is quite sure that the Old Testament Scriptures, as the Alexandrian Jews possessed them, were the literal and infallible word of God. He does not precisely explain how the writings were produced, nor does he apparently possess any systematic or carefully worked out theory of the nature of inspiration, but of the fact itself he has no doubt. Every word of the text is infallibly correct, and he never thinks of calling it in question in any essential particular. His reverence for the sacred Book is quite as complete and emphatic as was the later Protestant devotion to the same dogma in the days of the Counter-Reformation.

The idea of infallible inspiration conveyed through priests or prophets or seers was characteristic of Jewish religious thought from the days of Samuel, but it was by no means confined to the people of Israel. Practically every ancient tribe possessed certain shrines or holy places where the Deity was supposed to communicate with human beings through the medium of specially designated subordinates. The most famous of these oracles, as the Greeks styled them, was the one at Delphi where Apollo spoke through the trance possessions of his frenzied priestesses. At first the Delphian prophecies were looked upon as infallible and were preserved as such, but later on they came to be regarded as of more or less doubtful value. This was due to the fact that the prophecies were often couched in ambiguous language and not infrequently their predictions failed. Among the Romans there were the sacred Sibyline books which were supposed to contain prophetic material of supreme value for guiding the destinies of the state. Here too there was apparently much ambiguity, and the later guardians of the nation came to place little stress upon the dubious words of the Sibyl. Nations other than Greece and Rome had their sacred books, notably the Persians, Egyptians and Hindus, but we need not refer to them here. The point we wish to make is that the belief in verbal inspiration of sacred documents is of world-wide extent and not confined within the circle of Jewish or Christian theology.

To the mind of Philo, in common with practically all of his contemporaries, the problems raised by later criticism in connection with his theory of divine revelation did not possess special significance. The numerous textual variations, the possibility of error on the part of the copyist, the difficulty of eliminating entirely the personalities of the Scriptural authors in the production of their writings, the uncertainty concerning the inclusion or rejection of various books in the sacred canon,—all these things were inconsequential to him. He felt sure that in some way the Biblical text which he possessed was produced by the very Spirit of God and that this fact made every word of it absolute and infallible. He would no more have thought of questioning its authority than he would have dared to dispute the spoken word of Jehovah himself.

This unswerving acceptance of the dogma of verbal inspiration was destined to play a very large and important part in the history of the church. The early Christians who were of Jewish extraction believed in it unhesitatingly, but applied it to the Old Testament alone inasmuch as there was no accepted canon of the New Testament for several centuries after the church was founded. The Greek Christians, having no Jewish background, did not for the most part revere the Old Testament, and on this account began the formulation of the New Testament canon to take its place. They speedily invested the new writings with the same sanctity which the Jews had given to the old. Here again the doctrine of verbal inspiration quickly won the day even in the face of the fact that there was no standard text of the New Testament books and the numerous copies which were in existence all differed from one another in certain verbal particulars. The task of deciding which text represented the infallible word of inspiration was found to be an impossible one, with the result that most of the later Bibles which came to be used were redactions from a great number of texts and therefore corresponded exactly with no other manuscript whatever. Later Protestantism, as we shall see, had to wrestle with this problem and to a certain extent is still wrestling with it. The fundamentalist of the twentieth century goes back directly in his thinking to Philo. The difficulties which confronted the old Jewish scholar of Alexandria, but which failed to disturb his traditional belief in verbal inspiration, find a striking parallel in many threads and currents of our modern theology.

VII

The feature of Philo's teaching to which we have just referred carried with it another characteristic that was destined to become of great significance in the formulation of future theology. We refer to his emphasis upon the allegorical method of interpreting the Scriptures. Believing as he did in verbal inspiration and at the same time possessing a code of ethics which was on a level with the highest moral values of his day Philo found it difficult to reconcile all of the passages in the Old Testament with some of his most important ethical conceptions. Inasmuch as he could not and did not call in question the absolute infallibility of the sacred text he found it necessary to secure some means whereby the Scriptures could be adjusted to his ethical standards. He discovered this means, as the Greek thinkers in their dealings with their own Bible, the writings of Homer, had previously found it, in the method of allegorizing the unpleasant details. By the simple process of discovering a double meaning in the text it was quite easy to iron out the crassest moral inconsistencies. For example, the apparent endorsement of incest in the case of Lot's daughters, as recorded in the book of Genesis, was explained by Philo as an allegory which had no connection whatever with actual history. Other moral difficulties were glossed over in the same way, so that Philo eventually succeeded in bringing the Old Testament standards quite up to the level of the social conventions of his own day. It is interesting to note in this connection that he never entirely discarded the historical features of the text. He insisted that part of it was history and part of it was allegory, but he never seemed to be quite clear where the allegory began or where the history left off. Apparently the only guide which he possessed in the matter was his conviction that when any passage appeared to be morally wrong it must not be regarded as literal but must of necessity receive an allegorical interpretation. The result of this confusion is a somewhat ludicrous admixture of fact and fancy, of historical narration and poetical imagery, all mingled together in apparently helter-skelter and hopeless fashion. Philo himself does not seem to have been conscious of the situation, but it is quite apparent to the modern reader of his works. Later on the allegorical method, in the hands of Origen and others, received much more skilful expression. For many centuries it was the accepted means of interpreting the Scriptures, and it has not entirely lost its vogue at the present day. The Authorized Version of the Old Testament adopts it quite frequently in its chapter headings, the most notable example being found in the text of the book of Canticles. Saint Bernard was largely responsible for translating the Oriental voluptuousness of the Song of Solomon into highly refined Christian symbolism, and his exegesis was accepted almost universally for many centuries. Had it not been for this fact it is doubtful whether the church would have permitted a piquant romance of this character to remain in the canon. Under the skilful treatment of Bernard it became possible for even the most lofty-minded prioress or nun to read the pages without damage to her ascetic standards. This is only one out of many illustrations of the use of allegory in Biblical interpretation. Beyond any question the method was the important factor in saving the day for the theory of verbal inspiration, which, as we have observed, originally called it into existence. What its advocates failed to see was the fact that it practically nullified the authority of the text which they were seeking to honor. By making it possible to find other than the ordinary logical or historical meaning in the words, they opened the door to every species of imaginative embellishment which later ingenuity could devise. The extent to which this can be carried has been fully illustrated in the multitudinous and fantastic interpretations of the book of Revelation which every century has brought forth. Modern criticism has destroyed the necessity for adopting the allegorical method by showing the impossibility of holding to the old theory of verbal inspiration in which Philo and his followers believed so implicitly. Since this theory is unthinkable, at least in its original meaning, it is quite easy to interpret the Scriptures according to their plain and obvious significance without doing violence to our higher ethical standards. The recognition of the principle of development in the history of divine revelation solves the problem much more simply than the use of allegory and, in reality, does much more honor to the text. All this, however, was beyond Philo and remained beyond his followers for many centuries.

VIII

Summing up the work of Philo in its relation to the later development of theology we find that he made four outstanding contributions to the field. First, he introduced into Jewish and Christian thinking the doctrine of the divine immanence as a factor of controlling importance. Second, he formulated definitely the doctrine of the Logos as a means of explaining the way in which God is present in the world. Third, he confirmed and handed down the theory of verbal inspiration in connection with the text of the Scriptures, and fourth, he advocated the allegorical method of interpretation as a means of avoiding the ethical difficulties involved in his view of divine revelation. All four of these contributions were destined to play a very important part in the history of theology. Strangely enough, they became the basis of Christian speculation, although they were formulated by a Jew, who, as far as we know, never heard of Jesus or His teaching. The nexus between Philo and the early Christian thinkers is not definitely known. It seems obvious that the authors of the Gospel of John and of the Epistle to the Hebrews were acquainted with his writings, and it is quite possible that Paul also knew them. Their influence upon the development of the strictly Alexandrian school of Christian theology is indisputable. Of this we shall have more to write when we come to deal with Origen. Here we need go no further than to say that it is impossible to trace back the various threads of Greek Christian speculation without reaching the conviction that most of them owe their origin to Philo Judæus, or, if this be putting the case too emphatically, to say that to him at least they owe their first theological formulation.

CHAPTER II

PAUL OF TARSUS

IF PHILO represents the starting-point of Greek theology, Latin thinking must inevitably be traced back to Paul of Tarsus. Like the great Alexandrian he was a Jew, but unlike Philo he later became a Christian. His influence upon the development of Christianity in the Western World stands unchallenged and unrivaled. Aside from Jesus himself Western civilization probably owes more to him than to any other figure. In any list of the dozen, perhaps even half-dozen, outstanding characters in the drama of world history he would necessarily find a place. Great theological systems like those of Augustine, Luther and Calvin, have been founded upon brief and apparently casual passages abstracted from his writings. It is quite impossible accurately to estimate the extent of his influence upon the thought and life of humanity.

I

Paul resembles Philo in the fact that we know very few of the details of his life. Practically everything which we possess in the way of information is contained within the pages of the New Testament. There are, it is true, many legends concerning his career which have come down to us, but even the most uncritical reader could scarcely believe in their genuineness or authenticity. The most interesting of these stories, the apocryphal *Acts of Paul and Thecla,* we shall have occasion to refer to later, but there are other documents, such as the correspondence of Paul with Seneca, and numerous apocryphal letters, which purport to give side-lights upon the biography of the great Apostle. In the New Testament we have the material contained in the book of Acts and scattered allusions to his personal experiences in the epistles of Paul himself. When all of our source material is put together it is discovered to be of the briefest and most fragmentary character. It is true that later biographers have managed to expand the data to mammoth proportions, but such achievements are tributes to the imaginative skill of the authors rather than to the plenitude of material available for their purpose.

The actual facts·which we know concerning the life story of Paul may be told in a few words. He was born at Tarsus, the gateway city of Cilicia, of Jewish parentage but also possessing from his birth the rights of Roman citizenship. We know nothing further concerning his parents. It is perhaps unfair to base historical inferences upon the silence of biographers, and yet the consideration that Luke avoids so completely all reference to Paul's family or people can scarcely have been accidental. The Apostle himself, in one of his later prison epistles, refers to the fact that he had given up everything for his faith, counting it, as he says, but the vilest refuse in comparison with what he had gained by the exchange. The very impetuosity of the statement seems to indicate that he had given up what most of men would consider something worth retaining. Felix, the Roman Governor who doubtless knew the personal connections of his captive, kept Paul in prison for two years with the idea of securing a large sum for his release. It is, of course, possible that he hoped to squeeze this money out of the Christian associates and friends of the Apostle, but it seems more probable that he expected to get it from his wealthy relatives and most probable that he looked for the greater part of it to come from Paul's parents and immediate connections. In this he was disappointed, a fact which makes it reasonably clear that the break between Paul and his home ties because of his acceptance of Christianity was final and complete.. Internal evidence drawn from his writings furnishes conclusive proof that he was highly educated, not only in the rabbinical lore of his own people but also in the literature and philosophy of Greece. He tells us himself in one of his casual biographical references that he was a Hebrew of the Hebrews, tracing his lineage to the tribe of Benjamin, and in his political affiliations a Pharisee. Moreover, he had "sat at the feet" of the great rabbinical teacher, Gamaliel, the leading rabbi of his day. It was probably while studying under Gamaliel at Jerusalem that he first became acquainted with the new sect sometimes contemptuously referred to as the Nazarenes or, as the Greeks preferred to style them, Christians. Luke describes in detail the bitter animosity of the young zealot toward these heretics and the part which he had in their persecution. The story of his miraculous conversion on the Damascus highway, which Paul himself never tired of recounting, his retirement into Arabia, his later missionary labors concluding with his arrest in Jerusalem and his imprisonment in Rome are all matters of such familiar knowledge that we need not stop to repeat them here. Luke's fascinating biography breaks off abruptly with the Roman imprisonment. Tradition fills in the gap with the assertion that Paul perished in the first persecution under Nero, and there is nothing inherently improbable about such a statement. The great and magnificently imposing cathedral of St.-Paul's-without-the-Walls is built upon the spot where it is said that the Apostle was beheaded by a Roman executioner. This, however, proves nothing from the standpoint of actual history as every church of importance in southern Europe lays claim to some such pious background. In any event, Paul might as well have been beheaded on the highway to Ostia as elsewhere, and if the guardians of the cathedral are benefited by the legend why should we object to believing in it?

Naturally enough Paul's personal appearance and characteristics have been the subject of keen investigation. He has heightened the mystery by tantalizing references in his letters which are subject to the most varied interpretations. For example, his famous allusion to the so-called "thorn in the flesh" has become the starting-point of no end of learned disputation. Some commentators insist that the thorn, or more correctly the "stake," which tormented him was the physical affliction of epilepsy or malaria, while perhaps the majority refer it to blindness or to some disease of the eyes upon the basis of another casual statement in his letter to the Galatians, which, however, may have nothing to do with the matter. A well-known evangelist who practises faith-healing and who will not, therefore, admit that Paul suffered from any physical distemper which he was concededly unable to remove insists that the "stake" was not any sort of disease or ill health, but that it refers to some particular individual who belonged to the Judaizing party which opposed Paul, who followed the Apostle wherever he went and insisted on making things warm for him in every new location.

The references to the physical appearance of the Apostle which are contained in the epistles, are also somewhat annoying. Paul tells the Corinthians that certain slanderers have asserted that he writes great words but when you once see him, you recognize that his "bodily" presence is weak and his speech "contemptible." Although flatly denying this allegation, the Apostle still leaves us under the impression that there may have been some physical justification for the slander. Luke, indeed, tells us that when the people of Lycaonia were about to pay divine honors to Paul and Barnabas because of the exhibition of their miraculous powers they styled Barnabas "Jupiter" and his companion "Mercury," which would seem to indicate that Paul was the less imposing of the two figures. The record of his sermons and missionary addresses indicates that the Apostle must have been a speaker of remarkable power, but beyond this we know nothing. Whether he was tall or stout, ugly or handsome, whether his voice was resonant or the reverse, these and many other personal details which we would like to know about are all matters of pure speculation. The artists have pictured him as a somewhat elderly man with an abundance of whiskers, although there is no historical justification for these details. In his altar-piece entitled the *Madonna of San Antonio,* for which Mr. J. Pierpont Morgan paid an almost fabulous sum, Raphael has depicted the First Person of the Trinity along the same general lines so that Paul could not expect any better treatment. Despite the clerical antipathy to hirsute embellishments manifested in the shorn tonsure of the monks and other clergy, the Middle-Age artists, like the Mohammedans, regarded the beard as a necessary symbol of dignity. Among the many paintings of Paul and Peter which date from the Renaissance period we do not recall any one which depicts either of them without a beard. This fact, however, proves nothing as far as the actual physiognomy of the two distinguished worthies is concerned.

II

More important than his physical appearance, habits of speech or dress, we must consider the intellectual and spiritual background of the great Apostle. From this point of view he was the product of at least four outstanding and all-important forces.   The first was his Hebrew ancestry and early training, the second was the influence of the Greek culture in which the city of his birth was steeped and which must have played a great part in his early education, the third was the overshadowing political significance of the Roman Empire and the Roman law which was brought closer to Paul than to most Jews because of his privileges as a Roman citizen, and the fourth was his conversion to Christianity and the mystical experience which attended it. These four influences were unquestionably the outstanding factors in his life.   Probably the last came to be the dominant one in his conscious experience, but in the more uncertain realm of the subconscious the earlier educational influences must always have held sway.   It is these factors which explain many of the contradictions in the ordinary Pauline theology.

The first consideration to which we have just referred remained a strong motive in determining Paul's way of thinking, even to the end of his days.   Despite his battle for freedom on the part of the Gentile Christians he was always proud of his Jewish ancestry and of his Pharisaical training.   The Pharisees, it should be remembered, held implicitly to the doctrine of salvation by works; that is, by the observance of ceremonial rites, to a rigid fatalism, or predestination, and third, to the immortality of the human soul.   These convictions had much to do with shaping the Pauline theology in later years.   Under the influence of his mystical experience he repudiated salvation by works, but he never fully got away from predestination, and the belief in immortality guaranteed by the resurrection of Jesus became the very corner-stone of his gospel.

The Greek influence upon Paul's philosophy of life was scarcely less pronounced than the Hebrew.   As many writers have pointed out, he must have been very familiar with the great Stoics since he quotes from two of them in his sermon on Mars Hill, while the impress of the Stoic ethics is noticeable throughout his writings. Paul was born in a Greek community and his work as a Christian missionary was largely with the inhabitants of the Greek city states. He was familiar from the beginning of his career with the Hellenic point of view and always sympathized very extensively with it. How well he knew his Plato and Aristotle we can not, of course, determine, but there are traces of the influence of both philosophers in the Pauline writings, and in the nature of the case, the assiduous student of Gamaliel could not have missed reading the works of the supreme philosophers of the ancient world. Paul, it should always be remembered, wrote in Greek, and while his productions for the most part employ the colloquial Hellenistic language of his day there can be no question about his acquaintance with the classics.

The Roman influence is perhaps less marked from a surface point of view than either the Hebrew or the Greek, but it may be questioned whether it was any less important. The great imperialists of the church from Augustine to Aquinas drew their inspiration primarily from Paul, and while they probably misinterpreted him in certain respects there can be no doubt that they found many legitimate points of contact in his writings. Paul was too keen and sensitive a thinker not to appreciate the tremendous significance of Roman imperialism for the civilization of his age. He desired, above everything else, Luke tells us, to see Rome and was not satisfied until his wish was fulfilled, even though he entered the imperial city as a prisoner and suffered shipwreck while on the way to his destination. Paul thought of Christianity to no slight extent in terms of Roman imperialism. It was this larger vision which raised him above his Jewish provincialism and spurred him on to greater missionary activity. Paul's Roman background had not a little to do with the expansion of the Christian teaching in the Apostolic age.

All theological students have made much of the influence of his mystical experience at the time of his conversion upon the life and thought of the Apostle to the Gentiles. Unquestionably this factor was of great significance in shaping his later career. However modern psychology may interpret the Pauline experience, the Apostle himself never doubted its truth or reality. He believed that he had seen Jesus and that his interview was not a mere vision or hallucination. As far as we can discover from his letters, his faith in the veridical quality of his experience on the way to Damascus was never shaken. While he uses many other arguments to prove the truthfulness of Christianity it is apparent that his own convictions largely grew out of his immediate personal experience. All interpreters of Christian mysticism agree upon this point. However we may explain the fact, the fact itself remains. The mystical quality in Paul's religious life was one of the prime factors in determining his theology.

III

Out of the background which we have just depicted certain definite doctrines emerged and found expression in the Pauline teaching and practise. With the more important of these features we shall deal later. Here we wish to mention only a few of the lesser known and yet by no means insignificant characteristics. Among them may be included his views concerning women and the ascetic life, his premillenarian opinions, and his teaching upon the duty of subjection to the state. Although not of major importance in his own thinking each of these questions became a factor of tremendous significance in the later history of the church. His attitude toward women and marriage was largely responsible for the celibacy of the priesthood and for the Roman Catholic dogma that the virginal state is to be regarded as more honorable than matrimony, while his premillenarian views and especially his teaching concerning the Antichrist have been exploited by the Fundamentalists of every century, and his political dictum that every soul should be subject to the higher powers and that the powers that be are ordained of God was long the bulwark of the monarchical theory of the divine right of kings.

It seems probable that all of these inferences represent exaggerations of Pauline doctrine. The thirteenth chapter of Romans, for example, may teach passive obedience on the surface, but the fact that Paul himself defied the Roman law when it ran counter to his conscientious convictions proves that his words are not to be taken too literally. As for his premillenarianism, competent criticism of the epistles shows that he modified his attitude on this question as he grew older and that during his riper years of Christian experience it no longer played an especially important part in his thinking. His views as to the significance of celibacy have been especially misunderstood. The passages which his ascetic interpreters usually cite in defense of their doctrine are based almost entirely on his premillenarian convictions and were no doubt modified when he ceased to believe in the imminent second coming of Jesus. To use his own language, "the time is short," and this being true it made little difference in view of the approaching end of the world whether people married or not. Nevertheless, the idea of celibacy and of extreme asceticism in matters pertaining to sex fitted in well with the prevalent philosophy of the monastic period and for this reason came in the long run to dominate the church.   This tendency was manifested comparatively early in the history of Christianity, as we gather from such documents as *The Shepherd of Hermas,* which is largely a glorification of the monastic ideal and which probably dates from the middle of the second century.

We have already referred to the apocryphal story of Paul and Thecla as illustrating certain early conceptions of the Apostle's personal appearance and teaching.   The pamphlet entitled *The Acts of Paul and Thecla* is mentioned specifically by Tertullian, who lived about the close of the second century A.D., and by a host of other Christian writers who lived after his time.   Tertullian, it is true, attacks the book as a forgery, but the fact that it was produced at such an early date proves that the views which it promulgates as Pauline must have come into existence at any rate within a century after the great Apostle's death.   The story, despite its antiquity, possesses points of interest and is not devoid of dramatic quality.   The scene is laid in Iconium, where Paul has come to preach the new gospel of Christianity.   He is welcomed in the house of Onesiphorus, who is a resident of the city, and he is accompanied by Demas and Hermogenes, both of whom are depicted by the author as already traitors to the faith.   The description of Paul's personal appearance is interesting:

At length they saw a man coming (namely, Paul) of a low stature, bald (or shaved) on the head, crooked thighs, handsome legs, hollow-eyed; had a crooked nose; full of grace; for sometimes he appeared as a man, sometimes he had the countenance of an angel.   And Paul saw Onesiphorus and was glad.

Thecla, who is the daughter of one of the leading citizens, hears Paul preaching in the house of Onesiphorus from her adjoining home, and is so attracted by his manner and message that she is entirely won to the new gospel. What this gospel was is indicated by a brief synopsis of his sermon as this second-century writer gives it.

Blessed are the pure in heart; for they shall see God.

Blessed are they who keep their flesh undefiled (or pure); for they shall be the temples of God.

Blessed are the temperate (or chaste); for God will reveal himself to them.

Blessed are they who abandon their secular enjoyments; for they shall be accepted of God.

Blessed are they who have wives, as though they had them not; for they shall be made angels of God.

Blessed are they who tremble at the word of God; for they shall be comforted.

Blessed are they who keep their baptism pure; for they shall find peace with the Father, Son and Holy Ghost.

Blessed are they who pursue the wisdom (or doctrine) of Jesus Christ; for they shall be called the sons of the Most High.

Blessed are they who observe the instructions of Jesus Christ; for they shall dwell in eternal light.

Blessed are they, who for the love of Christ abandon the glories of the world; for they shall judge angels, and be placed at the right hand of Christ, and shall not suffer the bitterness of the last judgment.

Blessed are the bodies and souls of virgins; for they are acceptable to God, and shall not lose the reward of their virginity; for the word of their (heavenly) Father shall prove effectual to their salvation in the day of his son, and they shall enjoy rest forevermore.

In conformity with this teaching Thecla, who is betrothed to a noble of high rank in the city, tells her parents that she will not carry out her engagement. Her lover becomes enraged and at the suggestion of Demas has Paul arrested and thrown in prison. Thecla follows him thither and by bribing the jailer gains admission in order that she may listen to more of the new teaching. When she is discovered the Governor sentences her to be burned alive, while Paul is banished from the city. When the hour for her execution arrives Thecla is bound nude upon the funeral pile and a great fire is kindled around her. Nevertheless, upon her praying to the heavens for deliverance the earth opens and a great part of the fire disappears while a heavy rain from above puts out what is left of the flames. The people are astonished at the miracle, and Thecla is allowed to depart unharmed. Later she follows Paul and Onesiphorus, who had found refuge in a cave outside the city, and offers to accompany the Apostle throughout the world. Paul rejects this proposition because of his fear of scandal, and Thecla proceeds alone to another large city where she proclaims the new gospel and, after divers adventures, is arrested and sentenced to be thrown to the wild beasts in the arena. When the sentence is about to be carried out certain of the animals defend her against the others, and her life is thus preserved. Later on she establishes a species of convent and becomes renowned for her holy and pious way of living. The conclusion of her career is interesting. The Magistrate of the city determines that he will destroy her influence and her miraculous powers by employing certain base creatures to attack her and thus take away her reputation for stainless purity. Inflamed by drink these men start out on their impious mission. When they reach the cavern where Thecla lives alone she is not frightened by their declarations of violence. She prays for deliverance as she had done before on the funeral pyre and in the arena, and this time too her prayer is answered. The great rock wall of the cavern opens, to the astonishment of the onlookers, receives the holy martyr within its cleft side and then closes again as before. From this time forth the spot becomes holy ground and miracles are performed in its neighborhood. It may be interesting to add that the story tells us that Thecla was ninety years of age at the time of her miraculous deliverance.

It is obvious that throughout the exaggerated details of this second-century production there runs definite propaganda in behalf of the ascetic life. Celibacy and virginity are passports to heaven, and even married people are to remain as though they were not if they wish to secure salvation. The obvious contradiction of this teaching to the plain language of Paul himself in the seventh chapter of I Corinthians did not disturb the author of the story. The interesting fact is that within a century after Paul's death his example was already being used to promote views of extreme asceticism which he would certainly have been the last man to countenance during his lifetime. The Apostle was not an ascetic, although his missionary duties compelled him to practise more than ordinary self-denial in his way of living. But if he knew how to be abased, he knew also how to abound, and the idea that he looked upon all material pleasures as sinful is the height of absurdity.

IV

The chief contribution of Paul to Christian theology may be dealt with under four great conceptions: (1) his teaching concerning God; (2) his conception of the person of Christ; (3) his views of the essential nature of man and of the human soul; and (4) his doctrine of immortality. Four words, *God, Christ, Man* and *Immortality,* thus cover the entire range of the Pauline theology. It remains for us to deal very briefly and as untechnically as possible with his views upon these all-important subjects.

Paul's conception of the nature of God was largely derived from his Jewish ancestry and traditions. Unlike Philo, he never seems to have allowed the Platonic doctrine

of the divine immanence in all creation to change, in any
serious way, his older view.   It is true that in his sermon on
Mars Hill he makes use of the famous Stoic maxim concerning the Deity, "in him we live and move and have our
being," but there is nothing to indicate that he used the expression as in any sense a confession of his own pantheistic
inclinations.   In the Epistle to the Colossians and elsewhere
he refers to the Logos doctrine in terms which are decidedly
Greek, but even here he never really departs from his traditional Jewish point of view.   As we have already remarked,
this standpoint looked upon God as almost wholly transcendent, or separated from His world.   The Jews, during
the early Old Testament period, interpreted Jehovah as
most of the ancient peoples thought of their gods, that is,
in purely anthropomorphic terms.   To the mind of the
primitive savage the Deity is always simply the tribal chief-
tain magnified and with greatly extended powers.   He is
regarded as strictly personal and as maintaining the
simplest and most immediate personal relations with his
subjects.   He walks in the garden in the heat of the day, he
talks with man face to face, and when this conception becomes too naïve it is indicated that although he can not be
seen yet his voice can be heard and his presence recognized
by physical criteria.   Through all of these modes of expression runs the simple, forthright conviction of the reality
of a transcendent, personal Deity which was the supreme
and outstanding contribution of Jewish religious thought to
the human race.   It is true that in later times the Hebrew
interpreters became less naïve and anthropomorphic in their
pictures of Jehovah, but the general outlines always remain
the same.   Never once does the clear-cut vision of a personal God fade away into the confused and hazy metaphysic
of a mystical pantheism.   Even in a thinker like Philo the
transcendence of God is never wholly given up.   As for

Paul, there is nothing to indicate that he ever seriously modified his early Pharisaical conceptions of the essential nature of the Deity. Jehovah was always God to him, and it was Jehovah to whom he referred when he spoke of "the God and Father of our Lord Jesus Christ." Moreover, Jehovah meant to him the personal Deity who warned Adam concerning the Fall, appeared to Abraham on more than one occasion, conversed with Moses on the Mount, and made his presence known to Elijah through the still small voice heard amid the desert fastnesses of Mount Horeb. There is no doubt that Paul's conception of God was that of a transcendent, personal Creator and Ruler of the universe, and that he maintained this view throughout his career.

In the older Pharisaical teaching which constituted a part of Paul's university curriculum the doctrine of predestination had already been formulated as a necessary feature of the divine government of the world. The arguments in its favor were simple and direct. If God is the great Creator and Ruler of the world, if He possesses intelligence and knows what He is about, then of course He plans and foreknows everything which is to take place. To suppose that things happen without His being acquainted with the fact limits His divine knowledge. To suppose that He knows about them without willing that they shall occur is to limit His divine power or goodness. In any case, the only logical way out is to assume that God does know and does predetermine everything that happens in the universe over which He is sovereign. The Pharisees never worked out all the details of the theory of predestination as it afterward became embodied in such imposing systems as those of Augustine and Calvin, but the germ of the idea is in their teaching. When one understands this fact such passages as the famous reference, a quotation from the book of Jeremiah, to the potter and the clay in the ninth chapter of Romans, and the predestinarian implications of the first chapter of Ephesians become simple enough. Paul had learned all this from his Pharisaical teaching and had accepted it as a matter of course before he became a Christian. Afterward he appears never to have adjusted fully all the implications of his new position to the philosophical background of his past career. Hence arise certain contradictory view-points in his writings which he does not himself attempt to straighten out. They are readily understood and appraised when we comprehend clearly the theological biography of their author.

In regard to the matter of predestination what many of Paul's interpreters appear to have forgotten is that for every passage which teaches or infers the doctrine of election he has written at least two passages which can only be understood upon the assumption of human freedom. This is true of epistles like Romans and Ephesians where the predestinarian teaching is stressed most vigorously, and is also true of his other writings. Paul does not attempt to reconcile these divergences. Perhaps he never wrestled seriously with them. His practical turn of mind and the insistent demands which his work made upon him prevented him from spending much time upon mere theological subtleties. He never doubted the divine providence nor did he ever lose his faith in human responsibility. Just how the two things were to be hitched up together apparently did not disturb him. It was enough for him to recognize the facts and let some one else do the explaining. Others have been doing it ever since, with not altogether satisfactory results.

This practical turn of mind which demanded a clearcut and definitely personal conception of the Deity was not only Jewish but it was also preeminently Roman and Latin.

As the doctrine of the divine immanence, foreshadowed by Philo, became the corner-stone of Greek-Christian theology, so the doctrine of the divine transcendence, expressed with such force in the writings of Paul, became the corner-stone of the theology of the Latin church. The Roman mind, unlike the Greek, cared little for metaphysical subtleties or speculations. It was interested in practical things, in law courts and government, in public administration, in ethical conduct and in the personal behavior of its citizens. From such a point of view the old Jewish conception of the Deity as a personal being who could be best understood as a great king or emperor was most completely adapted to the necessities of life and religion. It is no wonder, therefore, that this idea became central in the thinking of Augustine, the greatest of Latin theologians, and that it remained central in the thought of his followers throughout the ages.

V

Paul's conception of the nature and person of Jesus Christ was doubtless the most immediate and outstanding feature of his theology. Unlike his view of Jehovah, his teaching concerning Jesus dates only from the period of his conversion to Christianity. Up until this time there is nothing to indicate that he thought of the Nazarene as other than a misguided enthusiast or impostor. After his experience on the highway to Damascus Jesus assumed an entirely different place in his thinking and life. The Galilean is now the King of kings and Lord of lords, the one through whom Jehovah is revealed to the human race in His perfection, the one to whom is committed all authority in heaven and in earth, the one who has conquered death and the grave, the one who has brought salvation from sin and the blessed hope of immortality to all who become His followers, in short, the one who fulfills completely and perfectly the highest Messianic ideals and traditions of the chosen people of Israel. In referring to Jesus, Paul's favorite expression is always "the Lord Jesus Christ." There is nothing to show that the subtle distinctions of the Nicene Second Person in the Trinity ever seriously occupied the Apostle's mind. What interested him was not the theoretical but the practical definition of Deity. Jesus was Lord, that is, His word, His will and His way were supremely authoritative, and after all these were the only things that mattered. There can be no doubt that Paul's position upon this much mooted point of the Deity of Jesus was the same as that of Peter and of the early Christians in general. They worshiped their Master as their Messiah and Lord without perceiving any incongruity whatever between this conception and their universally held Jewish monotheism. Jehovah was revealed in Jesus as far as He can be made known to man, and there was therefore no contradiction between the two ideas. It is true that the early Christian evangelists, like Paul, who went among the Gentiles preaching the new gospel, stressed the doctrine concerning Jesus so much that it alone gained the serious attention of their hearers. Not having any Jewish background, and not believing in the Old Testament, or in fact knowing anything about it, they dispensed with Jehovah, and Jesus became their sole Deity. We shall have to deal more directly with this point of view in the next chapter when we discuss the life and work of Marcion. Professor McGiffert, in his interesting little book entitled *The God of the Early Christians,* has shown how completely the Gentile converts worshiped Jesus as their only Deity while the Jewish Christians thought of Jehovah as the one ultimate God.

The Lordship of Jesus, understood not in a metaphysical or theological but always in a supremely practical sense, was the key-note of Paul's preaching. The unknown God whom the Greeks and Latins sought to find in vain is perfectly revealed in the life and teachings of the Man of Galilee. He has power to save, He offers salvation as a free gift and not as the price of endless ceremonial requirements, He brings the definite assurance of personal immortality and happiness, and only through Him can humanity as a whole or as individuals find the way of life. This was Paul's message, and it was this gospel which conquered the Western World. Later theology substituted all kinds of metaphysical and doctrinal interpretations of the Deity of Christ for the simple practical teaching of Paul, but the underlying idea was always the same. The authority of Jesus is central throughout the history of Christian theology just as it is central throughout the writings of Paul.

VI

Paul's teachings concerning man and the nature of the human soul were of the utmost consequence in the later development of Christian theology. One need only recall such terms as original sin, total depravity, justification by faith, and a host of others of similar import to recognize the tremendous part which the Pauline anthropology played in the development of theological speculation. Latin theology especially was indebted to the great Apostle to the Gentiles for its emphasis on the problems of sin and redemption. The reformers likewise, particularly Luther and Calvin, went back to Paul for the basis of their teaching. Much of these later speculations was no doubt read into the writings of the Apostle instead of being extracted from them, but the germ of what followed, at any rate, was undeniably present in the Pauline epistles.

Of the origin and of the essential nature of the human soul Paul says very little. In the course of centuries three distinct theories became recognized as explanatory of the appearance of the soul in time. The first, and perhaps the oldest, was the theory of preexistence, held by Plato and Socrates among the Greeks, and by Origen, the great Christian theologian. The second was the theory known as traducianism, which held that the soul is begotten and generated along with the body and develops side by side with it. This appears to have been Aristotle's view and was accepted in the main by Tertullian, Augustine, Luther and the Latins generally. It, of course, represents the modern scientific point of view. The third was the theory of creationism which held that the soul is created *de novo* at the time of birth and that it enters the body when the individual is born. This is the view entertained by many of the Eastern Fathers, by Saint Jerome and, during the time of the Reformation, by Calvin and Beza. In the writings of Paul we find no express endorsement of any one of these views. It is not at all certain that Paul accepted the prevailing Greek psychology with its threefold distinction of body, soul and spirit, although there are some interpreters who think that he did so. Later on we shall discuss his views concerning the persistence of the human personality after death. Even in dealing with this question we shall find that the Apostle was far from taking a dogmatic position.

What stands out as especially significant in Paul's thinking regarding the nature of man is his constant recognition of the fact and the destructive character of sin. Again and again in his writings we have the most striking emphasis upon the dangerous and deadly blight which the dark shadow of evil has cast upon the human race. The problem is obviously not a theoretical one with the Apostle but, on the contrary, with him as with Augustine the situation which he pictures has to do with the deepest springs of his personal life. Psychologists have long wrestled with the problem of the Pauline sensitiveness to sin. Some have held that it arose from the natural conflict of human desires with the rigid moral code imposed by the Jewish law, but the fact that the keenest and most sensitive expressions of the conflict appear to date from a period after Saul's conversion scarcely bears out this theory. In view of certain statements which he made long after he had become a Christian, such for example as his famous reference to himself as the chief of sinners, it seems probable that there was some one outstanding sin which was bound up with his personal career and the memory of which he was never able to efface from his mind. There can be little doubt but that this sin was his persecution of the people whom he afterward regarded as his brethren and co-workers. How far he went in the bitterness of his blind hatred for the Nazarene he never expressly tells us, but there is every reason for believing that he regarded himself as responsible for the direct martyrdom of some, at least, of the Christians and that later on he came to think of himself on this account as a murderer. Even the fact that he has found mercy and the further fact that he was conscientious in all that he did can not close his eyes to the enormity of his wrong-doing when the whole situation becomes clear to him. It is his reflections on this personal problem which led to his most profound theorizing concerning the true nature of sin. If a man so careful to observe the law as he had been from his youth up could nevertheless fall into such grievous sinfulness, how was it possible for any human being to escape the machinations of the evil one? Paul concludes, indeed, that it is not possible, and he explains the situation rather indefinitely, it is true, by a declaration of the universal depravity of the human race based in some way upon the original sin of Adam. The fact that he was unable to awaken to his sinful condition without the interposition of a miracle proved to him that only the divine grace could avail to save any human being from the deadly effects of wrong-doing. Hence arose in the later fabric of Latin theology the highly speculative conceptions of original sin, of total depravity and, above all, of the sovereign and irresistible grace of God.

Some of Paul's biographers feel that aside from the great sin to which we have referred the Apostle was subject, like Augustine, to certain temptations of the flesh to which he refers in the famous psychological conflict depicted in the seventh chapter of Romans. If there is any basis for such suppositions we are entirely without external evidence as to its reality. We know so little of the facts concerning Paul's personal life that it is quite impossible to dogmatize upon this point. What appears to be certain is that he possessed an almost morbid sensitiveness to sin and that this characteristic was destined to exert the most profound influence upon the theological views of later generations.

VII

The Pauline teaching concerning immortality is to be found almost in its entirety in the one great chapter which was later to be incorporated as a part of the burial service of practically all Christian bodies. The church at Corinth had written to him with regard to certain teachings which were being circulated in the congregation to the effect that there was to be no resurrection of the dead as Paul, in his original message, had obviously proclaimed. The situation touched the great Apostle to the quick and called out one of the most superb masterpieces in all the literature of eschatology, the famous fifteenth chapter of I Corinthians. Clear and unmistakable as are his references to the reality of the future life, the actual theory of the hereafter which he held appears not altogether certain. It is usually asserted that Paul accepted the Platonic doctrine of the natural immortality of the human spirit and that he regarded the Resurrection of Jesus as simply a demonstration of a fact which already existed but which had hitherto been only inadequately proved. Many interpreters, however, including especially such high authorities as Professors Stevens and Simpson, believe that Paul accepted the idea of conditional immortality,—the condition involved being the power of the Resurrection to confer eternal life upon those who avail themselves of it. Upon the basis of this theory all human beings are doomed to death, and eternal life is brought to them as a free gift through the Resurrection of Jesus Christ. As is the case with so many other speculative questions in the writings of Paul, it is not easy to reach an absolute decision with regard to his conception of the future. Probably here as elsewhere he held conflicting views. What seems clear is that he believed in the fact of eternal life for the Christian and that he regarded this fact as a matter of primary concern in his proclamation of the gospel. When we remember that Paul was a Pharisee, and that the Pharisaical teaching concerning immortality was, in the main, identical with the position of Plato, we have at least one clue to many of the Pauline expressions upon the subject. Some students have suggested that Paul's faith in the reality of a future life had largely faded before he became a Christian and because of this fact the good tidings of the Resurrection brought renewed cheerfulness and hope to his soul. Whatever considerations may have been present in his thinking the one outstanding fact which emerges is his absolute and unhesitating confidence in the survival of his own personality through the assurance furnished by the Resurrection of his Lord and Master.

Upon this fact we must be very clear. Paul's faith in a future life was the very corner-stone of the message which he proclaimed, and this faith influenced to an extraordinary degree the whole current of later Christian thought.

VIII

Paul's influence upon Christian teaching must not be reckoned by the few considerations which we have advanced in the present outline. There are many other points where he stimulated and even originated speculative questions of great importance. Nevertheless, we believe that we have indicated the outstanding characteristics of his contribution to theology. By virtue of his Jewish inheritance and his Roman citizenship he formulated his ideas in terms which became peculiarly appealing to the Latin type of mind. Hence Paul is the real patron saint of the Western World, as John has long been regarded as the inspirer of Eastern orthodoxy. The Roman Catholic allegiance to Peter is purely technical and hypothetical. Saint Paul was the real founder of the Western church and of the Western type of theology. It was not without warrant that Augustine and the Latin Fathers in general drew their inspiration from his pages. He was not entirely neglected by the Greek theologians, but it is useless to claim that he was their chief inspirer or master. He did influence the heretical Gnostics tremendously, as we shall see in the next chapter, but Gnosticism was speedily suppressed and the Greek orthodoxy which came in its place was conceived more in the tradition of the Johannine writings than in that of the Pauline. It was not until the appearance of Augustine that Paul assumed the preeminent position in the history of theology which he was destined to occupy for so many centuries.

CHAPTER III

MARCION

NOBODY knows the precise date of the death of Paul the Apostle. Tradition says that he was martyred under Nero some time during the seventh decade of the first century A.D., but this is mere conjecture. Assuming that it represents a measure of truth nothing is more obvious than the fact that the early Christian churches of the Gentile world were left to shift for themselves within a comparatively short time after they were founded. From the standpoint of theology the century between 50 A.D. and 150 A.D. presents the most puzzling problems upon which we are called to pronounce. During this period the church expanded over the Roman Empire, developed its ritual and organization, wrote most of its authoritative literature, and in almost every way laid the foundations of its future greatness. Practically every disputed question in the field of ecclesiastical history or discipline dates from this century. If we possessed clear, definite and comprehensive records of what actually occurred at this time most of the troubles of church historians would be over. Unfortunately, our information concerning what actually took place during this epoch-making interval is of the most meager and unsatisfactory character. The few contemporary records which have come down to us are obviously casual and do not represent the real thought or life of the times with which they deal. Perhaps much of the history was never written. Perhaps the best of what was produced, for one reason or

another, has perished.   Perhaps in some forgotten corners
of the Eastern World documents yet remain which, when
discovered, will cast a flood of light upon this obscure epoch
in the history of Christianity.

We can understand a little of what went on within the
circles of the church by recalling a few of the obvious facts
of the history of the Roman Empire itself.   With the death
of Saint John Christianity entered upon what we ordinarily
term its sub-Apostolic era.   It spread rapidly, especially
among the slaves and lower classes, and was so unobtrusive
in its methods of propagation that it speedily gained a foot-
hold in every section of the empire.   Persecution did not
check it because most Christians gloried in the privilege of
securing the martyr's crown and as fast as they were put
to death others stepped forward to take their places.   In
some strange way these fanatics, as Tacitus and Suetonius
styled them, had learned the secret of mastering the fear of
death, and everybody who witnessed their fortitude secretly
or openly desired to possess it.   As Tertullian, who lived a
century later, said, the blood of the martyrs is the seed of
the church, nor is his statement a mere rhetorical exaggeration.   The Roman Empire in the end was forced to capitu-
late to these unresisting enthusiasts.   Marcus Aurelius, one
of the greatest philosophers of the ancient world, was
totally at a loss to understand the secret of Christianity.
Although just and merciful by disposition, he persecuted
the Christians with the utmost severity because he considered their religious belief to be a pernicious superstition
which undermined the whole political and social structure of
the Empire.   This was in general the position of the Roman
rulers from Nero to Constantine.   In justice to these
potentates it is only fair to say that, from their point of
view, they made a remarkably acute appraisal of the
essential meaning and function of the Christian religion.

I

The earliest form which Christian theology assumed grew up during this period of subterranean development. Under the stress of persecution the Christians met in out-of-the-way places and developed a somewhat esoteric system of intercommunication and expression. They produced literature which was highly symbolic and which revealed its inner meaning only to the initiated. The Revelation of Saint John, which finally found a place in the New Testament canon, is perhaps the most striking representative of this class of writing that is accessible to the modern reader. So skilfully did the author of this revolutionary pamphlet disguise the purpose he had in mind that his work still puzzles the unenlightened and gives rise to all sorts of fantastic interpretations. No doubt the early Christians who understood the symbolic language read the book with enthusiasm and drew great comfort from its pages. The Roman overlords who were so mercilessly excoriated by its author apparently never once suspected the true nature of its contents. It was well that they did not, for otherwise every copy of this brilliant and scintillating impeachment would long since have been destroyed, and like so many contemporary documents, the book would have been buried forever beneath the débris of the centuries.

The tendency to conceal theological polemics under the form of imaginative literature no doubt had much to do with the development of Gnostic speculation. The Gnostics were the founders of Christian theology, in the full sense of the word. For ten or more decades they dominated the field of religious thought. This fact helps us to understand why our records of the first and second centuries of Christian history are so meager. With the rise of orthodox theology Gnosticism was put under the ban, and its productions were sought out and destroyed with all the enthusiasm of a

religious crusade. So effectually was the work done that
only a mere scrap of one of the most trivial Gnostic documents now survives as the sole memento of a literature
which must have been of the most extensive character. Even
this fragment was discovered only recently and obviously
escaped the rage of its pursuers by the barest accident. All
that we know about Gnosticism is derived from the writings of its bitterest enemies. These critics were not always
distinguished by moderation or fairness in their treatment
of what they considered to be heresy. Irenæus, Hippolytus
and Tertullian, who have furnished the bulk of our information concerning the Gnostics, were all intense partizans.
They do not aim at presenting an impartial view of the subject with which they deal. They looked upon heresy as the
most deadly of all sins, and they were quite sure that their
Gnostic enemies were the most damnable heretics.

II

What did the Gnostics teach, and why were they so
severely condemned by their orthodox opponents? One
peruses the musty volumes of Irenæus and Hippolytus and
reads the strange jargon which they attribute to the Gnostic
teachers with a certain sense of unreality. Obviously, there
is some truth in the absurd picture of Gnosticism but even
a novice in the field of criticism can discern the fact that it
is not the whole truth. Basilides, Saturninus, Valentinus
and Marcion doubtless indulged in much fantastic speculation, but there must have been some rational appeal
which gave life to their imaginative figments. In Antioch,
in Alexandria, in Rome, these men, even under the shadow
of persecution, dared to establish great schools which bore
the Christian name and which attracted multitudes of
disciples. As we have observed, the one protection which

Christian thought possessed at this time was to assume the garb of figurative and imaginative language. How far this consideration entered into the Gnostic literature we can not say. It is not improbable that a great many of their published absurdities can thus be explained.

Even Tertullian, who was in some respects the most bitter enemy of Gnosticism in every form, admits that his opponents were motived in their speculations by a desire to solve certain fundamental problems. Among the questions involved were: (1) the origin and nature of evil, (2) the peculiar ethical standards of the Old Testament, (3) the sufferings and death of Christ, and (4) the method of redemption. These problems were solved by highly imaginative methods, it is true, but even upon the testimony of their enemies, the Gnostic theologians made a desperate effort to save the moral issues which were involved. A brief investigation of their answers to the questions we have just cited will help to make this fact clearer. With regard to the problem of evil they preferred a dualistic interpretation of the universe rather than to make the God they worshiped responsible for everything. Their orthodox opponents took the other horn of the dilemma with consequences to which we shall have occasion to refer many times later. If we attribute cruelty, hatred and injustice to the Deity we shall speedily strive to emulate Him in all these particulars. The early Gnostics held that the Demiurge, whom they identified with the God of the Old Testament, was responsible for the mixture of good and evil in the world. This God they refused to worship, giving their homage to Jesus alone, whom they considered to be the embodiment of the true God of goodness, beauty and love. Whatever we may say about their philosophy no one can dispute the fact that Marcion and his associates saved their ethics by espousing dualism.

The identification of the Demiurge, or architect of the world, with the God of the Old Testament, helped to explain some of the ethical problems which the Jewish Scriptures presented to these intelligent representatives of the Greek Christian world.   They could not understand how to reconcile the slaughter of the Canaanites with the Sermon on the Mount.   Moreover, the ethical motive was so dominant with them that they rejected all mere casuistical explanations.   They were not anxious to safeguard any particular dogma, but they were eager to preserve their moral and religious distinctions.   They had accepted Jesus Christ as God, and His way of life as an expression of the will of the Deity.   They took these beliefs too seriously to permit them to compromise their convictions in the interest of traditional authority.   Of course, they had never been Jews and therefore had no particular sense of the sanctity of the Old Testament.   They lacked historical perspective in their understanding of the true relationship of Judaism and Christianity, but even their enemies can not deny that their ethical motives were sound.   They were close to firsthand information concerning the original gospel preached by the early Christian missionaries and evangelists.   They may have wandered afield a great deal in their interpretation of this teaching, but modern students of their work can detect a sincerity of moral purpose underlying it which was unrecognized for centuries.

The Gnostic dualism helped to explain the mystery of the sufferings and death of Christ.   The powers of evil triumphed temporarily on Calvary, but the true God, represented by Jesus, won the victory in the hour of resurrection.   Here again it was not necessary to twist one's moral sentiments by laying the responsibility for the cross upon the God and Father of Jesus.   In the same way the process of redemption became a climb upward in fellowship with Jesus through the circles of the eons to the throne of eternal goodness and truth. Plotinus worked this all out much more skilfully two centuries later in the Neo-Platonic doctrine of emanations which has aroused such enthusiastic admiration on the part of Dean Inge. How much of his system the Egyptian philosopher borrowed from Gnostic Christianity no one can say. It is true that Plotinus rejected the earlier dualism, but he retained the idea of emanations and much of the Gnostic scheme of redemption.

III

The details of the life of Marcion which have come down to us are meager and unsatisfactory. We do not know when he was born nor when he died. By casual references in the writings of his opponents we learn that he came to Rome from Pontus shortly after 140 A.D., bringing with him a sum of money amounting to over two hundred thousand sesterces, or fifty thousand denarii. It is difficult to convert these figures into a correct money reckoning for our own time inasmuch as the purchasing power of currency changes so largely from age to age. As nearly as we can estimate Marcion's capital it must have amounted to approximately ten thousand dollars. Upon arriving in Rome he associated himself at once with the Christian congregation worshiping in that city and speedily obtained a position of prominence. This may have been due in part to the fact that without solicitation he gave his entire fortune to the church. His teaching soon aroused vehement opposition on the part of the orthodox leaders with the result that he was excommunicated and his money returned to him,—an example which has not always been followed by the ecclesiastics of later ages. Driven out of Rome, he apparently kept up his propaganda and caused no slight disturbance in the ranks of the faithful. Tertullian, who appears to have been an elder in the church of the metropolis at the time when the great controversy arose, took a special hand in the proceedings and wrote one of his best known works against the arch-heretic. There is a tradition that Marcion professed penitence in order to get back into the fold, and that he was offered reconciliation, to quote the old record itself, "on condition that he brought back to the church the rest also whom he had trained up for perdition." The charitable old chronicler who gives us these details adds further that the would-be penitent was prevented by death from fulfilling his contract. Apparently this consummation was a matter of high glee to the orthodox party inasmuch as it prevented the worst of all the early heretics from escaping the hell-fire which he deserved. Tertullian gives a graphic picture at the beginning of his treatise against Marcion of the homeland and also of the personal character of the heretic. This passage is so characteristic both of the rhetorical ability and the partizan prejudice of its author that we are constrained to quote rather extensively from it.

The Euxine Sea, as it is called, is self-contradictory in its nature and deceptive in its name. As you would not account it hospitable from its situation, so it is severed from our more civilized waters by a certain stigma which attaches to its barbarous character. The fiercest nations inhabit it, if indeed it can be called *habitation,* when life is passed in waggons. They have no fixed abode; their life has no germ of civilization; they indulge their libidinous desires without restraint, and for the most part naked. Moreover, when they gratify secret (and unlawful) lust, they hang up their quivers on their car-yokes, to warn off the curious and rash observer. Thus without a blush do they prostitute their weapons of war. The dead bodies of their parents they cut up with their sheep, and devour at their feasts. They who have not died so as to become food for others are

thought to have died an accursed death. Their women are
not by their sex softened to modesty. They uncover the
breast, from which they suspend their battle-axes, and pre-
fer warfare to marriage. In their climate, too, there is the
same rude nature. The day-time is never clear, the sun
never cheerful; the sky is uniformly cloudy; the whole year
is wintry; the only wind that blows is the angry North.
Waters melt only by [the application of] fires; their rivers
flow not by reason of the ice; their mountains are covered
with heaps of snow. All things are torpid, all stiff with
cold. Nothing there has the glow of life, but that ferocity
which has given to scenic plays their stories of the sacrifices
of the Tauri, and the loves of the Colchi, and the crosses
of the Caucasi.

Nothing, however, in Pontus is so barbarous and sad as
the fact that Marcion was born there, fouler than any
Scythian, more roving than the [waggon-life of the]
Sarmatian, more inhuman than the Massagete, more
audacious than an Amazon, darker than the [Pontic] cloud,
colder than its winter, more brittle than its ice, more deceit-
ful than the Ister, more craggy than Caucasus. Nay more,
the true Prometheus, Almighty God, is mangled by Marcion's blasphemies. Marcion is more savage than even the
beasts of that barbarous region. For what beaver was
ever a greater emasculator than he who has abolished the
nuptial bond? What Pontic mouse ever had such gnawing
powers as he who has gnawed the Gospels to pieces?
Verily, O Euxine, thou hast produced a monster more credi-
ble to philosophers than to Christians. For the cynic
Diogenes used to go about, lantern in hand, at mid-day to
find a man; whereas Marcion has quenched the light of his
faith, and so lost the God whom he had found.

Most of the above brilliant diatribe is obviously
rhetorical buncombe. Marcion, by the testimony of his own
enemies, was not a Scythian but a native of Sinope, in Pontus, which was a Roman province and was considered a
civilized section of the Empire. His father, we are told by
Epiphanius, was bishop of his native city and had a high
reputation both for his orthodoxy and his exemplary char-

acter. Marcion himself must have been a man of intellectual ability and moral fervor. The proof that he possessed both characteristics is to be found in the lasting impression which he made on the whole future of Christianity. Few men have been responsible for so many significant departures in the history of religion. It was this arch-heretic, whom Tertullian and Irenæus denounced with such ferocity, who was responsible for the formation of our New Testament canon, for the adoption of the Old Roman Symbol, the first Christian creed, and who had not a little to do with the later overthrow of the allegorical or accepted method of interpreting the Scriptures. These are all matters of prime importance, and the first two especially are of such significance that they demand something more than a mere casual reference.

IV

The books which comprise our present-day New Testament have been accepted for so long a time and with such complete universality by all types of orthodox Christians that it is difficult for us to realize that for at least a century after the church was founded there was not even the semblance of a New Testament in existence. The documents which make it up were written, of course, but they were scattered throughout the Empire and were not collected in a single volume. The Jewish Christians, in common with their Hebrew brethren, accepted the Old Testament as Scripture, that is, as the infallible word of God, but no one thought of attaching such sanctity to the new writings. As far as we can see, not a single document which later helped to constitute the new covenant was written with this purpose in mind. Luke tells us that he composed his Gospel for his friend Theophilus, and with the idea of conveying an accu-

rate account of the life of Jesus to those who were not otherwise familiar with the source material so well known to the
historian. The author of the Fourth Gospel also tells us
that he prepared his book as a definite apologetic and apparently with no thought that it would be regarded as
Scripture. Matthew and Mark represent earlier Jewish
records which must have been compiled with even less conception of the ultimate position which they were to assume.
Luke wrote the Acts of the Apostles as a sequel to the Third
Gospel. There is good reason for thinking that he carried
the history further, but if this is true the record which he
produced has been lost. One-half of the New Testament is
made up of the correspondence of Paul. Modern scholars
like Deissmann and Ramsay have shown that beyond the
slightest scintilla of doubt these letters were practically all
relics of a rather hasty and busy personal correspondence
and that the author had apparently no conception that he
was producing works of permanent value. The same thing
was doubtless true of the shorter letters of Peter and John.
Hebrews is a rather carefully finished literary production,
and this observation also holds good of the book of James.
Revelation is of course an apocalyptic essay written under
the stress of persecution and preserved to the present time
largely because no one understood what the author was
driving at.

A typical illustration of how the Pauline documents
were produced may be found by a critical examination of
the material contained in I Corinthians. Obviously, this
letter was a reply to a series of questions propounded by the
church at Corinth to the Apostle while he was engaged in
his ministry at Ephesus. Paul answers the questions in very
considerable detail and adds a few personal observations of
his own. The whole letter must have been dashed off at
white heat, and was probably dictated in a few hours. This

is all the more remarkable because it is in the thirteenth and fifteenth chapters of I Corinthians that the Pauline inspiration rises to its sublimest heights. It seems quite likely that Paul and the other Apostles wrote a great deal more than has come down to us. If this surmise is correct the letters which have been lost must have perished within a few decades after they were written, for apparently Marcion, who lived less than a hundred years later, knew only the documents that are contained in our New Testament. Beyond any question, there were many other books dealing with the life of Christ and the early history of the church which have entirely passed out of existence. It is possible to make a long catalogue of the titles of such books extracted from casual references in the ancient Fathers. Among them may be mentioned the *Gospel of the Egyptians,* the *Gospel of the Hebrews,* the *Acts of Philip,* the *Acts of Thomas,* and a multitude of others which we can not take the time to name. None of these books was looked upon as Scripture by the early Christians or by their immediate followers. The writings of Paul and the documents which constitute our present New Testament must have possessed superior claims from the first, but even these books were not considered by the generality of Christians as being on a par with the Old Testament.

It should be remembered that Scripture, even at this early period, was universally considered as verbally inspired and as the absolutely inerrant word of God. Philo, as we have observed elsewhere, held steadfastly to this view, and his position was universally accepted by Jews and Christians alike. The citations from the Old Testament which are contained in the New Testament records are obviously quoted with this theory in mind. Paul, it is true, cites the Greek Septuagint text very freely, and apparently from memory most of the time, but he always uses it with the authoritative significance which Philo would have given it. When the famous passage in II Timothy was written, "all scripture is given by inspiration of God, and is profitable for doctrine, for reproof, for correction, for instruction in righteousness," the reference must have been entirely to the Old Testament record. No doubt the early churches to which Paul ministered prized his letters very highly and used them as practical mentors, or codes of discipline, but such usage was entirely local and was not designed to supplant the real Bible, which was, of course, the Old Covenant.

Marcion upset all of this. Not having been a Jew he had no religious inheritance which predisposed him to give any special consideration to the Bible of the Hebrews. Christianity he knew from the Pauline standpoint of freedom from the Law, and in common with most Greek Christians he recognized Jesus as his only Deity. His conception of the character and message of the great Teacher was evidently based upon much the same information as we possess to-day. He seems to have been whole-hearted in his acceptance of the ethics of the Sermon on the Mount and the gospel of good-will in general. He found this teaching quite out of line with the picture of Jehovah as revealed in certain portions of the Old Testament. It appears likely that, in common with many other Gentiles, he felt a certain prejudice against the Jews and was unwilling to make a fair examination of their records. However this may be, he seems to have turned with avidity to the more speculative suggestions of the great Gnostic teachers, like Saturninus and Basilides, who attracted throngs of citizens to their lectures in the busy metropolitan centers of the empire. With Valentinus, perhaps the most famous and brilliant of them all, he appears to have established rather close personal contacts after he moved to Rome. Marcion never seems to have understood or cared anything about the fantastic speculations of the Gnostic exponents. He was a practical man above everything else and his chief interest in Gnosticism arose from the fact that it enabled him to get rid of the moral difficulties involved in an acceptance of the current Old Testament traditions. He was not long in seeing that if he intended to eliminate the old Bible he must find something to take its place. Accordingly, he boldly proceeded to construct a New Testament, or Scripture, which he proposed to use in the place of the Hebrew version. This first edition of the New Testament appears to have been made up of eleven books, the Gospel of Luke, and ten of the letters of Paul. No copy of Marcion's New Testament has come down to us, but the testimony of contemporaries is to the effect that he used the text very freely, cutting out sundry passages which did not fit his theories and entirely rejecting any documents which appeared to have a Jewish flavor about them. Of course, we have only Marcion's enemies as witnesses to this free handling of Scripture, but it is not at all impossible that the tradition is correct. The arch-heretic of Pontus was a bold and original innovator, and centuries later, when the New Testament canon had been authoritatively established for a thousand years, Martin Luther was daring enough to imitate his example.

The orthodox party could not afford to yield the New Testament field to Marcion. Speedily other books were added to the eleven originally suggested, and in the course of two centuries our present canon became fairly well established. Some apocryphal books, like *The Shepherd of Hermas* and the Epistles of Clement and Barnabas, held on for a long time, but were ultimately discarded. Other books now in the text, especially Hebrews, II Peter, Jude and Revelation, had a difficult time maintaining their places. Some writers looked askance at James, and Martin Luther

shared this view even at the time of the Reformation. Ultimately the New Testament became *the* Bible of the Christians as the Old Testament previously had been and is the
Bible of the Jews. The church authorities held on to both
Scriptures, apparently without being much disturbed by the
moral scruples which perplexed the soul of Marcion. For
a thousand years Christianity was much more sympathetic
with the Old Testament standards than those of the Sermon
on the Mount. The leaders of the Crusades liked to read
of the heroic deeds of Joshua and David and to emulate
their example. Even Cromwell and his Ironsides chanted
Psalms and used the Old Covenant almost exclusively for
purposes of worship. They yielded a nominal homage to
the new covenant, but the idea of turning the other cheek
and of practising the law of love was too much for them.
They preferred the sword of the Lord and of Gideon, and
they had no scruples about hewing Amalek to pieces.
Marcion's Bible would not have suited them at all. It is
doubtful whether any considerable number of them would
have been able to accept Christianity if it had not been for
the comforting enormities of the Old Testament.

V

We are indebted to Professor A. C. McGiffert for the
suggestion that Marcion was responsible for the Old
Roman Symbol, which was the true germ of the Apostles'
Creed. Throughout the first century the early Christian
churches apparently got along without any formal doctrinal
statements. The only confession of faith required for
baptism was a simple statement of belief in the Messiahship
of Jesus Christ. Probably most of the Gentiles did not use
or appreciate the Jewish term Messiah, and therefore made
their confession with the understanding that they took Jesus
as their actual Deity. Professor McGiffert again, in his

volume entitled *The God of the Early Christians,* has made this point perfectly clear. The Jewish converts confessed Jesus as the Messiah, the Gentiles acknowledged him as their Lord or God, but both groups meant substantially the same thing. The Gentile formula was simpler because it had no background of a distant Deity like the Jewish Jehovah, and yet Jew and Greek alike acknowledged the absolute authority and lordship of Jesus over their lives. The primitive confession, therefore, secured a homogeneity of ethical values which was the prime consideration in the early life of the church. The Christians were united in their pledge of unswerving loyalty to Jesus and to His way of life. Other considerations did not disturb them because at this early period other considerations did not matter.

By the middle of the second century theological speculation had begun to take the place of ethical content in the thought and life of the church. Justin Martyr, the foremost of the early apologists, was beginning to put forth his speculative union of Christian dogma with Greek philosophy. Irenæus, the great Bishop of Gaul, was using his extraordinary administrative talents in stemming the tide of Gnostic teaching which for a time threatened to sweep everything before it. The salvation of the church, to these orthodox interpreters, appeared to lie in rigid conformity to their own philosophical and theological dogmas. The influence of Roman imperialism, as we shall see later, gave renewed power to the concept of monism in theology, and it was difficult for the average man at this time to think of the Deity as other than a highly amplified and glorified Cæsar. This imperializing tendency soon came to dominate the church, and led to the most bitter attacks upon advocates of Gnostic dualism, like Marcion. The strife between the two factions became so bitter that the original conception of Christianity as an ethical doctrine, rather than a system of theological dogma, was almost entirely forgotten. Especially was this true of the dominant party, as we shall discover when we come to tell the story of Nicæa.

When Marcion arrived in Rome, about the middle of the second century A.D., the church in that city must have been predominantly Jewish and imperialistic in its theology. The new teacher from Pontus speedily ran afoul of this majority sentiment, and was promptly excommunicated. In order to keep him permanently out of the fellowship his opponents bethought themselves and devised the first of the long line of historic Christian creeds. This was styled the Old Roman Symbol, and served as the nucleus of the later document known as the Apostles' Creed. The latter in its present form, it should be remembered, is not older than the seventh or eighth century A.D. The precise character of the Old Roman Symbol when it was first written can not be determined. It doubtless contained at least the earliest sections of the present Apostles' Creed, but it is difficult to say just where it stopped. Certainly, it must have affirmed, over against the heresy of the Marcionites to the effect that the God of the Old Testament was not the God of the New, that challenging expression of monism, "I believe in God the Father Almighty, maker of heaven and earth."

Later on, when the Creed of Nicæa was formulated, the orthodox adherents made this affirmation still more water-tight by adding the words, "and of all things visible and invisible," which, of course, makes the Deity responsible for evil as well as good, for Caligula and Nero as well as for Paul and Francis, for the bubonic plague baccilus and the cotton boll-weevil, to speak of no other contradictory features which modern scientific investigation has disclosed in the universe. Most of the ancient theologians shied off a little from the proposition that God created the devil and all his works. Nevertheless, if the evil one actually exists he must be either visible or invisible, and therefore must have been created by some one. This difficulty seriously troubled certain of the more thoughtful, like Augustine and Origen, but most of their contemporaries simply classified it as a "mystery" and let it go at that. We shall have occasion to refer to this mystery more than once hereafter.

With the formulation of the Old Roman Symbol the era of creed-making had begun. It was not until the Nicene dogma was put forth in 325 A.D. that any of these theological formularies could fairly claim the title of ecumenical or universal. Long before Nicæa, however, the great city churches of the empire had adopted creeds and had used them freely for the purpose of excommunicating heretics. The process of exclusion, which has written so many sad chapters in the history of the church, had been inaugurated and was soon to become the established custom.

Curiously enough, these cast-iron tests of fellowship were practically all of a highly speculative or theological character. Unlike the criteria which Jesus himself put forth in the Sermon on the Mount, and wherever His teaching is recorded in the New Testament, these confessions of faith said nothing about ethical conduct or the building of the Kingdom of God either in the hearts of individuals or in the world at large. Instead of this they stressed subtle metaphysical distinctions which even those who wrote them could not explain in any intelligible way. The Athanasian Creed, for example, was presumably written to clarify the Nicene, but it would require a genius of supernormal power to clarify the Athanasian. Presumably, the creeds are rational statements, and yet the only orthodox interpretation of their meaning involves a denial of rationality. Everybody who attempted to explain the dogma so that it would make sense was a heretic, the true orthodoxy consisting in avoiding all such explanations.

VI

Aside from being primarily responsible for the New Testament and the Apostles' Creed, Marcion stirred up considerable ferment in theological circles by his methods of Scriptural exegesis. He refused outright to accept the allegorical system of Philo, and insisted that the sacred books should be subject to the ordinary canons of interpretation. This was the easier for him because he rejected the Old Testament entirely, and the New Testament which he formulated was slight in content and lacked the sanctity of age. The striking impression which Saul of Tarsus made upon the Gentile world is illustrated by the fact that Marcion constructed his entire Bible out of his writings and the companion Gospel of Luke, who was Paul's associate and biographer. Marcion must have known about Matthew and Mark, but appears to have rejected their testimony because of the Jewish coloring of both books. The other writings of the New Testament may or may not have been familiar to him, but if he was acquainted with them he did not regard them as of especial importance. Of course, he was separated by little more than half a century from the time of the Apostles, and the Apostolic tradition must have exerted a great influence at this time. It is not inconceivable that Marcion's father, or his grandfather at the utmost, had heard Paul preach—perhaps had even been converted by him. Under such circumstances the necessity for written Scripture was less apparent than it speedily afterward became. Marcion himself recognized the desirability of the written formulation, and it was for this reason that he began to organize the New Testament canon. The Jewish-Christian churches which looked upon the Old Testament as Scripture did not feel this need in the same way. Nevertheless, the bold innovation of Marcion speedily put them on the defensive and they too were obliged to construct a

New Testament supplement to their Scriptures in order to compete with his heretical Bible.

In still another way the heretic of Pontus interfered with the established data of orthodoxy. Nearly all the Christian apologists, from the New Testament times onward, were accustomed to use predictive prophecy as one of the major lines of argument for their position. Many of them were not agreed as to the interpretation of particular Scriptures, and some of the conclusions reached were exceedingly fanciful. This imaginative use of Scripture fitted in rather well with the allegorical method, and we find the two in constant use in the writings of the ante-Nicene Fathers. The predictive character of ancient prophecy proved not only its own inspiration but also the divine government of the world. This naturally led to the formulation of the doctrine of predestination as we discover it in the writings of Augustine and his successors. The great Roman theologian argues for election upon the ground that only through this conception is predictive prophecy possible. Unless God has made sure that everything must happen in a certain way no one could certainly predict the course of future events. On the other hand, if the Deity had actually predestined and predetermined everything which was to come to pass, it became a very simple matter to establish the principle of predictive prophecy. All that was necessary was for the Omnipotent to disclose faint inklings of His plan to certain favored individuals, and the work was accomplished. Professor Fullerton, of Oberlin, in his fascinating little study entitled *Prophecy and Authority,* has explained the history of predictive prophecy in detail so far as it relates to the story of Christianity. Its vogue continued for a long time and still exists in certain quarters, but the disappearance of the allegorical method of interpretation and the rise of modern historical criticism have largely destroyed its utility. As Professor Fullerton correctly indicates, there were certain respects in which Marcion antedated the modern findings by some seventeen or eighteen centuries. He was not so much a modernist in these particulars as his distinguished successor, Theodore of Mopsuestia, but in his matter-of-fact way of interpreting the Scriptures he was unquestionably the forerunner of the great Antiochean.

VII

Marcion was not without his faults, and some of them were of the most serious character. He was never a scholar, and his crude and uncritical acceptance of Gnosticism laid him open to the barbed shafts of more competent theologians like Irenæus and Tertullian. Even in his ethical teaching he was led astray by the rigid dualism of the Gnostic schools. Clement of Alexandria, as well as Tertullian, denounced his asceticism and especially his advocacy of the celibate ideal. It was not long, however, before orthodoxy veered around to the same position. Catholic and Gnostic alike looked upon all material objects as sinful, and the ghost of the most morbid phase of Platonic speculation fell like a pall upon the civilized world. Strange fictions were devised to give a romantic coloring to the abnormalities of asceticism. By retiring to a convent and remaining aloof from the world of human beings young women were led to believe that they might become the brides of Christ, and young men were promised the unspeakable beatitudes of Paradise as reward for their voluntary crucifixion of all human pleasures or desires. Certain of the results of this singularly abnormal philosophy will come up again when we shall have to deal with the theology of mysticism. Here we need only remark that, however ahead of his age Marcion may have been in certain particulars in this matter of ascetic dualism, he trailed far behind so sane and balanced an interpreter of orthodoxy as Saint Clement of Alexandria.

With all his faults Marcion stood for a certain ethical idealism which was superior to the more subtle philosophy of his opponents.   He wanted to establish the goodness of God, no matter at what cost, and his ethical instincts at this point were sound.   If his teaching had prevailed there would have been no *autos da fé,* no Inquisition, and no burning of heretics by either Catholics or Protestants.   It was the triumph of the imperialistic God of Tertullian and Augustine which led to most of the later horrors in the history of the church.   The idea that the Deity could do anything which he himself regarded as unjust or cruel seemed unthinkable to Marcion, but this was not the case with his opponents.   There are passages in Tertullian in which the grim old Roman orator challenges his enemies to do their worst with rack or fagot or sword, being well assured that his persecutors will suffer infinitely more in the eternal flames of hell.   The satisfaction which this reflection apparently gives him makes the thought of his own torments trivial and insignificant.   It was the common belief of the period, at least in orthodox circles, that the joys of Paradise would be enhanced by the possibility of witnessing the torments of the damned.   Augustine has a great deal to say about this somewhat gruesome topic later on, but neither Augustine nor Tertullian represented anything unusual from the orthodox point of view.   As Marcion saw all too clearly, no human being will ever rise to a higher moral level than the ethical plane of the Deity he worships.   A God who could condemn little children to the unending flames of perdition simply because some of their remote ancestors disobeyed his commands represents an ethical ideal which was later to write history in the torture chambers of Torquemada, the flames which consumed the bodies of Huss and Servetus, and which broke Jean Calas on the wheel only two centuries ago. Marcion's theology at the worst would never have permitted such things as these. He was close enough to the original message of Jesus to recognize its incongruity with the idea of a Cruel Omnipotence. His theological gropings were grotesque and absurd enough, but his moral sense was sound, and the world might have been better off if his heresy had prevailed.

CHAPTER IV

THE first really great name in Christian thought is that of Origen. One has certain reservations in making this pronouncement, especially when one thinks of Clement of Alexandria, but nevertheless the dictum holds good. Origen has been styled the founder of systematic theology, and there appears to be no valid reason for disputing the statement. While a less attractive figure than Clement in many respects and teaching certain views of life which are obsolete to-day, Origen none the less stands out as one of the three or four most influential figures in the history of theological discussion. For the last half-century there has been something approaching an Origenian revival in religious circles, and the great Alexandrian was perhaps never more influential than he is to-day. The reasons for this situation will receive due attention a little farther on in this volume.

I

One of the mysteries of early Christian history is the founding of the church at Alexandria. There was an old tradition to the effect that John Mark, the companion and amanuensis of the Apostle Peter, was responsible for the first proclamation of the Gospel in the great commercial metropolis of North Africa. Later on the Venetians capitalized this legend by bringing the bones of Mark from Alexandria to Venice and by making the author of the

Second Gospel the patron saint of their community. One of the most magnificent temples in Christendom arose in his honor, and the great square of the city was called after his name. The Alexandrian records supply no foundation for the Venetian tradition. If Mark actually lived or preached in Alexandria we know nothing about it. All that we do know is that by the middle of the second century there was a strong and influential church in the Egyptian metropolis and that by the beginning of the third century it had become the most significant religious community in Christendom. For many years the Bishop of Alexandria was the leading personage in the ancient church. He was the first to receive the title of "papa" or "pope," which was later taken over by the Bishop of Rome and which the latter wears to this day.

Toward the close of the second century a school for the instruction of Christian workers and laymen was developed in Alexandria under the direction of a certain philosopher named Pantænus. Of this individual but little is known, the principal fact of importance in his career being that he had a pupil named Clement who succeeded him. Of Clement's life we are likewise not very well informed. We have two large volumes of his works which have been handed down to posterity, but these books contain very few details concerning the biography of their author. They are chiefly made up of lectures or lecture notes covering the curriculum of the school which Clement taught. They are exceedingly valuable because they not only give us a reasonably accurate conception of what Christianity was during the second century A.D., but they also afford a splendid picture of the prevailing customs of the age. In the volume designated *The Instructor*, for example, we have the following under the section entitled "The Hair":

Since cropping is to be adopted not for the sake of elegance but on account of the necessity of the case; the hair of the head, that it may not grow so long as to come down and interfere with the eyes, and that of the moustache similarly, which is dirtied in eating, is to be cut round, not by the razor, for that were ungenteel, but by a pair of cropping scissors.   But the hair on the chin is not to be disturbed, as it gives no trouble, and lends to the face dignity and paternal terror.

In much the same vein *The Instructor* goes on to say that a cropped head not only shows a man to be grave and dignified but also renders the cranium less liable to injury by accustoming it to the presence of both cold and heat, and further averts the mischiefs which arise from changes in temperature since the hair is like a sponge which absorbs poisonous vapors and so "inflicts on the brain constant mischief from the moisture."   Were it not for the fact that it is quite impossible to suspect the college youth of the present age of any familiarity with the pages of Clement one might be led to conclude that *The Instructor* had set the fashion in headgear, or the absence of it, in our modern universities.

In the matter of feminine styles Clement is also decidedly *à la mode*.   He says, for example:

It is enough for women to protect their locks, and bind up their hair simply along the neck with a plain hair-pin, nourishing chaste locks with simple care to true beauty. For meretricious plaiting of the hair, and putting it up in tresses, contribute to make them look ugly, cutting the hair and plucking off it those treacherous braidings; on account of which do not touch their head, being afraid of disordering their hair.   Sleep, too, comes on, not without fear lest they pull down without knowing the shape of the braid. But additions of other people's hair are entirely to be rejected, and it is a most sacrilegious thing for spurious hair to shade the head, covering the skull with dead locks.

Evidently the old Alexandrian pedagogue would have been a strenuous advocate of bobbed hair if he had lived during the present age. Upon the matter of cosmetics he was perhaps a little more conservative. Under the caption "Painting the Face" he says:

Nor are the women to smear their faces with the ensnaring devices of wily cunning. But let us show to them the decoration of sobriety. For, in the first place, the best beauty is that which is spiritual, as we have often pointed out. For when the soul is adorned by the Holy Spirit, and inspired with the radiant charms which proceed from Him,—righteousness, wisdom, fortitude, temperance, love of the good, modesty, than which no more blooming colour was ever seen,—then let corporeal beauty be cultivated too, symmetry of limbs and members, with a fair complexion. The adornment of health is here in place, through which the transition of the artificial image to the truth, in accordance with the form which has been given by God, is effected. But temperance in drinks, and moderation in articles of food, are effectual in producing beauty according to nature; for not only does the body maintain its health from these, but they also make beauty to appear. For from what is fiery arises a gleam and sparkle; and from moisture, brightness and grace; and from dryness, strength and firmness; and from what is aërial, free-breathing and equipoise; from which this well-proportioned and beautiful image of the Word is adorned. Beauty is the free flower of health;

which passage Mr. Bernarr Macfadden would certainly have appropriated for his *Physical Culture Magazine* if he had possessed the slightest knowledge of its existence. Certainly he would have regarded as choice meat the following description of the model maiden:

Zeno the Cittiæan thought fit to represent the image of a young maid, and executed the statue thus: "Let her face be clean, her eyebrows not let down, nor her eyelids open nor turned back. Let her neck not be stretched back, nor the members of her body be loose. But let the parts that hang from the body look as if they were well strung; let there be the keenness of a well-regulated mind for discourse, and retention of what has been rightly spoken; and let her attitudes and movements give no ground of hope to the licentious; but let there be the bloom of modesty, and an expression of firmness. But far from her be the wearisome trouble that comes from the shops of perfumers, and goldsmiths, and dealers in wool, that which comes from the other shops where women, meretriciously dressed, pass whole days as if sitting in the stews."

Nothing is too insignificant for Clement to pass upon in the matter of human behavior. A man is to walk neither furiously nor with a lingering step nor swaggering nor effeminately, but gravely and leisurely as becomes a gentleman. Neither is he "to spend his time in barber shops and taverns babbling nonsense." He is to amuse himself by going to church with his wife and he may also indulge in the "kiss of charity," which evidently was a species of ordinance in the Alexandrian religious community. In respect to the latter *The Instructor* wisely enjoins caution.

And if we are called to the kingdom of God, let us walk worthy of the kingdom, loving God and our neighbour. But love is not tested by a kiss, but by kindly feeling. But there are those, that do nothing but make the churches resound with a kiss, not having love itself within. For this very thing, the shameless use of the kiss, which ought to be mystic, occasions foul suspicions and evil reports. The apostle calls the kiss holy.

When the kingdom is worthily tasted, we dispense the affection of the soul by a chaste and closed mouth, by which chiefly gentle manners are expressed.

Clement would probably have been in favor of the Volstead Act if he had been living at the present time, although he refers to Paul's advice to Timothy concerning the use of wine and appears to regard it as a perfectly legitimate medicine. "The natural temperate and necessary beverage for the thirsty is water. . . . I therefore admire those who have adopted an austere life and who are fond of water, the medicine of temperance, and flee as far as possible from wine, shunning it as they would the danger of fire." There are very precise instructions in regard to behavior in the public baths so as not to provide scandal. Christian women are especially exhorted to be modest in the presence of their slaves, a practise which the heathen appear to have entirely ignored.

Clement was in no sense of the term an ascetic. He believed in marriage, both for the clergy and the laity, although he admitted it might not be suitable for everybody. He denounced gluttony and immoderate eating, but he had no objection to attending banquets were due decorum practised. He thought it perfectly legitimate for a Christian to acquire wealth provided he did it honestly and used it in the right way. He is occasionally very frank in his advice and there are whole chapters in the English version of the ante-Nicene Fathers containing his works, which the Reverend William Wilson deemed inadvisable to render in English. The Latin superscription of one of these chapters sufficiently indicates its general character: *Quaenam de procreatione liberorum tractanda sint.* Instructors in the language of Tully and Seneca have missed a great opportunity for inducing interest in their favorite study by omitting from their repertoire the works of the great Alexandrian.

II

The theology of Clement possesses many points of affinity with that of his Jewish predecessor, Philo. Like the latter, he believed in the divine immanence, and had no patience with the view that God is far away from the world and is not interested in it. He accepted the Logos doctrine of Philo as adapted to the Christian message by the author of the Fourth Gospel, and made it a central feature of his speculation. He placed particular emphasis upon the incarnation, and he thought of salvation as a matter of education rather than of sudden or catastrophic conversion. He was especially emphatic in his advocacy of the harmony of Greek culture with Christian doctrine. He must have been a scholar, for he quotes frequently from most of the classical writers, and appears to be thoroughly familiar with their productions. He was a great deal of an eclectic in his general theological attitude, and this fact tends to make his teaching more popular at the present time. He honors the church and occasionally refers to its ordinances and rites, but it is easy to see that his interest is not primarily in the field of ecclesiology. In many respects he is the freest, frankest, most modern of all the Fathers of Alexandria.

Clement died some time during the second decade of the third century A.D. His works were long regarded as models of their kind, and he himself was held in the highest estimation. Later, along with his great pupil, Origen, he fell under the suspicion of heresy and was eliminated from the circle of the orthodox Fathers. Nevertheless, he received the title of Saint, which distinction he maintained until the beginning of our modern age when one of the popes dropped his prefix, alleging that he was not significant enough to justify his possession of the appellation. Maybe so, but it seems queer that less distinguished men have worn it and still are wearing it to-day. We trust that this making and unmaking of sainthood did not trouble the spirit of the immortal Alexandrian on the other side of the Great Divide. Perhaps it amused him as it diverts those of us who read the story to-day.

We are unfamiliar with the circumstances which surrounded either the beginning or the close of Clement's career. Persecutions came on apace at Alexandria, and it may well be that he met the death of a martyr. His temper was irenic and tactful, and this trait may have enabled him to escape the fate of so many of his companions. One would like to know the facts, but it is not probable that they will ever be discovered. All that is certain is that he concluded his work somewhere between 211 and 216 A.D., and that he was succeeded in the principalship of the catechetical school at Alexandria by his great pupil and companion, Origen.

III

Some day a competent authority will write a history of the great eunuchs of the world. The list is sufficiently impressive: Origen, Abelard, Bagoas, Narses, the Treasurer of Candace, Mesrour, and many others come readily to mind. Of the number Origen is probably first in fame and importance. The advocacy of ascetic practises in the early church had grown steadily since the days of the Apostles, and the Greek theologian's literal application of a well-known passage in the Gospel of Saint Matthew was quite in line with the traditions of his age. There may have been some justification for the radical step which he took in the peculiar surroundings of his early life. Alexandria was a gay and dissolute community, and temptations of the most lurid character were everywhere present. Charles Kingsley's picture of the night life of the Egyptian metropolis in the pages of *Hypatia* is not an exaggeration. Tradition avers that when Origen succeeded to the position of Clement at the head of the catechetical school he was only eighteen years of age. This fact and the heavy responsibilities which his new position carried with it may have had not a little to do with the decision which has puzzled so many of his biographers.

Origen Adamantinus, as his contemporaries styled him because of his adamantine courage and firmness, assumed the leadership of the Christians at a time of great persecution. His father, Leonidas, received the martyr's crown, Origen encouraging him to go to his death, and had it not been for the entreaties of his mother and a sense of responsibility to the Christian cause the boy himself would have shared the same fate. Later on in the Decian persecution, about the middle of the third century, Origen was imprisoned and tortured and treated so cruelly that he later died as a result of his injuries. Throughout his career he never shrank from teaching and preaching the Gospel in the presence of both friends and foes. He was perhaps the most indefatigable worker in ecclesiastical history. He wrote incessantly, and one of his biographers informs us that he produced in all some six thousand volumes. Doubtless these books were for the most part brief essays and sermonettes, but even this consideration leaves him as an author of prodigious industry. He wrote three distinct commentaries upon the whole Bible, elaborating each section at length. Most of his productions are lost, but what remains constitutes one of the most imposing contributions to Christian theology. He was the first systematic theologian, and his work entitled *De Principiis* is still a model of scholarly speculation, although it probably was written before he reached the age of thirty. It is interesting to note that two of the greatest treatises in the history of theology, this work of Origen's and the *Institutes* of Calvin, were both produced before their authors had passed out of their twenties. It is possible that Origen changed his mind concerning some of the views expressed in this early work, but if so we have no record of the fact. In his treatise written in opposition to the Roman skeptic, Celsus, Origen has made a valuable contribution to Christian apologetics and to the contemporary history of his age. Celsus was the most brilliant and caustic critic which Christianity has ever had to face. Later skeptics, such as Hume, Gibbon, Voltaire, Paine and Ingersoll have done little more than to steal his thunder. Origen sets a model for other disputants by quoting the arguments of Celsus practically entire before making his answer to them. In this way his readers have an opportunity to scan both sides of the situation before reaching a conclusion. Had it not been for this rather unusual disposition to be fair to his opponent on the part of Origen it is not probable that the work of Celsus would ever have come down to posterity.

IV

The Greek theology, in many respects, reached its highest point in the speculations of Origen. It is true that Athanasius and other teachers carried his thought farther, but in comprehensiveness and mental grasp he stands out above all of them. He was not content to confine his investigations to one particular field or to touch only one side of Christian dogma. Like Augustine and Aquinas after him, his province was the entire range of Christian doctrine. As a result, in any list of the half-dozen greatest figures in theology which could be made his name would perforce have to be included.

Origen, like Clement, believed in the divine immanence, but he probably qualified the idea a little more fully than his predecessor. It is quite easy for the conception of immanence to pass over into pantheism, as it did in the thought of Plotinus, the great contemporary and rival of the theologian. The hypothesis of theism affirms that God must be both transcendent and immanent, and Origen sought to guard this doctrine with the utmost dialectical skill at his command. He never went so far in the direction of transcendence as did the Latin school, and especially Augustine, but he went far enough to make it clear that no tinge of pantheism attached to his thinking.

It was probably in the field of Christology, or the doctrine concerning the divine nature of the Logos, that Origen made his greatest contribution to later thought. Leaders of all schools a century later appealed to his works in order to confirm their theories. The Arians seized upon one passage in his writings in which he appeared to affirm that the Son was subordinate to the Father in order to justify their position, while Athanasius and his companions just as confidently went back to Origen and borrowed his doctrine of the eternal generation of the Son in order to make good their contention of the equality of the First and Second Persons in the Trinity.

What was Origen's real position upon the question? It is difficult to say. In all probability he had not himself worked out all of the details to his own satisfaction. Had he done so he might have expressed more heretical views than the church credits him with to-day. He was a brilliant, sparkling and highly stimulating thinker, and such men are apt to close their speculations as they begin them, with a riddle.

Origen, like Clement and the Greeks in general, believed in the freedom of the will and in the educational method of salvation. He had a keener consciousness of sin than Clement, and was much more of an ascetic, but in the main he agreed with his teacher as to the essential doctrines of the church. Like Clement, he was not interested in ecclesiology, and he was an independent in his conception of church government and authority. He was a great believer in the infallibility of the Scriptures, and carried the allegorical method of Philo to its complete and thoroughgoing conclusion. All Scripture, Origen said, is capable of three different kinds of interpretation: the historical, the ethical and the mystical. The first is simply the plain statement of the text. Some passages require no other elucidation. The second is the moral and ethical truth which lies beneath the ordinary meaning and which only the conscientious and diligent student will recognize. The third, or mystical, lies deeper still, and is revealed only to those who are genuine initiates in the more profound truths of religion. By following this threefold method of exegesis, Origen was, of course, easily able to get rid of all the moral contradictions and difficulties of the Old Testament. His emphasis upon this altogether fallacious method of interpretation became a great stumbling-block in the development of modern critical analysis. At the same time, the Alexandrian theologian saved his moral idealism by his use of allegory. He makes this fact clear by calling attention to the absurdity of taking the text at all times in its literal significance. He ridicules the conception of God walking with Adam in the Garden of Eden and says that no man with sense would think of accepting the words in their literal significance. He resolved the difficulties in the New Testament in the same way, especially the apparent contradictions in the Four Gospels. While the allegorical method is hopelessly impossible from a critical standpoint it was infinitely better than the literal acceptance of immoral attributes as pertaining to the actions of the Deity and His followers. It was better to explain away the slaughter of the Canaanites and the execution of Rizpah's children than it was to attempt to excuse them as the actions of an all-loving Father. Like Marcion, Origen was morally superior to the Latin theologians who followed him and who manifested no squeamishness about accepting the cruelties of the Almighty. Both Marcion and Origen were

Greeks, and all students of the Hellenic peoples have remarked upon their extraordinary freedom from the taint
of inhumanity which was so characteristic of both the Phœ-
nicians and the Romans. The conception of an eternal hell
of torment did not spring from the Greek mind. It appears
to have been Oriental in the first place, and it fitted readily
enough into the Roman appetite for horrors. Epicurus advocated his philosophy of atheism in order to rid his
countrymen of the nightmare caused by the fear of hell.
Obviously in his day faith in the future inferno was real
enough and was the basis of not a little exploitation by the
established order of priests. Compared with the lurid
anticipations of future damnation held by most people during his own day Epicurus felt that his promise of an eternal
sleep would bring great comfort and relief. The Jews, prior
to the Exile, knew nothing of the conception of future
torment. After they became acquainted with the Zara-
thustrian lake of fire and the Greek conceptions of the
underworld they began to formulate somewhat ghastly in-
fernos on their own account. The literature of the period
between the Old and New Testaments contains many illustrations of this tendency. The book of Enoch is a typical
example. No one knows who wrote it or when it was
written, but if Dante did not get some inspiration from its
pages he ought to have done so. The idea of burning endlessly is reiterated again and again. Miss Lily Dougall, in
her interesting volume entitled *The Lord of Thought,* has
covered this field with accuracy and insight. In the ancient
world the conception of hell arose primarily from the desire
of the under dogs to get even with their oppressors. They
could not do it in this world so they balanced things up by
consigning their tyrannical overlords to everlasting fire in
the next. When one reflects that slaves and other underlings
were crucified and tortured in every conceivable manner with-

out the slightest compunction by their masters one can appreciate the natural quality of the feeling of vengeance. In the book of Revelation the saints who have been martyred cry out to the Lord to avenge them upon their oppressors and tormentors, and the assurance is given that this will be done. The examples of Jesus forgiving the men who crucified Him, and Stephen praying for his executioners, are difficult to duplicate even in the lives of their followers. For the most part, especially in Latin theology, the idea of eternal torture for the wicked is one of the chief consolations of the righteous. The ghastly and lurid cruelties of the medieval age spring largely from this type of dogma. Men found it quite easy to burn others at the stake, to break them on the wheel, to dislocate their joints on the rack and to torture them in every other conceivable way when they thought of the eternal burning in hell which the Lord himself had authorized and was to superintend. The Spanish Inquisition arose primarily because a tender-hearted monk wanted to save the wicked from the eternal torture of perdition by tormenting them a little in this world to the end that they might abjure their heresies and be saved.

Origen and the Greek theologians in general were disinclined to believe in the doctrine of eternal torment. It was this fact which later caused the church to place the great Alexandrian upon its list of heretical Fathers. Instead of an eternal hell Origen taught the doctrine of restitution, that is, that all souls will ultimately be saved and come to a knowledge of the truth. He believed in the purgation of sins in the next world and appears to have regarded the process as necessarily painful but felt sure that it would have a happy ending and that in no case was any suffering to be undergone except in the interest of the final reformation of the sinner. The idea of endless torture without any possibility of repentance or reformation was totally foreign to his conception of the Deity. As we have already indicated, this doctrine became the accepted teaching of the church, but it was never advocated by the great theologians of Alexandria. It was the Latin line which accepted it, and it was derived from Oriental sources rather than Christian. The conception was somewhat softened during the Middle Ages by the doctrine of purgatory, but at the time of the Reformation Protestantism revived the old dogma with all its horrors. The Calvinistic hell, which was borrowed directly from Augustine, is as grotesquely lurid as anything which it is possible to conceive in this particular field. Not that it was any worse than Dante, but it was more inclusive, for the Geneva reformer, like the other Protestants, consolidated purgatory and perdition under the single heading of the latter. Doubtless the scandal over indulgences which precipitated Luther's revolt had something to do with the discarding of the Middle State, but in any case the action taken was a step backward. It was many years before Protestantism emancipated itself from "the dark shadow of Augustine" and went back to the simple New Testament teaching upon the subject. The idea that Jesus would condemn any one to eternal torture entirely without meaning or hope is, of course, unthinkable. The whole subject constitutes a dark nightmare in the history of the human race. Nevertheless, it has been scarcely half a century since Canon Farrar was dubbed a heretic because he sought to revive the teaching of Clement and Origen instead of blindly following the Latin Fathers. To-day few Christians would dispute his perspicacity. Origen has more followers than Augustine, and the world is all the better for this fact.

V

Alexandrianism in Christian theology reached the climax of its influence when, under Athanasius, it dominated the first great council of the church at Nicæa in 325 A.D. This is matter for a separate chapter and can not be discussed here. After the days of Athanasius the school became more and more spiritualistic and fanatical until the Arabs swept down in the seventh century and wiped it out of existence. Paganism and the old Greek culture had flared up in one final magnificent expression in the teachings of Plotinus and his Neo-Platonist companions. Tradition asserts that Origen and Plotinus were both students in the same school, but if this is correct there is no record of the fact in the writings of either of them. It is possible that they never met, although they had many things in common. Origen was a thoroughgoing Christian, and for the most part he was associated with the lower classes of the people, who constituted the vast majority of the followers of the Nazarene. Plotinus, on the other hand, mingled with the nobles and appears to have been on good terms with the Emperor himself. His philosophy was intended for intellectual highbrows only, and he cared nothing about the common people or their fate. He was an eclectic thinker who borrowed freely and judiciously from all the philosophers who preceded him. Much of his doctrine of divine emanations appears to have been derived from the Gnostics, although he makes no acknowledgment of the fact. Like most of the Hellenes, he appears to have despised Christianity, looking upon it as a vulgar superstition fit only for slaves and the lower classes of workmen. Naturally enough, the philosophy of Plotinus appealed to the higher classes, especially at the Roman court, and during the latter part of the third century it loomed up as the most formidable rival of the Christian teaching. There was in it much genuine religion, highly intellectualized mysticism, and many other features which are still appealing after the lapse of nearly twenty centuries. Dean Inge, in his Gifford Lectures on the *Phil-*

osophy of Plotinus has reintroduced the Alexandrian thinker to our modern age. Unquestionably, Augustine and practically all later Christian theologians drew considerable inspiration from Plotinus. He was probably the only first-rate intellect in the field of philosophy proper from Aristotle to Descartes.

Neo-Platonism, while pagan and hostile to Christianity, was saturated with the spirit of the Alexandrian theology. It taught a doctrine of salvation by reabsorption in the Deity, which resembles much of the mystical coloring of the Fourth Gospel. Likewise, in its emphasis upon the divine immanence it partakes of the thought of Clement and Origen. It is difficult to classify Plotinus, but it seems more reasonable to regard him as a pantheist than a theist. To him the whole universe was simply the overflowing of the divine nature, so that in a very true sense everything may be said to come from God and of necessity must ultimately return to Him. St. Augustine absorbed a great deal of the Neo-Platonic thought prior to his conversion, and although his transcendent Deity was very different from the pantheistic World Soul of Plotinus there are many points of resemblance between the two. The oft-quoted saying of the Bishop of Hippo, "We have come from Thee, O God, and our souls shall find no rest until we return to Thee again," seems a direct echo of the great Alexandrian. Augustine was Roman to the core and could only interpret the divine nature in terms of imperial sovereignty, but in so far as he had a Greek master that teacher was Plotinus.

There was one respect in which the Neo-Platonic philosophy found no parallel in Christian thought. This feature was its negative theory of sin and evil. There was really no place in the system of Plotinus for evil and, like other metaphysicians, he was hard put to it to explain the presence of sin in the world. Since everything which exists emanates from the Deity, if evil is real at all it must likewise come from God. It is, upon this hypothesis, only another form of good, a conclusion which the facts of life have never warranted. In the face of these difficulties Neo-Platonism simply withdrew itself from the world at large and made no attempt to deal seriously with the problem of reforming humanity. In the hands of later teachers, like Proclus, Iamblichus and Porphyry, it sought to develop a rival cult with a priesthood and other ritualistic features. Bitterly hostile to Christianity, it drew the support of all those who for one reason or another wanted to crush out the new faith, but there was no real vitality in it and in less than a century it had lost the battle. It possessed attractive features for the upper-class intellectuals, but it had no word for the great downtrodden masses of the Empire, and therefore failed in the competition. Nevertheless, it remains as one of the outstanding achievements of human thought, and it will always make an appeal to the intellectuals of every age. There is reason to believe that Plotinus influenced Hegel and, indeed, most of the absolutists of modern time. Even to-day his works are still read with much interest. A new edition of his complete writings has been announced, and it is improbable that the human race will ever forget him. It is only fair, however, to say that he was the originator of a philosophy and not the founder of a religion. It is true that he was a thoroughgoing mystic and claimed to have experienced the divine ecstasy at least two or three times, but this circumstance was not sufficient to make him a great prophet in the religious sense of the term.

Plotinus died in 269 A.D., fifteen years after the death of Origen. His last words were an epitome of his teaching: "Now the divine in me is struggling to reunite with the Divine in the All." Only half a century remained before

Constantine was to make Christianity ·the state religion of
the empire. Neo-Platonism allied itself with the old pagan
cults in a last effort to prevent the inevitable. Swinburne,
in his *Ode to Proserpine,* has interpreted with singular
beauty and truthfulness the attitude of the votaries of the
old tradition. Doubtless many a follower of Plotinus, no
less than of Zeus and of Proserpine, echoed, at least in
spirit, the famous stanza:

> Thou hast conquered, O pale Galilean;
> The world has grown gray from thy breath.
> We have drunken of things Lethean,
> And fed of the fulness of death.

Compared with the sunny, easy-going optimism of the older
religion Christianity seemed to the followers of Plotinus
like something exceedingly drab and drear. It was concerned much about death, and its Savior was pictured as a
Man of Sorrows. But the new faith had power to deal with
facts as they are, while the older cults lived only in a world
of dreams. The gray era of the Middle Ages was at hand.

VI

After Athanasius the theology of Alexandria degenerated into ascetic extravagances and mere mystical moonshine. All kinds of monastic communities grew up in the
Egyptian desert and morbid asceticism ran riot throughout
the land. Out of this situation grew such erotic and sensual
romances as found expression, among others, in the story of
Thais, which has made such an appeal to the lovers of the
footlights in our own generation. Charles Kingsley, in
Hypatia, has pictured the conflicting currents of the age.
Hypatia herself represented the final incarnation of the
spirit of Plotinus. She was opposed and eventually done to

death by the adherents of Cyril, the Bishop of Alexandria, who likewise represents the degenerate outcome of the nobler theology of Origen. Fanatical, prejudiced and superstitious as he was, Cyril foreshadowed the final decay of Alexandrian theology. As far as Greek thought was concerned the scepter had passed to the rival school of Antioch. Only a few centuries were to elapse before the Mohammedan armies were to subjugate the Eastern World and to plant the banner of Islam where the cross had ruled before. The Greek Orthodox church remained, but in Alexandria, Antioch and Constantinople it degenerated into a mere incarnation of ritual without the semblance of intellectual energy or speculative power. Such a doom was inevitable where fanaticism was substituted for reason, and magic for the ethical content of religion. One catches a clear vision of all this when one reads Kingsley's dramatic story of the death of Hypatia at the hands of the Christian mob of Alexandria:

Yes. On into the church itself! Into the cool dim shadow, with its fretted pillars, and lowering domes, and candles, and incense, and blazing altar, and great pictures looking from the walls athwart the gorgeous gloom. And right in front, above the altar, the colossal Christ, watching unmoved from off the wall, his right hand raised to give a blessing—or a curse?

On, up the nave, fresh shreds of her dress strewing the holy pavement—up the chancel steps themselves—up to the altar—right underneath the great still Christ: and there even those hell-hounds paused. . . .

She shook herself free from her tormentors, and springing back, rose for one moment to her full height, naked, snow-white against the dusky mass around—shame and indignation in those wide clear eyes, but not a stain of fear. With one hand she clasped her golden locks around her, the other long white arm was stretched upward toward the great still Christ appealing—and who dare say, in vain?—

from man to God. Her lips were opened to speak; but the words that should have come from them reached God's ear alone; for an instant Peter struck her down, the dark mass closed over her again . . . and then wail on wail, long, wild, ear-piercing, rang along the vaulted roofs, and thrilled like the trumpet of avenging angels through Philammon's ears.

Crushed against a pillar, unable to move in the dense mass, he pressed his hand over his ears. He could not shut out those shrieks! When would they end? What in the name of the God of mercy were they doing? Tearing her piecemeal? Yes, and worse than that. And still the shrieks rang on, and still the great Christ looked down on Philammon with that calm, intolerable eye, and would not turn away. And over his head was written in the rainbow, "I am the same, yesterday, today, and forever!" The same as he was in Judea of old, Philammon? Then what are these, and in whose temple? And he covered his face with his hands, and longed to die.

It was over. The shrieks had died away into moans; the moans into silence. How long had he been there? An hour, or an eternity? Thank God it was over! For her sake—but for theirs? But they thought not of that as a new cry rose through the dome.

"To the Cinaron! Burn the bones to ashes! Scatter them into the sea!" . . . And the mob poured past him again. . . .

It was only natural that the mob which tore Hypatia to pieces before the high altar of the cathedral should manifest the same insane fanaticism in every avenue of life. The fine moderation of the first great Alexandrian, Clement, with his broad and tolerant approach to every form of human endeavor, had been buried past the hope of resurrection. The morbid asceticism which we find foreshadowed in the life of Origen grew to full fruition in the days of Cyril. Men were concerned with abstruse theological subtleties and withdrew into the desert to mortify the flesh and to seek for celestial visions to compensate them

for the earthly joys which they cast aside. The monks became mystics and dreamed strange visions which the common folk were wont to accept as the very voice of God.
The vague heresy of the old monk Eutyches found special
favor with the later Alexandrians because it fitted in well
with the fabric of their dreams. In the technical language
of the schools, this belief is called by a long Greek word,
Monophysitism, and means literally the doctrine of one
soul. As we shall see later, it referred to the teaching that
Christ did not possess a human soul but was simply the
Divine Logos inhabiting a human body. He thus was removed from the circle of ordinary humanity and came to
be regarded as a being so divine that he could not be
worshiped without recourse to some human mediator like
the Virgin Mary or one of the saints. While the church
condemned this view it nevertheless persisted for centuries.
It is only in modern times that Christ has regained His
humanity and is once more thought of as an historical personage. During the Middle Ages He was "Very God," as
the old creed put it, but in no real sense did He partake
of our common humanity.

The morbid asceticism of the Egyptian monks was
matched by similar performances in other parts of the
Christian world. Whether we are to attach credence to the
theory of Professor James H. Leuba, in his *Psychology of
Religious Mysticism,* or not, there can be no doubt that the
monastic life fostered many mental delusions. Professor
Leuba, it will be recalled, holds that all of the phenomena
of mysticism can be explained on the basis of misdirected or
thwarted sexual desire. We do not think that he has made
his case, but he has accumulated enough evidence to prove
that a great many of the visions of monasticism arose from
this source. When one adds the fasting, scourging and other
forms of self-torture which were parts of the ascetic routine

one can realize that this sort of physical basis might easily give rise to every species of mental hallucination. In any event, Alexandrianism, under the successors of Cyril, represented a far cry from the noble intellectual idealism of Clement and Origen. Between the times of the two schools, however, we must deal with the high tide of Greek theology in the person of Athanasius.

CHAPTER V

ATHANASIUS

FOR more than a thousand years the name of Athanasius has remained the symbol of orthodoxy in Christian theology. Along with Augustine and Aquinas, he helps to constitute the great trinity of dogmatic thinkers down to the period of the Reformation. It seems a little strange that all three of these illustrious dignitaries should be honored with names beginning with the first letter of the alphabet. In this respect they are by no means alone. At least three more figures of first-rate importance in the history of speculation share the same peculiarity. The men to whom we refer are Anselm, Abelard and Arminius. Each of these is entitled to a chapter in this book, and there are others belonging to the same noble family which space considerations will not permit us to discuss.

I

In order to understand the life and work of Athanasius it is necessary for us to have a clear conception of the circumstances under which Christianity was proclaimed in the different sections of the Roman world. The first adherents of the new faith were, of course, Jews, and as we have already indicated under the chapter on Marcion, these believed in Jehovah as the one God of all the earth. They thought of Jesus as the Messiah, or the Son of God, but never conceived of Him as taking the place of Jehovah. The simple, primitive monotheism of Israel passed over

113

without a break into the thought of Jewish Christianity.
While this was true of the Hebrew Christians it did not at
all represent the position of the Gentiles. The latter had
never been Jews and knew nothing about any allegiance to
Jehovah. Prior to becoming Christians they had worshiped
Zeus, or Apollo, or Artemis, or perhaps all of them put
together, but the strange God of the Jews was entirely
foreign to them. They listened to the preaching of Paul
and other Christian evangelists and were glad to exchange
their old Deities for a new God who was called Jesus Christ.
They accepted Him and His way of life and based their
hopes of immortality upon the story of His resurrection.
They had no difficulty about receiving Him as God, since
their previous religious background made such a theological
attitude quite simple and natural. So long as they did not
come into close relationship with Jewish Christians it was
possible to maintain an amicable attitude. Sooner or later,
however, it was inevitable that the two points of view should
conflict. The first battle occurred when the Jewish influence
routed the Gnostics; the second when the more moderate
Greek party routed the Arians. It is this latter performance which must occupy our attention in the present chapter.

The Trinitarian idea of the Deity is very old. We find
it in ancient Egypt, in India, in Greece, and in nearly every
other mythology under the sun. It is true that the trinities
are not all alike and that most of them have but little resemblance to the doctrine formulated by Athanasius. In
Egypt, for example, the Trinity of Osiris, Isis and Horus
represented the natural family group of father, mother and
child. In India Brahma is the creator, Vishnu the pre-
server, and Siva the destroyer. Sundry triads among other
peoples reflected similar conceptions. As far as we can see,
there is no relationship between these traditions and the
highly wrought, metaphysical speculations of Nicæa. The

practical problem with which Athanasius had to deal, as Professor McGiffert has shown in his volume entitled *The God of the Early Christians,* was how to weld the Jewish and Gentile conceptions of the divine nature into one unitary and harmonious doctrine. It should be remembered that Christians of all classes were monotheists. They believed in one God, but unfortunately he was not always the same God. The Jews accepted Jehovah; the Greeks accepted Jesus. Both agreed that there could be only one Deity. To reconcile these opposing views became the task of the Council of Nicæa.

II

The controversy came to a head during the first quarter of the fourth century. Arius, a presbyter of North Africa, had been educated in the school of Lucian at Antioch and had there imbibed views which combined the traditional monotheism of the Jews with the metaphysical ideas of Aristotle. The heretical Bishop, Paul of Samosata, had originated the position held by Lucian and later by Arius, and had taught long before the doctrine of subordination which the Arian apostles borrowed from Origen. According to this cult, the Son is the Logos or Eternal Wisdom of the Father but was created by Him and is in no correct sense to be described as of the same essence or substance. In the forthright language of Athanasius, Arius declared that there was a time when the Son was not, that is, a time when the Father alone existed. The Son, therefore, was not God in the same sense as the Father. It was not difficult for Arius to cite Scriptural passages in support of his position. The fact is, that it represented the fairly consistent tradition of Jewish Christianity. If the Apostle Peter could have come back to earth at the beginning of the fourth century it is probable that, if he had understood the controversy at all, he would have been an Arian. Moreover, it is not improbable that even Paul himself might have been ranged on the side of the arch-heretic. Paul's views upon the question are not exactly clear, but he was a Jew and no Jew ever thought of there being any God, in the true sense of that word, except Jehovah. The terms of the first commandment were dinned into the ears of every child of Israel from the time of his infancy, and he never forgot them nor did he ever presume to compromise with them.

Arius came into conflict with Alexander, the Bishop of Alexandria, during the second decade of the fourth century, and as a result of the Bishop's orders he was excommunicated and driven out of Egypt. He fled to Cæsarea, where he was received kindly by Eusebius, the Bishop, who later became the author of the first Church History and who had been educated in the school of Lucian at Antioch. The African heretic found a still warmer friend and supporter in another Eusebius who was at this time a Bishop of Nicomedia in Asia Minor and who likewise had been a classmate and fellow-student in the school of Lucian. This Eusebius took up the cudgels in behalf of Arius and the two addressed letters to many bishops, with the result that a very considerable party accepted the views of the new teacher. Alexander wrote letters also, some of them decidedly intemperate in tone. In one of the few which have survived the ravages of time he styles Arius a murderer of the divinity of Christ, a villain worse even than Judas, and sundry other things which it is not necessary to detail here. Judging from the tone of his correspondence he must have been somewhat excited when he wrote. It was not long before the whole Eastern World was aflame with the contention. Clergy and laity alike began to take sides, and it became obvious that the unity of the church was seriously threatened.

In the meantime, Constantine the Great had defeated Lucinius and had become the sole Emperor of Rome. From the day that he had seen the cross in the heavens with the words beneath, "In this sign shalt thou conquer," he had made up his mind to accept the Christian religion. Although he was not baptized until shortly before his death he considered himself a Christian throughout his reign, and his chief counselor and adviser was Hosius, the old Bishop of Cordova in Spain. Many historians have inferred that Constantine became a Christian solely from considerations of state policy. They tell us that he was anxious for some unifying force which could be used to bind his discordant empire together; that he recognized the value of Christianity in this connection, and that this consideration was the dominant motive in his conversion. Whether this criticism is just or not, the fact remains that when the Roman Emperor became sole monarch in 323 A.D. he was much distressed because of the threatened schism between Alexander and Arius. The spiritual force which he counted upon as the means of unifying his empire was itself in danger of being rent into fragments. The situation irritated him, especially in view of the fact that, like Mr. Wells after him, he could not understand what all the fuss was about. He dispatched a letter to the two contesting parties and sent it to Alexander by the hands of Hosius. It is a thoroughly human document and gives us a tolerably fair insight into the way in which the Emperor's mind worked. He says, in substance, that the whole contest is over unimportant matters and that it should at once be abandoned. Nobody can understand the terms in dispute and probably if they could understand them they would be no better off. The thing for both Alexander and Arius to do is to shake hands and make up.

It has never been quite clear whether Hosius really tried

to reconcile the two contestants on any sort of impartial basis. For some reason he seems to have espoused the cause of Alexander from the start, and it is not likely that Arius received much consideration from him. Possibly he felt that in matters of this kind bishops ought to stand together. Possibly his Gentile sympathies were with the Greek party as opposed to the Jewish. Possibly there were personal considerations involved which have not come down to us in the record. Whatever the solution may be, the outcome of his mission was not in doubt. He returned to Rome and reported to Constantine that it was impossible to reconcile the parties. The Emperor asked his advice, and the Bishop recommended the calling of a general council of all the ecclesiastical dignitaries in the Empire in order to decide whether Arius or Alexander should triumph. The Emperor wanted peace at any price. He acquiesced in the suggestion and in a short time couriers were dispatched throughout the Empire, notifying all the bishops that there would be a general council at the small town of Nicæa, near Nicomedia, in Asia Minor, and that the imperial court would pay the expenses of all who would attend the meeting. The time was fixed for the early summer of 325 A.D.

III

Out of the eighteen hundred or more bishops who were urged to attend the council less than a fourth were interested enough to take the trip. Of these by far the greater proportion came from the East. The western dioceses appear to have taken no interest whatever in the matter. Less than two per cent. of their full representation put in an appearance when the council was called to order, and not all of these stayed until the close. The old Bishop of Rome refused to undertake the journey but sent two presbyters to fill his place. Notwithstanding this fact the Latins unanimously accepted the dogmas formulated at Nicæa without the slightest pretense of rebellion. They have always been orthodox Trinitarians but have never attempted to throw any light of their own upon the doctrine.

Nicæa is located just across the Hellespont from Constantinople. It was hot when the council began its sessions in June, and the weather did not become any cooler in July and August. The Emperor himself, sitting on a golden throne, formally opened the council. The debate began at once and continued for many weeks. There were three parties: the extreme left wing, championed by Arius and by the Bishop of the district where the assembly was being held, Eusebius of Nicomedia; the extreme right wing, led by Athanasius and Alexander, the Bishop of Alexandria; and the center, led for the most part by Eusebius, the Bishop of Cæsarea, who later wrote up the story of the proceedings in his Church History. At the beginning, the majority of those present belonged to the middle group, but the turmoil which ensued led to a tightening of party lines and eventually the right wing secured the victory. The watchword of Athanasius was a Greek term which meant "of the same substance." The slogan of the center was another word which meant "of like substance." The Arians were disposed to accept the center position, provided they could not do any better, but the right wing stood firm and refused to abate a jot of its contentions. The two watchwords were exactly alike with the exception of an *iota,* the smallest letter in the alphabet, which separated them. Gibbon has made merry about raising so much pother over an *iota,* but his sarcasm is beside the point. The insertion of a very small letter in a word may radically change its meaning— and so it was in the present instance. The skeptics, from Constantine to Mr. Wells, have been wrong about the insignificance of the issue. There was a great underlying principle involved, as the succeeding history of the church has fully demonstrated.

The burden of the debate in behalf of the orthodox conservatives fell upon Athanasius. He is described at this time as a rather slight figure with a bullet-shaped head, black hair and eyes, an olive complexion, and with a remarkably keen and expressive countenance. Arius was tall and rather handsome in his own way, although apparently much older than his antagonist. There was considerable excitement during the discussion, and some of the orthodox party stuffed their fingers in their ears whenever Arius arose to speak in order that their minds might not be polluted by listening to his blasphemous arguments. Occasionally the proceedings threatened to develop into a free-for-all prize-fight, but the presiding officer, fortunately, averted this scandal. Constantine grew tired of the interminable discussion and turned over the gavel to Hosius. Not being accustomed to the jargon of the schools it was no wonder that the Emperor failed to see the point. After many weeks had passed in debate he instructed his spokesman that it was time for the contestants to get together. As usual, he did not care what the basis of unity might be just so that some basis could be secured. Hosius busied himself about the matter but found it difficult to handle. At first he tried to work out a compromise, under the leadership of Eusebius of Cæsarea, but Athanasius stood firm so the only option left was to declare in his favor. This was accordingly done, and under the pressure of the imperial ban the bishops were won over from the party of opposition until, with one notable exception, Eusebius of Nicomedia, the original supporter of Arius, the decision was unanimous. The first ecumenical creed in the history of Christendom was formulated and was put forth as the only standard of faith for the use of the churches. Constantine was delighted with the outcome. He had at last brought the wrangling church-men together, and he felt quite competent to enforce unity now that he had a definite basis upon which to act. He banished Arians right and left and let it be understood that the Nicene Creed must be everywhere respected. At the same time, he disclosed his personal indifference to the issues involved by protecting Arius himself and by showing favors to the followers of the heretic as long as they were willing to yield outward conformity. The fact is that Constantine never had the slightest conception of what the creed was about, in which respect he differed but slightly from millions of other people who have lived since his time. It is not improbable that a great many of the bishops who signed the document were in the same predicament, and yet we are assured that whatever it may mean it is the Christian faith without the acceptance of which we must be infallibly damned.

IV

What is the real meaning of the Athanasian formula? In reading the bulky pages of the ante-Nicene Fathers we find the works of Athanasius peculiarly difficult to elucidate. He actually appears to be trying to formulate a rational interpretation of the Trinity, but one is never able to get hold of it clearly. Later experience proved, of course, that the attempt was impossible. Any reasonable explanation of the Trinity is and always has been heresy. The orthodox view and the only orthodox one is that the relationship is beyond reason and must therefore be relegated to the realm of mystery. The Athanasian Creed, which was formulated later just in order to explain more fully the orthodox mean-ing of Nicæa, makes this fact perfectly clear. Take, for example, a few citations from this ancient document, which still appears in the Anglican prayer-book as one of the three ecumenical symbols of the church:

Whosoever will be saved: before all things it is necessary that he hold the Catholic Faith:

Which Faith except every one do keep whole and undefiled: without doubt he shall perish everlastingly.

And the Catholic Faith is this: That we worship one God in Trinity, and Trinity in Unity;

Neither confounding the Persons: nor dividing the Substance (Essence).

For there is one Person of the Father: another of the Son: and another of the Holy Ghost.

But the Godhead of the Father, of the Son, and of the Holy Ghost, is all one: the Glory equal, the Majesty coeternal.

Such as the Father is: such is the Son: and such is the Holy Ghost.

The Father uncreate (uncreated): the Son uncreate (uncreated): and the Holy Ghost uncreate (uncreated).

The Father incomprehensible (unlimited): the Son incomprehensible (unlimited): and the Holy Ghost incomprehensible (unlimited, or infinite).

The Father eternal: the Son eternal: and the Holy Ghost eternal.

And yet they are not three eternals: but one eternal.

As also there are not three uncreated: nor three incomprehensibles (infinites), but one uncreated: and one incomprehensible (infinite).

. . . . .

He therefore that will be saved, must (let him) thus think of the Trinity.

One is tempted to suggest, after reading this ancient and hoary document that its authors might have added a fourth incomprehensible, to wit, the creed itself. Nevertheless, the Athanasian formula, which was written somewhere from four hundred to eight hundred A.D. and of course had no direct relation to Athanasius himself, does correctly interpret the orthodox doctrine of the Trinity.

It is the very essence of the dogma that it can not be made rational. To assert that three are one, in the absolute sense of both words, is obviously a contradiction in thought. It is just like speaking of a triangle with two of its angles right angles, or the old jest about an irresistible force meeting an immovable body. Such statements can not be considered seriously in the realm of science since they involve essential contradictions. They may serve as the basis of pleasantries, but even in this case it is their very absurdity which makes them useful. No one would think of suggesting them for any other purpose.

In the history of dogma the situation is altogether different. There, as the Athanasian Creed witnesses, logical contradiction is made the center of orthodoxy. Irrationality constitutes the very heart of faith. On the basis of the common reason we know that one simply can not be three nor three one, if we are to use the words without juggling their meaning. Nevertheless, we are instructed under penalty of damnation that we *must* believe that this contradictory thing is true, and that, in fact, it constitutes the most important consideration in determining our salvation. It is not much wonder that modern science has occasionally felt a disposition to quarrel with theology. If any botanist or chemist were to introduce the Athanasian principle into his science he would speedily be relegated to a madhouse. Of course, the theologian can justly claim that his discipline deals with far more lofty themes than those which engross the attention of the ordinary scientific workman. Even conceding this superiority, the latter may be pardoned for showing some measure of indifference to the more exalted methods of investigation employed by the purveyor of the higher mysteries.

The utility of the principle embodied in the orthodox conception of the Trinity can not be disputed. No teaching could have been more valuable from the standpoint of ecclesiastical authority. Let it be once conceded that the doctrines of the church may be full of contradictions and nevertheless the embodiment of divine truth, that the basis of faith may be hostile to reason and still essential to religion, that, in a single word, the dogmas of the church are absolutely immune to intelligent criticism, and any ecclesiasticism which can hold its membership to these principles is securely intrenched in its position. No matter how false or ridiculous or absurd may be its pretensions it can always take refuge behind the Mystery of the sacred Trinity. Having disarmed all rational criticism it is at liberty to go any length it may please without the fear of rebellion. It was no wonder that the church took kindly to such a useful bit of armor. As we have already observed, there is at least a strong probability that Athanasius himself desired to rationalize the doctrine, and certainly many efforts were made in this direction by others. All such attempts were of necessity heretical, since they were set to overthrow the very thing which gave the dogma its value, that is to say, the Mystery. With the latter to help them the ecclesiastical authorities felt free to go ahead and formulate other useful dogmas and regulations without the fear of meddling on the part of outside critics.

It was thus that the gates were opened to many Mysteries. First came the person of Christ, with which we shall deal in the next chapter, then the sacrifice of the mass, and last of all, the crowning Mystery of transubstantiation. In every case, reason is politely relegated to the rear and is requested to withdraw in the presence of the Incomprehensible. During the period of scholasticism a nice adjustment between the preserves where reason could roam at large and the domain of the church, where Mysteries hold sway, was worked out with much care by subtle minds like those of Saint Thomas and his companions. Even these loyal sons of the church found difficulty in drawing the exact line of demarcation, but they were all quite sure that such a boundary exists. The ecclesiastical authorities could not afford to throw over reason entirely. There were times when it could be made a very useful servant. The important thing was to prevent its intruding upon the field where their own authority would otherwise rule supreme. Hence the elaborately wrought systems of Bonaventura and Aquinas, which are still the pride of the church that gave them birth.

V

The triumph of the Mystery interpretation of the Trinity was not achieved without a struggle. It is perhaps impossible to ascertain how many efforts were made to rationalize the doctrine, but judging from the testimony of Eusebius and others there must have been some scores of them. All of these gained adherents but were ultimately suppressed by the iron heel of orthodoxy. Perhaps the most significant attempt was that of Sabellius, who lived in the third century and whose influence appears to have been very considerable, although being a heretic none of his works has come down to us. Tradition avers that he was a Lybian by birth and spent some time in Rome, but the details of his biography which we possess are scanty indeed. He asserted that the Mystery of the Trinity was to be interpreted through the conception of a unitary substance with a trinity of manifestation. In other words, there is but one God, but He is manifested to humanity through three forms or modes. At one time he is the Father, at another time the Son, and at still another the Holy Spirit. This position was certainly logical enough, but was speedily shot full of holes by the orthodox champions. Inasmuch as the theory involved the idea that the Deity perished by crucifixion its advocates were frequently called Patripassians. It was not difficult for keen logicians like Tertullian to call attention to the absurdity of expressions like those of Jesus upon the cross, "My God, my God, why hast thou forsaken me?" when he himself was, according to the theory, the God to whom he prayed. Sabellianism was especially disliked by the Arians, and they made a point of calling attention to the logical superiority of their own theory. The Athanasian party, likewise, attacked it but the simplicity of the doctrine attracted many adherents until the Council of Nicæa definitely placed it under the ban. Nevertheless, it has frequently appeared in various disguises throughout the later history of the church. Many a modern curate, in his efforts to rationalize the dogma of the Trinity, without being conscious of the fact has made use of the simple formula of Sabellius. Perhaps most people who try to think of the Trinity at all visualize the subject from the standpoint of the old Lybian heretic. The Greek Christians were attracted to it when it was first proclaimed because it did give vital expression to their belief in the Deity of Christ. When Athanasius formulated the orthodox doctrine these men went over to him because they found the same dogma expressed in his interpretation without many of the objections which were inherent in Sabellianism.

It should always be kept in mind that the real purpose of Athanasius was to safeguard the essential Deity of Jesus. To concede that the founder of the Christian faith was nothing more than a man, or, as Arius asserted, a demi-God, was to destroy his authority and ultimately to eliminate him as the central figure of the faith. Unless Jesus really was "Very God," as the terms of the creed put it, He was shorn of His power as one who could save unto the uttermost. Athanasius was right in his refusal to give up this central fact in his religion. Had Arianism triumphed Christianity would have become only another form of Judaism or Mohammedanism. Orthodoxy has its faults, but it at least preserved the essential authority of Jesus unimpaired. It may be doubted whether the ethical implications of this conception were even partly grasped for centuries, but to-day we can recognize their value. Perhaps most Christians during these early years thought of their formula in the somewhat amusing terms of Gwatkin: "Sooner or later every Arian nation had to purge itself of heresy or vanish from the earth. Even the distant Visigoths were forced to see that Arians could not hold Spain. . . . Of continental Teutons the Franks alone escaped the plague of Arianism. It was in the strength of orthodoxy that they drove the conquerors of Rome before them on the field of Vouglé, and brought the green standard of the Prophet to a halt upon the Loire." Perhaps Richard the Lion-Hearted and the other crusaders thought the same thing when they chased their Mohammedan enemies from the field. Unfortunately, the God of battles did not always decide in favor of orthodoxy. More than once the Arian Moslems triumphed over their Christian foes. Especially was this true when, after many vicissitudes, Mohammed II planted the banner of the crescent upon the walls of Constantinople, where it has remained practically without interruption until the present hour.

To the modern mind the truth which Athanasius sought to conserve might have been safeguarded without recourse to the logical contradictions of the orthodox dogma. It was not necessary to assert that Jesus exhausted the total meaning of the Deity in order to give Him a position of absolute authority. All that was needed was simply to take Him at His own word. He never proclaimed that He was co-substantial with the Father, but rather that He embodied a true and perfect revelation of the divine nature. In other words, He represented all that men can know and understand of the nature and will of God. That there is much in the Divine Being which goes far beyond the reaches of human thought every intelligent student must concede. Jesus is Very God as far as He goes, but He does not exhaust the meaning of omnipotence. Some such truth as this, a truth essential to the very being of Christianity, was doubtless inherent in the thought and purpose of Athanasius. We may readily concede that the metaphysical atmosphere of his age required some formulation like the Nicene symbol. The men of the fourth century delighted in philosophical subtleties and in theological hair-splitting. In our modern age, with its marvelous scientific and mechanical development, the old scholastic jargon seems strangely out of place. The authority of Jesus as the highest revelation of God, as the one who is the Way, the Truth and the Life, as the one who furnishes the only solution of the great mysteries of birth and death, is still eagerly accepted and cherished. The orthodox formula is out of step with the demands and needs of a scientific age. The truth which it sought to enshrine is still needed, but it must be separated from the husks of outworn speculation in order to live. Lazarus must unwrap his grave clothes and come forth. The thought of the twentieth century can not remain forever enchained by the speculative forms originated by theologians of the fourth.

Even before Athanasius had passed from earth the center of interest in theology had shifted from the Mystery of the Trinity to that of the person of Christ. How Jesus could be completely divine and completely human at the same time was a problem which presented as many difficulties in its own way as the Trinitarian dogma itself. In the next chapter we shall discuss more in detail the implications involved in this statement.

VI

The Council of Nicæa was called for the purpose of establishing unity in the church. Hosius had suggested that the will of the bishops as expressed in a world council might well be regarded as the voice of the Holy Spirit upon the question under discussion. Constantine apparently shared his opinion. When the Nicene formula was put forth the Emperor expected universal acquiescence in its pronouncements. He used the power of the empire to secure acceptance of the creed. Bishops who ventured to express dissent were threatened with loss of position, and if they persisted in their attitude they were deposed from their sees. At the same time, the royal guardian of the church took pains to show that he had no inherent prejudice against Arianism. He befriended Arius himself and restrained any disposition on the part of the authorities to inflict unnecessary punishment upon the heretics.

After the death of Constantine, in spite of the Nicene formulary, Arianism raised its head again and again. Not infrequently it invaded the imperial court and controlled the destinies of the empire. Upon occasions of this kind Athanasius was banished from Alexandria and was forced to retire into the desert until a new emperor took the helm of state. The fluctuations involved in this seesaw program of the court continued throughout the fourth century. During one of the most reactionary periods Arius was brought back in great pomp, and under the pressure of the Emperor the church was compelled to cancel his excommunication and to receive him again into its membership. Great preparations were made for the occasion, although the orthodox communicants who could not look upon the ceremony as anything short of sacrilege gnashed their teeth with rage and despair. At the last moment destiny interfered to prevent so great a disgrace. The ancient heretic, for he was now eighty years of age, the night before his formal induction was seized with violent hemorrhages and died within a few hours. Gibbon, in reviewing the circumstances attending his demise, asserts that only two hypotheses are adequate to explain the situation. The two from which he says one must make a choice are miracle and poison. The contemporaries did not hesitate between these alternatives. The orthodox party everywhere asserted that the Lord had personally intervened to prevent His church from being signally disgraced. They recalled how Judas had perished and were not slow to draw a parallel between the physical circumstances which attended the death of the heretic and those which Luke refers to as having been present at the death of Judas. Such gentle amenities have not infrequently given color to the theological combats of the centuries.

In the end the Nicene formula triumphed. The great Emperor Theodosius called a new council to meet at Constantinople in 381 A.D., and the final formulation of the Trinitarian position dates from this event. The creed which we usually denominate the Nicene was not drawn up until after the adjournment of the Council of Constantinople. It was once believed that it emanated from the ecumenical gathering itself, but later research has shown it was formulated after the council had closed its sessions, and appears to have been the work, at least in large measure, of Cyril of Jerusalem, who had been the dominating figure in the council. The additions contained in the Constantinopolitan statement deal chiefly with the nature and work of the Third Person of the Trinity. The creed of 325 A. D. had closed with the ambiguous expression, "I believe in the Holy Spirit." These words were susceptible of different interpretations, and many diverse conclusions were drawn from them. Macedonius, the Bishop of Constantinople, asserted that the Third Person was not co-substantial with the First and the Second, and for this reason the party in the church which denied the Deity of the Holy Spirit was styled the Macedonian. Athanasius and his followers took the position that the Third Person was on an equality with the First and the Second in the Holy Trinity. This interpretation was indeed inherent in the orthodox theology from the beginning, but it had not been made explicit at Nicæa. There had been such long and bitter discussion over the Second Person that Athanasius and his associates did not regard it as wise to introduce another problem into the conflict. It was for this reason that the matter was left unsettled and ambiguous.

The ultimate triumph of orthodoxy was not entirely due to the intellectual and moral vigor of Athanasius. During the latter part of the fourth century his efforts were ably seconded by three men who constitute what is known as the Cappadocian school in the history of theology. These three men were Gregory Nazianzus, Gregory of Nyssa and Basil. Of the three, the second named was the greatest theologian, while the other two were better known for their gifts as orators and as ecclesiastical statesmen. All three of these eminent churchmen held stoutly to the orthodox Nicene doctrine and opposed the Arian position to such an extent that they were accused by their enemies of tritheism, that is, of a belief in three gods instead of one. This they of course denied, insisting upon their adherence to the unity of the Godhead. The Cappadocians, and especially Gregory of Nyssa, were among the first to formulate the view of the atonement which looks upon the death of Christ as a ransom paid to Satan for the salvation of mankind. This view became exceedingly popular and held the field in orthodox circles until the time of Anselm. Although the Nicene Creed had expressly declared that the Deity was the maker of all things visible and invisible practically none of its adherents was willing to eliminate Satan from the horizon of religion. Just why the Lord should have created the devil and later have paid him a ransom by sacrificing His own Son was never fully clarified by the dispensers of the Mysteries. This oversight, it is true, was not entirely unique in the history of thought.

Gregory's explanation of the atonement seems somewhat naïve at the present time but appears fully to have met the intellectual and spiritual needs of his day. Satan, he tells us, had enslaved the whole human race through the fall of Adam and it was necessary that a ransom should be paid in order that mankind might once again be set free. These terms meant much more in an age when slavery was a universal institution than they can possibly mean to us. The word "redeemer" itself is derived from the Latin and means literally one who buys back in the slave markets an individual who thus secures his freedom. The devil, as the Cappadocian theologian expresses it, had made the whole human race his slaves. Christ went into the market and by His death on the cross purchased freedom for humanity. The whole transaction seemed perfectly intelligible to slave owners and bondsmen alike during the period of the later Roman empire.

It was reserved for another Gregory, the great Bishop of Rome who lived two hundred years later, to suggest that Satan had been cheated in the bargain made in the atonement. He had anticipated that Jesus would remain his subject after He had been put to death on the cross, but when his victim rose from the dead he lost his prey. In this way, by a process of clever dealing, the arch-enemy of mankind was entirely outwitted and was presumed to have given way to despair. The somewhat primitive ethics of the period considered it no sin whatever to cheat the devil, and it added a spice of humor to the somber coloring of the faith when the priests who proclaimed the new evangel to the northern barbarians enlarged upon this aspect of their message.

The Council of Constantinople was attended by only one-half the number of bishops who were enrolled at Nicæa. Those who were present were all from the Orient, not a single Western representative considering it worth while to make the trip to the imperial city. Nevertheless, its formulations were termed ecumenical, that is, universal, and have been so accepted by the church until the present time. Advocates of the historical creeds are accustomed to style the Nicene-Constantinopolitan, which is the one used in all modern churches under the name of the Nicene, as ecumenical. The truth is that it was not formulated by the council at all but as we have seen was put forth after the assembly had adjourned and therefore possessed no official standing. Had it been the product of the council it would have embodied the collective wisdom of less than a tenth of the higher representatives of the church. Nevertheless, we are told that this ancient symbol is the only correct and infallible statement of the essential faith of Christendom. Moreover, the Eastern and Western churches are not even agreed upon the text of the document. The Western formula states explicitly that the Holy Spirit proceeds from the Father and the Son, while the Eastern text affirms that He proceeds from the Father alone. Nobody has ever explained precisely what is comprehended in the idea of "procession," and it is difficult to see what important considerations are involved in the rival statements. Notwithstanding this fact, the Greek Orthodox churches separated from the church of Rome on account of this distinction and remain apart until the present hour.

Athanasius, in thought and life, embodies the climax of Alexandrianism. His name became the symbol of orthodoxy throughout the centuries which followed and was not inappropriately attached to the last of the three ecumenical symbols. As the sponsor of orthodox Trinitarianism he has achieved undying fame. Without possessing the penetrating intellect of Origen he was able in a time of crisis to stamp his name and his fame indelibly upon the church. No taint of heresy has ever been attached to him. He remains embalmed in the odor of sanctity wherever Nicene Christianity is revered. A man of force and clearness of vision, he possessed rather unusual executive abilities and was consequently greater as a bishop than as a theologian. He was tolerant and kindly in his attitude toward others, and his biographers never weary in emphasizing his personal charm. No breath of scandal attaches to his name. From birth to death he was wedded to the church. It is therefore fitting and proper that the church should honor him as one of the most saintly of all its heroes, and one of the most heroic of all its saints.

CHAPTER VI

THEODORE

THEODORE is the most modern of all the ancient theologians. In reading the pages of this fifth-century scholar one is impressed again and again by the freshness and permanence of his point of view. Like his master, Aristotle, he anticipated the theory of evolution centuries before Darwin, and modern historical criticism has not greatly improved upon his standards of exegesis. Of course, he was dubbed a heretic by the ecclesiastical nobodies who followed him, but this fact no longer detracts from his fame. As the years pass on his reputation grows, and it is safe to say that it has not yet reached its zenith. There is a human touch about him which appeals to the modern mind. One of the old chroniclers tells us that when a youth he was much in love with a beautiful damsel who lived near his own home. He had determined to give his life to the church, and inasmuch as the two objects of his affection could not be reconciled according to the ecclesiastical rules of the day he was at last constrained to bury the romance of his earlier years. Unlike Augustine, no suspicion of scandal attaches to the brief idyl of Theodore. His was a gentle life, straightforward, clear and limpid as the sparkling streams of Hellas. The volcanic eruptions which rent the soul of the tempestuous Bishop of Hippo found no place in the stately decorum of his Greek contemporary. From first to last he embodied the Aristotelian conception of virtue as the Golden Mean. His life was harmonious and

135

his teaching scientific and clear. If it were possible for him to be reincarnated for the benefit of our modern age we can imagine him lecturing with brilliancy and power before the students of our own universities. He would scarcely need to revise his teaching to meet the requirements of our time. Assuredly this almost magically prophetic power is the supreme test of genius and skill.

I

The school of Antioch, to which Theodore of Mopsuestia belonged, was the great rival of Alexandria in the field of early theology. The New Testament itself tells the story of the founding of this early Christian community, and informs us that the followers of Jesus were first called Christians at Antioch. The inhabitants of the city were especially given to satire, and some commentators have thought that the title, like so many other religious appellations, was attached to its followers in derision. Whether or not this view is correct the name speedily became universal and has remained so throughout the centuries.

Antioch was founded by Seleucus, one of the four captains of Alexander the Great who divided his Empire after his death. It was situated on the river Orontes in the most beautiful section of Syria, and soon became one of the very cultured and populous cities of the ancient world. It was especially famous for the architectural beauty of its buildings and for the luxurious coloring of its surroundings. One or more of its suburban groves achieved fame throughout the length and breadth of the Roman world. The citizens of Antioch were fickle, pleasure-loving, and at times disposed to be cynical, but the general level of intelligence was probably higher than in any other city of the ancient world with the possible exception of Athens. They did 'not hesitate to hurl shafts of ridicule at the Roman Emperors who visited them, and it is said that they owed their final destruction to the fact that they attempted to exercise this ancient prerogative upon one of their conquerors who was unable to see the point of the joke and reduced the city to ashes in consequence.

It was characteristic of the practical temper of Antioch that the idol of its schools was the Greek philosopher, Aristotle. Just as Alexandria erected a shrine to Plato so Antioch burned incense to his great successor. The distinction between the two masters of Hellenic thought was emphasized in the habits of mind of their worshipers. The Alexandrians were poetical, dreamy, mystical idealists, while their rivals were witty, practical, scientific realists. This distinction which obtained in all the activities of life was especially noticeable in the field of theology. The great masters of Alexandria—Clement, Origen, Athanasius, Cyril—were all highly speculative and mystical in their interpretation of doctrine. The great masters of Antioch—Diodorus, John Chrysostom and Theodore—were all practical men, scientific in temper, and would be classed today as intellectualists rather than mystics. Without being willing to break with orthodoxy they rationalized its irrationalities as far as the human intellect could achieve such a result. In consequence they were not infrequently accused of heresy, and Theodore, the greatest of them all, was finally placed under the ban.

Long before the time of the Antiochene thinkers the city had become suspect in orthodox Christian circles. Arius, the arch-heretic, as we have already seen, secured his schooling at Antioch, and his chief supporters were also products of the same intellectual environment. Lucian, the teacher of Arius, was generally regarded as hostile to the true faith, and his martyrdom, in the minds of many contemporaries, scarcely atoned for his heresy. Before his time the great Bishop, Paul of Samosata, had openly proclaimed views concerning the humanity of Jesus which scandalized the true defenders of the faith. People were apt to say that the evil taint which was present in the teaching of Paul passed from him to Lucian and from Lucian to Arius and his successors. It was no wonder that this ancient stigma was revived and applied to Theodore and his companions who lived a century later than Arius.

II

After the final word concerning the place of the Third Person in the Trinity had been written in the Nicene-Constantinopolitan Creed of 381 A.D. the chief interest in theology centered around the discussion of the person of Christ. The creed affirmed that He was "very God of very God, of one substance with the Father," and in all respects identical with Deity. At the same time it likewise affirmed that He was born of the Virgin Mary and that He was as truly human in this aspect of His nature as He was divine in the other. How could the two conceptions be regarded without negating each other? Humanity and Deity are dissimilar terms. The one apparently excludes the other. It is quite easy to see how Jesus could have been perfectly divine or perfectly human, but it is not easy to see how He could possess both characteristics at the same time. The skilful dialecticians who were estopped from further speculation by the final declaration of the Mystery of the Trinity found a no less fertile field for their ingenuity in the equally baffling problem of the person of Christ.

This second enigma of the ancient theology occupied the special attention of the school of Antioch. The four most distinguished members of this school, Diodorus,

Theodore of Mopsuestia, John Chrysostom, and Theodoret, all discuss the person of Christ at greater length than any other theme in theology. In the main their teaching is much the same. In substance, they follow their master, Aristotle, in their emphasis upon the ethical, practical and scientific aspects of the situation. They are primarily concerned in establishing the complete humanity of Jesus without, of course, desiring to sacrifice His Divinity. Theodore teaches the doctrine that humanity is on the road to perfection and that Jesus, through His perfect life and above all through His resurrection and His triumph over death, points the way to the ultimate consummation. The Divine Logos is separate from the human Jesus and yet the two are united in a single person. Theodore does not attempt to explain this contradiction by the orthodox Mystery route. On the contrary, he uses figurative expressions in an endeavor to rationalize the situation. The union of the divine and the human in Christ, he says, is like the union of two people who are married and become one. Or, it is like the spiritual and physical natures united in one human being. Such figures do not, of course, get rid of the difficulty, but they are at least efforts in the direction of a solution.

The teaching of Theodore and his companions concerning the complete humanity of Jesus and the necessity for maintaining a sharp distinction between the human and the divine natures led to the famous heresy of Nestorius. The latter had studied under the great Antiochene, and when he became Bishop of Constantinople in the early part of the fifth century he delivered an address in which he stressed the distinction between the human and the divine natures to such an extent that the orthodox became alarmed. They accused him of destroying the unity of Christ's person and after many bitter struggles in which the Alexandrians, led by Cyril, took the lead, Nestorius was finally deposed and banished. He was an active and vigorous man and his excommunication did not destroy his influence. He preached his gospel far and wide, and his converts became zealous missionaries of the faith. They pushed out across the borders of India into Burma and Tibet, and for the first time in human history they carried the banner of the cross not only into the secluded empire of China but into the distant islands of Japan. In all of these countries Nestorian Christianity attracted multitudes of converts. Competent critics tell us that there was a time when the Nestorians were the most numerous of all the sects of Christendom. Their glory has long since faded, but they still exist in the East and will probably continue to do so until the great consummation of all things.

Opposed to the heresy of the Nestorians was the strange mystical doctrine of the Monophysites. The term comes from a Greek word which means "one soul," and was attached to a group of Christians of this early period who asserted that Christ had really only one soul which was in its essence divine and was united at the Incarnation with a human body. This is perhaps not quite technically accurate as a description of Monophysitism, but it is close enough to express the essential point of view. What is stressed is the Divine Christ to the utter neglect of the human element in His nature. The founder of Monophysitism was an old Archimandrite named Eutychus who lived in a monastery near Constantinople. He fussed and fumed and mooned around until he became half addled and began to see visions with the result that he started the most formidable heresy between Arius and Pelagius. His highly mystical and imaginative theory was especially pleasing to the Alexandrians and to the dwellers along the banks of the Nile in general. It penetrated even to Abyssinia and Ethiopia,

and to this day the Greek churches in this distant part of
the world, including the Copts and sundry other groups,
are Monophysite in their theology.

From the standpoint of orthodoxy Eutychus was quite
as much of a heretic as was Nestorius, and his system was
eventually put under the ban. Nevertheless, the cloistered
life of the Middle Ages was loath to give up the old monk's
theory and actually retained it in many points. The humanity of Christ was forgotten and the Virgin Mary and the
saints took its place. Any one who studies the art of the
Renaissance can not fail to be impressed by the utter disregard of the humanity of Jesus which is manifested in the
paintings. It is always the Virgin who furnishes the con-
necting link between human beings and the Divine. One of
the charges made against Nestorius was that he refused to
style Mary the Mother of God, in this respect following
the lead of Theodore. In justifying his position the heretic
asserted that Mary was the mother of the human Jesus but
not of the Divine Christ. This attitude was thoroughly
repugnant to the medieval worship of the Virgin and was
one of the reasons why Nestorianism was especially taboo
in the West. There the reverence done Mary became more
and more pronounced until she, like her son, was declared
immaculate in conception and by this means was effectually
removed from the circle of humanity.

Divers and sundry varieties of heresy bobbed up concerning this much mooted question of the person of Christ
during the first two centuries after Nicæa. The very names
of most of them are tedious to recall and the theories
possess little merit when they are studied and interpreted.
The first of them all in point of time has a sort of Vichy
flavor about its title, and the average man can perhaps
remember it on that account. A certain bishop named
Apollonaris argued that the spirit of Jesus was divine while

his soul and body were human. This theory rested upon the current Greek psychology which divided the normal individual into three segments denominated body, soul and spirit. Apollonaris said that the human spirit constituting the third segment was removed and the divine spirit replaced it in the personality of Jesus. The Antiochenes were especially scandalized by this procedure which they asserted completely destroyed the equilibrium between the two natures. As divine, they maintained, Jesus had a body, soul and spirit which were all superhuman. As a man he likewise had a body, soul and spirit which were perfect in their kind. Apollonarianism, put in the baldest mathematical language, made Jesus four-thirds divine and two-thirds human. It seems probable that Nestorianism arose largely as a protest against this effort to overthrow the humanity of Christ.

After the Monophysites arose the Monothelites who asserted that Jesus had only one will and that will was not human but divine. They did not cut very much figure and were excommunicated in due form as soon as the orthodox could reach their case on the docket. There were so many heresies these days that it kept the true defenders of the faith busy calling councils and hurling anathemas at the sons of perdition who were forever disturbing the peace of Zion. Always, however, the essential irrationality of the Catholic dogma won out. As was the case with the doctrine of the Trinity so in the end it was the Mystery solution which decided what should be the orthodox view of the person of Christ. Not two distinct persons, as Nestorius seemed to affirm, nor one divine person, as Eutychus believed, but two and one at the same time, both perfectly human and perfectly divine, "neither dividing the Person nor confounding the Natures," this was the last word of the infallible majority upon the subject.

It was an appealing word to the Dark Ages upon which humanity was soon to enter. Even the rudiments of science were not in existence, since Greek culture had been buried and nothing had taken its place. Men were ruled by superstition, fanaticism and fear. They delighted in mysteries, miracles, mysticism and magic. The more irrational and fantastic a dogma appeared the more readily and faithfully was it accepted. Anything simple, easy or reasonable seemed to them to be of the devil. Like the aborigines of certain lands they esteemed their medicines as valueless unless the draft was exceedingly bitter and difficult to engorge. The ecclesiastical authorities were glad to minister to the popular taste. People who like this sort of thing are easy to lead around by the nose.

III

The interest of the Antiochenes, and of Theodore in particular, was directed primarily to a study of the human element in religion. Hence, they were much more concerned with anthropology, or the theological treatment of man and his problems, than with any other feature of doctrine. In this respect they approached nearer the Latins than was true of the Alexandrian teachers. There is a vast difference, however, between Latin anthropology as illustrated in the writings of Augustine and Greek anthropology as embodied in the thought of Theodore. The former was built around the idea of predestination while the latter always put free will at the center of its thinking. Strangely enough, Augustine magnified the enormity and seriousness of sin to an extent which was not at all true of his Greek predecessors. It would appear to be of the very essence of the conception of sin that the will of the sinner should be free to choose his evil way. The peculiar kind of logic which enabled Augustine to reverse this simple dictum of experience will occupy our attention later. Here we need only observe that Theodore, quite intelligently, emphasized the necessity of freedom for the development of the moral life. In this respect he was followed by Immanuel Kant, the great German philosopher, nearly fourteen centuries later.

Theodore makes some reference to predestination in his writings, but he always interprets the term in such a way as to get rid of its real implications. In doing this he followed the same tactics to which Augustine, Calvin and Jonathan Edwards resorted later on the other side. All of these worthies talk about freedom and extol its merits to the skies, but when we come to close quarters with what they mean by the word we discover that we are concerned with the shadow rather than the substance. In this particular field, the orthodox way of dealing with the Trinity and the person of Christ appears not to have been seriously considered as a dogma. We have creeds which support predestination and creeds which support free will, but we have no creed which lays emphasis upon absolute predestination and absolute and unmitigated freedom at the same time. Obviously, this appears to have been a serious oversight on the part of the masters of theology. There were reasons for the situation with which we can not deal at present but which were doubtless sufficiently important to justify what actually happened. In any event, the Mystery interpretation never got as far in the field of anthropology as it did in Christology and the allied departments of doctrine.

Theodore and the other members of the school of Antioch were also profoundly concerned with the future of the human spirit. Like Origen, with whom they differed on most other points, they believed in the ultimate restitution of all sinful beings to a state of holiness and of salvation. The Bishop of Mopsuestia, in common with his teacher

Diodorus, argues against the rationality of the belief in eternal torment and insists that unless the wicked are ultimately to be saved there would be no reason for continuing their existence. Like Origen, he looked upon hell as purely disciplinary and in no sense as a punitive institution. The cruelty and vindictiveness which run riot throughout the whole course of Latin theology find no place in the sweet reasonableness of the teaching of Theodore. Here again he is ahead of his age. After the long nightmare of medieval barbarism both in thought and fact the modern mind turns again with delight to the clear and yet profound testimony of the teacher of Mopsuestia.

IV

It is in the matter of Biblical interpretation that the Antiochenes come nearest the thought of the twentieth century. It seems astonishing that men with so little critical apparatus in their hands could achieve such remarkable results. Theodore, for example, appears to have had no technical knowledge of Hebrew, and yet his criticism of the Old Testament is as keen and penetrating as the best modern scholarship of our age. Take, for example, his estimate of the Song of Solomon. He tells us that it is an Eastern idyl which really has no place in a collection of religious books inasmuch as its interest is primarily romantic rather than ethical. He rejects entirely the allegorical method of getting rid of difficulties which was utilized by so great a thinker as Origen. Theodore correctly sees that this method really destroys the authoritative value of the Scriptures instead of preserving it. Since the nature of the allegory must always be left to individual speculation the Bible may be used to prove anything and therefore must in the end come to be of no use whatever for evidential purposes.

In his analysis of the value of the different books Theodore hews to the line with remarkable daring and discernment. Job, he tells us, is a poetical drama written not by a Jew but by a later Edomite. Very few of the Psalms can be rightfully attributed to David. The Proverbs are also of very doubtful value and not a great deal of historical significance can be attached to the books of Chronicles or those of Ezra, Nehemiah and Esther. He does not appear to have hit upon the documentary theory of the Pentateuch, but this was doubtless because of his lack of acquaintance with the Hebrew text. Had he possessed the evidence which modern scholarship has made available, he would probably have anticipated this point also. We are not here concerned with any defense of the critical position of Theodore. What we are interested in is the disclosure of his essentially intellectual point of view. Whether we agree with his conclusions or not, we can scarcely dispute the fact that his method of approach was infinitely superior to that of Origen or any of his Latin contemporaries like Augustine or Jerome.

When Theodore lived, that is to say during the latter part of the fourth century, the New Testament canon was not yet authoritatively determined. The text which he accepted appears to have excluded II Peter, II and III John, Jude and Revelation, and possibly the Epistle of James. Here he does not differ widely from many of his contemporaries and followers. It took centuries for the New Testament to crystallize into its present authoritative form. Even so late as the time of the Reformation Luther was ready to exclude the Epistle of James because of his quite unjustified conclusion that the book denies the value of faith and teaches the doctrine of salvation by works. In this connection it is interesting to note that with all of his radical critical views Theodore was never censored by the church for anything except his Christological teaching. Unfortunately for him, in his attempt to rationalize the relationship between the two natures in the person of Christ he seemed to come dangerously near to a denial of the Mystery. This could not be tolerated, so he was definitely anathematized and turned over to perdition by the Third Council of Constantinople which met somewhere about the middle of the sixth century. His pupil and follower, Nestorius, had long before received his quietus, so that the result in his own case had been anticipated. By a strange coincidence, the same council which denounced Theodore likewise stigmatized the supreme representative of the rival Alexandrian school, Origen Adamantinus. Inasmuch as both teachers were safely dead and to the minds of the orthodox consigned to perdition long before the official verdict was passed on earth, the pronouncements of the council would seem to have had little immediate significance. Their only purport was doubtless to warn the minds of unthinking laymen not to traffic with the damnable heresies proclaimed by the masters of Greek theology but to stick to the safe and authoritative absurdities of Augustine and Gregory. These latter prophets dispensed hell-fire in abundance and knew enough to teach people always to obey the church. The itch for freedom was not in their bones. They could be depended on, while men like Origen and Theodore were always capable of inciting some heresy or other even after they were dead.

V

After the time of Theodore, Greek theology speedily went to seed. There is a great deal of the touch of the old master in his disciple, Theodoret, but nothing that is distinctively original or advanced. John Chrysostom, the great contemporary of the latter, was so renowned as an orator that his heretical views have never brought him to book. As a matter of fact, he appears to have shared fully whatever heresies were possessed by Diodorus and Theodore. As perhaps the world's greatest preacher, at least since the days of the New Testament, he was too imposing a figure to unfrock lightly, so he escaped while the unlucky Theodore went to perdition which all shows the advantage of being a great pulpiteer instead of a mere teacher or theologian.

Theodoret was the last of the really great names in Greek theology. John of Damascus, with whom we shall deal presently, is generally regarded as the man who put the capstone upon Eastern thought, but John, in spite of his ponderous dulness, was a great deal of a dunderhead and bears no resemblance to the sparkling lucidity of the great Antiochenes. In between John and Theodoret we must deal with the mythical figure of Dionysius the Areopagite, whose works date from this period and, while of no consequence whatever during his own age, became tremendously influential in succeeding centuries.

The pseudo Dionysius, as he is usually styled, appears to have been an Eastern monk who lived somewhere in Asia, possibly in Edessa, during the fifth or sixth centuries. For divers unaccountable reasons this unknown worthy took it into his head to let loose his imagination upon things in general and after achieving a respectable number of pages he came to a halt and signed the name of Dionysius the Areopagite at the bottom of the last roll of parchment. This was the only brilliant thing that a modern reader can detect in the entire production, and it really was a stroke of genius. Dionysius the Areopagite is mentioned but once in the New Testament, but he occurs in the most dramatic portrayal of the missionary work of Paul and his name is sufficiently striking to keep it from being forgotten. He is, it will be recalled, one of the two converts whose names are given by

Luke as having followed the Apostle after his famous discourse on Mars Hill. Who he was or what became of him are questions to which history returns no answers, but in an age when critical investigation was unknown it was quite easy to use his name as a means for boosting the circulation of a document dealing with religion. Down until comparatively recent times people believed that the work attributed to Dionysius was genuine, but it required only the faintest knowledge of internal criticism to prove that this was impossible. The book can not be older than the fourth century, and as we have already indicated most probably belongs to the fifth or sixth.

The philosophy of Dionysius is a species of Neo-Platonic pantheism with emphasis upon the mystical side of religion. He deals familiarily with the angels, naming the different orders and going into details concerning their history. John Milton drew somewhat heavily upon his pages in the production of *Paradise Lost*. There was a time during the Middle Ages when he possessed an authority almost equal to Holy Writ itself. He inspired the one great thinker between Augustine and Anselm, Scotus Erigena, or John the Scot. The mystics all acknowledge their indebtedness to him. His conclusions, while not very carefully thought out, inevitably lead in the direction of the negative theory of evil. His general position was contradictory to the normal course of Latin thought but in spite of this fact he retained his ascendency in the Western church for centuries. The truth of the matter appears to be that very few of the ecclesiastics had the slightest conception of what he was driving at and gave him their endorsement only because they wished to appear learned and to pose as patrons of scholarship. Scotus himself, as we shall see later, would unquestionably have been burned at the stake if the gentle ecclesiastics of his time had understood what he was talking about. Not understanding him they gave him a clean bill of health. A hundred years after his death they discovered the infernal nature of his heresy and were much piqued because they could not make him the centerpiece in an *auto da fé*. Under the circumstances they had to be satisfied with sending him to Gehenna, which they did with much gusto and with a proper appreciation of the gravity of the case.

VI

The chief interest in the closing period of Greek theology arose from the subject of the worship of images. Our modern term "iconoclast" comes from this controversy, which lasted for several centuries. The Emperor, Leo the Syrian, was known as an iconoclast, that is, as literally a breaker of images, because he insisted upon destroying what he regarded as objects of superstitious veneration in the churches. In general, the emperors and the upper classes, both in church and state, opposed the use of the ikons, but the peasants were devoted to them and in the long run the peasants won. In the early development of Christianity the idea of image worship would have seemed the height of absurdity. Even as late as the time of Eusebius, that is during the fourth century, the use of paintings in the church was regarded as improper. Epiphanius, who lived about the same period, likewise refers to the impropriety of adoring such objects. Wherever Christianity retained the slightest flavor of its Jewish ancestry anything even approaching image worship was obviously impossible.

At the Second Council of Nicæa, which was held in 787 A.D. and was the last of the so-called ecumenical or general councils, a decree was passed which authorized the worship of ikons in the churches. From that day to the present time the Greek Orthodox communion has permitted and indeed emphasized the practise. In the Western church the tendency was more particularly toward the veneration of relics rather than of images. Nearly every city had its patron saint, and it was considered an essential of the proper reverence due this individual that his bones should repose in the municipality. They were usually entrusted to the authorities of the church and were commonly used for the purpose of working miracles. In a day when the science of medicine was unknown while diseases were rife and abundant, the universal recourse for protection from illness was to come in contact with the bones of a saint. Generally speaking, the medicine worked well enough and while the fees of the clergy were apt to be high they were probably no more than the customary toll exacted by the leeches of our modern age. It is true that in times of emergency, as for example when the Black Death nearly depopulated Europe, the saints were not so satisfactory as could have been desired, but it is only fair to say that scientific treatment has frequently been helpless in the presence of plague.

The progressive paganization of Christianity by the superstitious influences which surrounded it was a process that occupied centuries. So persistent and gradual were the changes that it is difficult for the historian to trace any of them to its source. The old Greek mysteries, the pagan practises and festivals of Teutons, Celts, Tartars and Slavs, the relics of Roman superstition, occasionally a touch of mystical magic from the Orient, were all engulfed in the capacious maw of the church and, after a fashion, devoured. In the long contest, whether Christianity really swallowed paganism or paganism Christianity may serve as a question for debate. Certain it is that the resultant ecclesiasticism bears slight resemblance to the church of the Apostolic age. No stretch of imagination can picture Peter, the fisherman of Galilee, wearing the triple tiara of Hildebrand or Boniface.

One of the most striking developments of paganized Christian theology was the substitution of the worship of the Virgin Mary for the old Mother goddess cult of the Mediterranean seaboard. Professor Farnell has traced the development of this feature and we need not recapitulate his argument here. Gradually the doctrines of the perpetual virginity of Mary, of her sinlessness, of her mediatorial powers, finally of her immaculate conception, all became articles of faith and essential features of dogma. One of these doctrinal points even so late as the last century inspired the Soubrise visions which led to the establishment of the shrine of Lourdes.

VII

The last great name in Greek theology is that of John Damascene. In his works the dogmatic thought of the East was finally filtered, bottled, corked and hermetically sealed, to remain unchanged and unalterable until the day of judgment. We know very little about the personal history of John. He lived during the eighth century A.D., and his home was apparently in Damascus, which still enjoys the distinction of being the oldest city in the world. It was entirely appropriate that this ancient worthy should inhabit such a locality. Everything about John is old—his style, his thought, his theological method, his tendency to repeat and stumble around and moralize over the records of the past. He developed some kind of idea of the relation between the two natures in the person of Christ which he styled enhypostatic or anhypostatic and which he interpreted as the conception of an impersonal human nature in Christ. He potters around endlessly in his efforts to elucidate his subject, but each succeeding page involves the reader in a deeper atmosphere of dulness until, completely befogged, he withdraws and allows the Damascene to rest peacefully beneath the accumulated dust of the centuries.

In justice to John it must be remembered that he wrote as an alien in a land under the domination of the Moslem conquerors of orthodoxy. It may well be that the loss of political independence played no slight part in the destruction of Eastern theology. The tendency to monastic mysticism, or mystical monasticism, which was developing in Alexandria even as early as the days of Cyril, found renewed encouragement in the thought of escape from the external oppression of Mohammedanism. Since the world without was going to rack and ruin it seemed best to withdraw to some lonely sanctuary and to forget the outer in contemplating the inner realities. Thus everywhere throughout the domain of Oriental Christianity the men who might have become leaders of thought surrendered themselves to the imperious claims of an all embracing mysticism. They meditated and dreamed, but thought no more. Once, indeed, they were spurred to some show of polemical spirit when the Franks dared to amend the Nicene-Constantinopolitan formula by adding the detested Filioque clause to the doctrine of the procession of the Holy Spirit. They fulminated and anathematized in the good old-time way, but their contributions lack the depth of Origen, the driving power of Athanasius, and the sparkling brilliancy of Theodore. It is evident that they had lost the formula for producing theology. The best of which they are now capable is to denounce their enemies as heretics and to exclude them from the true and Apostolic church. Accordingly, from this day forth Eastern and Western Christianity were divided into different camps. The East pursued its mystical way untouched by any desire to reopen the musty intellectual flagons of John Damascene. Hermetically sealed, they remain the symbol of philosophical stagnation and decay. From this time forward whatever pathway is left to theology must be sought for in the open spaces of the West. There the rediscovery of ancient learning made possible the further development of speculative thought. Later still the fiery avalanche of the Reformation rent the church in twain but gave theology a new lease upon life in the speculative systems of Protestantism. None of these things disturbed the quiet meditation of the orthodox monastic in the dull monotony of his cloistered life. Half drugged into somnolence by ritual and ascetic prayer the external world no longer exists for him, and why should he care to waste the time he might spend upon meditation in the writing of books? So he meditates and writes no more. The fall of the Eastern empire, the invention of printing, the discovery of the Western World, the Protestant Reformation, the rise of modern capitalism, even the tragic downfall of his greatest protectors, the historic dynasty of the Romanoffs, all take place without disturbing his repose.

Will he ever awaken from his slumber? Is there some day to be a rebirth of Greek theology which will bring back the intellectual glory and life of the great Alexandrians and the great Antiochenes? If the West can have its renaissance why may not the awakening also come to the East? Perhaps it is already on its way, and to use our modern parlance is around the turn of the road. Who knows?

CHAPTER VII

AUGUSTINE

AUGUSTINE is undoubtedly the foremost figure in theology. Omitting consideration of Jesus and Paul, no other personage in the annals of Christianity has so caught the imagination of the multitude. For centuries his has been a name to conjure with. The Roman Catholics class him as one of the four great doctors of the church and have instituted an order of monks which bears his name, while Protestantism owes most of its theology to his writings. Luther was his devoted admirer, and Calvin did little more than slavishly to imitate his teaching. For centuries the works of Augustine have been regarded as scarcely less authoritative than Holy Writ itself, and any teacher who could cite his words to point an argument felt he needed nothing more to overwhelm his opponents. He has attained the dignity of a fetish and the spell of his influence is not yet broken. There are indications that his power is waning, but the magic quality of his name will doubtless remain for centuries after his erratic teachings have been pitched into the discard.

I

Aurelius Augustinus was born at Tagaste, a little town in the province of Numidia, North Africa, on November 13, 354 A.D. His father, Patricius, had been a magistrate of the city but was apparently possessed of limited means.

We gather from the statements of Augustine himself that Patricius was gifted with a violent and ungovernable temper and that he was occasionally subject to lapses of an even more serious order. His wife, Monica, has survived as the model of an obedient spouse who submits to the tyranny of her husband with pious resignation. Orthodoxy has immortalized the name of this incarnation of meekness, and there are few places in the world where there is not a foundling asylum or home for unfortunate girls or some other such institution which bears the cognomen of Saint Monica. Analyzed under the careful and dispassionate light of reason the mother of Augustine appears to have been a woman of very mediocre ability with a distinctly superstitious quality in her make-up and a fondness for taking refuge, from what must have been an unhappy mating, in mystical quietism. Her piety was so extraordinary that she finally succeeded in winning both her husband and her son to Christianity, although it required many years before this result could be achieved. More extraordinary still, she won over her mother-in-law, who was at first violently prejudiced against her, and during their later years Augustine tells us in his *Confessions,* "They lived together with a wonderful sweetness of mutual good will."

According to the records, Patricius and Monica had three children. One was a daughter whose name and history are entirely unknown. The brother of Augustine was styled Navigius, but aside from this fact we have substantially no other record concerning him. Augustine was sent to school very early. His father desired him to become a scholar, with the idea that he who learns to work with his head does not need to work so much with his hands. His mother acquiesced, as she usually did in her husband's wishes, with the pious reflection that "his studies might hereafter lead him to God." As was customary, the lad was early instructed in the Latin and Greek classics. He tells us that he liked Virgil but that he had no taste whatever for Homer. The reason for this is obvious, since the language of Virgil was his native tongue, while he was required to master an alien dialect in order to appreciate the poet of Hellas. By his own testimony he was anything but industrious during his school-days. As was the case with Luther many centuries later, his masters attempted to instil the bacillus of industry by vigorous and unsparing use of the rod. Augustine had received some instructions in the power of prayer from his mother, and he made his first use of them in an attempt to escape from corporal punishment. The formula did not work, although he tells us that he used no little earnestness about it and caused much merriment because of his failure. It is interesting to note that his mother refused to have him christened when a child because it was the general belief at that time that while baptism washed out all sins that preceded it, any transgression which followed it acquired the greater enormity on that account. For this reason it became customary to postpone the ordinance until just before death in order that its full benefits might accrue to the sinner. Augustine himself did not favor this practise, inasmuch as it involved taking great chances in the matter of original sin. Without baptism the fall of Adam must unquestionably condemn every human being to eternal damnation, and therefore it was desirable to eliminate this danger as early as possible and take a chance on doing something else with the actual sins which might be committed later. From the time of Augustine down to the present his views concerning the desirability of early baptism have prevailed through large sections of the Christian world.

When he was sixteen years of age Augustine moved from Tagaste to Madaura, a larger town about twenty miles away where he had better opportunities for education and where he tells us he studied grammar and rhetoric but passed much more of his time, to use his own language, "walking in the streets of Babylon in whose filth I was rolled as if in cinnamon and precious ointments." It is possible that he exaggerated his own sensuality in the morbid self-revelations which we find in the *Confessions,* but there can be little doubt that he was something of a rake at this time. He did not stay at Madaura very long, but shortly after his father's death in 371 he moved to Carthage, where he tells us he plunged still further into the mire of vice. To quote his own language:

I befouled the spring of friendship with the lust of concupiscence, and I dimmed its luster with the hell of lustfulness; and yet, foul and dishonorable as I was, I craved through an excess of vanity to be thought elegant and urbane. I fell precipitously then into the love in which I longed to be ensnared. My God, my mercy, with how much bitterness didst Thou out of Thy infinite goodness besprinkle me for that sweetness.

He tells us that when he was only eighteen years of age he took a concubine who lived with him for thirteen years and who bore him a son to whom he gave the name of Adeodatus (given by God). Later on he deserted the mother of his child after he became converted to the true faith. During all this time he was troubled with scruples of conscience which must have made him a great bore. He would study Cicero for a while and then turn to the Bible. Again he would react and announce sententiously that the Sacred Writings were "unworthy to be compared with the dignity of Tully." Later on he remembered these lapses with much regret and self-condemnation. As nearly as we can judge from the *Confessions* there was a tinge of morbidity which attached to his entire career. His sensuality

was always colored with pessimism and his excessive mega-
lomania removed him from the ranks of normal humanity.
He was a simpering devotee of the stews, and the world
had to wait for more than a thousand years, until the time
of Jean Jacques Rousseau, to discover his equal in the field
of sickening sentimentality.

II

While he was at Carthage he experienced his first conversion. He was the kind of individual, as our modern
psychologists are fully aware, who might be counted on to
have a special predisposition toward the phenomena of re-
generation. Among the many rivals of Christianity which
were contending for mastery at this time the sect of the
Manicheans was especially influential. It had been founded
by Manes, a Persian reformer who combined certain
features of Gnostic Christianity with the Zoroastrian traditions of his people and produced a composite religion
which spread rapidly throughout the Empire. One of its
chief tenets was the doctrine of dualism, according to which
evil is the product of a principle co-equal with good. Human
responsibility was practically eliminated, a proposition
which was always especially pleasing to Augustine. There
were different grades or circles among the Manicheans, and
the new convert never appears to have achieved any very
high position with them, probably because he was unwilling
to break off his life of sensuality in order to do so. Despite
this fact he continued to be a disciple of Manes for nine
years, that is, from the nineteenth to the twenty-eighth year
of his life. His mother was very much distressed by his
apostasy but was comforted by a dream wherein was foreshadowed his conversion to the true orthodox faith. In
spite of this vision she went to a certain learned Bishop

whose name is not given to us to entreat him to reason with her son in order to bring him back to the pathway of truth. The Bishop declined to undertake such a task, saying that he would come back of himself in due season. It was about this time that Augustine, while teaching rhetoric in Tagaste, formed a close attachment with a young man of his own age who was later stricken by the fever and, according to the custom, was baptized just before death, as it appeared, and while in a state of complete unconsciousness. Contrary to expectation the young man revived, but when he did so turned violently against his former friend and admonished him to leave his evil ways. Shortly afterward he suffered a relapse and died. Augustine was in utter distress because, as he tells us, his friend was one "without whom his soul could not live." The passing of this youth was such a grievous sorrow that, to quote his language again, "my heart was utterly darkened, and whatever I looked upon was death."

Under the circumstances, it was no wonder that Tagaste became intolerable to him. He left his home and moved to Carthage, where he taught rhetoric with great success. He contended for the prize in poetry and was the winner in the civic contest. About this time he wrote his first book, a treatise on the Beautiful and the Appropriate. This work has been lost, and Augustine himself speaks of it in disparaging terms because it was built in large measure on the Manichean philosophy. At this period he tells us that he read the works of Aristotle, but it seems obvious that they made no very pronounced impression upon him

Although a Manichean, Augustine was not satisfied with his religious status. He never attained to anything more than the position of hearer or auditor, the lowest rank in the fellowship. He gives various reasons for his failure to climb higher, but the probability, as we have previously noted, seems to be that his moral conduct was such that the Manicheans, although not extraordinarily strict, found themselves unable to promote him. He sought and obtained an interview with Faustus, the Manichean Bishop of Mileve, who was the leading authority of the sect in North Africa. He found the Bishop a man of culture and eloquence but was not satisfied with his arguments. Probably no purely rational considerations would have brought him peace at this time. He was a neurotic, a psychopath, a nervous, irritable sensualist who was incapable of calmness or self-control. In 383 he went to Rome, where he attained success as a teacher with the sole exception that his numerous scholars refused to pay their bills. It may be imagined that this state of affairs did not improve his nervous condition. He heard of a new job at Milan and forthwith departed for that city in 384 A.D. His mother followed him there from Africa and continued to inform him, as she had done constantly since his infancy, that she was praying for his conversion. If there is anything in the value of suggestion it is not necessary to assume supernatural intervention in the future answer to her prayers.

At Milan the young neurotic came under the influence of Saint Ambrose, the greatest preacher of his day. The Milanese Bishop was a man of striking personality and speedily attracted the enthusiastic admiration of Augustine. Throughout his life the latter was a hero worshiper of the most pronounced type. He always wanted to be in subjection to somebody or some thing. Between the time when he first met Ambrose and the day of his conversion elapsed a period of tortuous doubt and despair. With almost morbid introspection he retails his experiences in the *Confessions*. He plunged from doubt to faith and from faith back to doubt and was unable to settle on anything. He was chiefly concerned with the cause of evil. He had given up

Manicheanism and was much inclined toward the monistic theology of Ambrose. Evil, however, stood in the way. If God is indeed all-powerful and all-good then whence comes evil? During this time he read the works of Plato in the Latin translation of Victorinus. From Plato he passed to a further study of Paul and especially of the Epistle to the Romans. Eventually he reached the conclusion that God could not be the author of evil, but that since He was the author of all substantial existence evil could not possess any genuine reality. To quote his own language, he ascertained it "not to be a substance but a perversion of the will, bent aside from Thee, O God, the supreme substance towards these lower things." He does not explain what caused the perversion of the will nor what he means by "lower things," but it was not logic that he needed at this time. His philosophy at this point was reechoed fifteen centuries later in the teaching of Mary Baker Glover Eddy.

While fumbling around among the philosophers in order to get the kinks straightened out of his system he continued his habits of debauchery. His mother persuaded him that he ought to give up his irregular living and consent to enter into the marriage state. She selected a young girl who was not yet of marriageable age and betrothed her wayward son to her. In anticipation of approaching wedlock he sent his concubine back to Africa, retaining, however, her natural son, Adeodatus. One feels a little curious about this woman whom he and Saint Monica cast off like old shoes. By the testimony of Augustine himself, after she had been sent back to Africa "she spent the rest of her life in retirement and purity." As far as we can learn the great theologian, while terribly smitten with remorse because of his relations with her, never felt the slightest tinge of repentance on account of separating her from her son and from the man to whom she had given the flower of her life.

The program of Monica did not work out well, even after she had disposed of her son's first attachment. Augustine found it impossible to wait two years for the bride his mother had arranged for him and therefore took another concubine. His action in this particular caused him deep and poignant remorse. Like Luther later on, the fear of death and the dread of hell were ever before his eyes. He felt that to go on in his carnal pleasures would inevitably mean that he would be plunged into the fires of perdition, and yet he owned himself incapable of breaking off his sensual attachments. He had reached the time when he needed a real conversion. It came. Listen to the story as he tells it himself in the pages of his *Confessions,* for it is one of the classics in the drama of biography.

I flung myself down under a fig tree, giving free course to my tears, and the streams of mine eyes gushed out, an acceptable sacrifice. I sent up these sorrowful cries, "How long? how long? To-morrow, and to-morrow? Why not now? Why is there not this hour an end to my uncleanness?"

I was saying these things, and weeping in the most bitter contrition of my heart, when, lo, I heard the voice of a boy or a girl, I know not which, coming from a neighboring house, chanting, and oft repeating, "Take up and read; take up and read." So quickly I returned to the place where Alypius was sitting; for there had I put down the volume of the Apostles when I rose thence. I grasped, opened, and in silence read that paragraph on which my eyes first fell: "Not in rioting and drunkenness, not in chambering and wantonness, not in strife and envying; but put ye on the Lord Jesus Christ, and make not provision for the flesh, to fulfil the lusts thereof." No further would I read, nor did I need; for instantly as the sentence ended, by a light, as it were, of security infused into my heart, all the gloom of doubt vanished away.

Closing the book, then, and putting either my finger between, or some other mark, I now with a tranquil countenance made it known to Alypius. And he thus disclosed to me what was wrought in him, which I knew not. He asked to look at what I read. I showed him; and looked even further than I had read, and I knew not what followed. This it was verily, "Him that is weak in the faith receive ye;" which he applied to himself and discovered to me. By this admonition was he strengthened; and by a good resolution and purpose, very much in accord with his character (wherein, for the better, he was always far different from me), without any restless delay he joined me. Thence we go in to my mother. We make it known to her, she rejoiceth. We relate how it came to pass, she leapeth for joy, and triumpheth, and blesseth Thee, Who are "able to do exceeding abundantly above all that we ask or think;" for she perceived that Thou hadst given her more for me than she was wont to ask by her pitiful, and most doleful groanings.

III

Augustine's conversion to Christianity proved to be permanent. From the time when it occurred, in 387, down to his death, in 430, he never seems to have wavered in his faith. He immediately adopted a celibate career and from this time forth was exceptionally careful in his relations with women. Throughout his long life as a Christian he never allowed any female to lodge in his house, and if the record be correct he never spoke to one of the sinful creatures except in the presence of some faithful representative of his clergy. He dressed with neatness and care and lived frugally in other respects. It is on record that he was considerate of the poor and that his benefactions were numerous.

The same year which witnessed his conversion marks also the end of the earthly life of Saint Monica. The *Confessions* practically close with the story of her passing, and this narrative is perhaps the most touching and eloquent in the book. The simple woman said, quite unostentatiously, that with the conversion of her husband and her son she had nothing else to desire in this world and was therefore ready to give up her life. Augustine writes in a style which has rarely been surpassed concerning his emotions when he realized that she was no more. Nevertheless, he refused to mourn her loss, thinking it unbecoming to the faith of a Christian.

Toward the end of the summer of 388, when he was thirty-four years of age, he set sail for Africa and landed at Carthage. He stayed there for a brief time and then went back to his home at Tagaste where he disposed of the property left him by his mother. He sold most of his inheritance and gave the proceeds to the church. Out of what remained he reserved a modest dwelling where he started a communal colony modeled after his conception of the original church at Jerusalem. This experiment did not last very long, but it was lengthy enough to start him on his career as an author. Not having much else to do at this time he began to write doctrinal tracts, especially against heretics. The taste which he acquired for this sort of thing continued throughout the remainder of his life and was chiefly responsible for his fame. He was ordained a priest in 391, and became Bishop of Hippo in 395. As far as we know, the sole celebrity which this place has acquired in history arises from the fact that it once had the spiritual ministration of Saint Augustine. It was a little town which appears to have possessed a reasonably good harbor but nothing else of consequence. The fact that so great a man as the father of Latin theology should have occupied so mean a position throughout his career has given rise to much speculation. As a matter of fact, it was the salvation of Augustine. It gave him ample time to write, which would not have been true in a position of greater importance. Had he occupied a see

of any considerable size or significance John Calvin might
have been put to the trouble of working out his own theory
of predestination a thousand years later.

During Augustine's long residence at Hippo he was constantly busy with doctrinal discussions. The death of his
illegitimate son, Adeodatus, while he was living at Tagaste
removed the last earthly attachment of his early life and
caused him to turn with singleness of purpose to his theological career. The lad, who died when he was seventeen
years of age, appears to have been peculiarly gifted, and
his loss was a matter of great sorrow to his father.
Augustine makes no reference to what it may have meant
to his mother.

Three great controversies kept the Bishop of Hippo
from thinking too attentively of the sinful pleasures of his
early life. The first was his warfare on the Manicheans,
the second was his conflict with the Donatists, and the third
was his historic combat with Pelagius. When he got
through with these things he fulminated tract after tract
against various types of heresy and composed a long ram-
bling treatise called *The City of God* which is interesting
for two reasons. First, it appears to have furnished the
theoretical starting-point of the Holy Roman Empire, and
second, it sums up in convenient fashion practically the entire
theology of Augustine. This work and his *Confessions* constitute about all that the average man cares to read of the
writings attributed to the greatest of the Latin Fathers. Of
these two works *The City of God* is by far the more difficult
to peruse. It is hopelessly involved and illogical, but he who
desires to understand Augustine would do well to read it
from first to last.

The controversy with the Manicheans came about
naturally enough. As we have already seen, in his early
years Augustine himself had been attached to this sect. He

had found it unsatisfactory and was anxious to prove to others the genuineness of his conversion. Moreover, the Manicheans were the most vigorous rivals of Christianity who disturbed the peace of the North African dioceses. Augustine went after them with hammer and tongs. He tells us there were five points in dispute between the two parties, to wit: (1) whether faith or knowledge is the way to holiness, (2) what is evil—its nature, possibility and reality, (3) the nature of free will, with special regard to the possibility of evil, (4) the compatibility of the free will of man and the foreknowledge of God, and (5) the compatibility of evil with the idea of a divine providence. Augustine was wrong in his attitude toward practically all of these questions, but he was such a vehement rhetorician and his views were so thoroughly in harmony with the prevailing thought currents of his day that he easily bore off the palm in the contest. Moreover, Manicheanism was just as far wrong in many of its positions, and Augustine was not the sort of antagonist who missed weak spots in his opponent's armor.

The controversy with the Donatists belongs primarily to church history and does not have any special significance in the development of thought. It did have a great deal of influence in the evolution of the papacy and the centralization of authority in Rome. The Donatists were fanatics and while doubtless conscientious were irrational and occupied an impossible theological position. Augustine acquired fame by taking the right side on this question. His position gave great satisfaction to the papal authorities and has had much to do with the extraordinarily generous attitude which the church has always manifested toward him. Donatism continued to be a real force in North Africa for a considerable length of time, but it eventually disappeared. It was built upon an idealization of the martyr spirit, and

the time of the martyrs was practically over. The underlying principle of the controversy bobs up every few centuries in the appearance of parties who claim to be superior
in morals and doctrine to all others and who will have no
fellowship with those whom they consider to be unclean.
Regarded from this standpoint Donatism will probably
never quite pass from the earth.

By far the most important of the theological duels of
Augustine was his controversy with Pelagius. The latter
was an Irish monk who had been led by his observation of
the effects of the doctrine of fatalism on moral conduct to
espouse the theory of absolute free will. In taking this
position he was not asserting anything new. The Greek
Fathers from Origen to Theodore were all believers in
human freedom and had no hesitancy about expressing their
views. Augustine was the first really great name in the
history of theology to accept the doctrine of predestination.
It was no wonder, therefore, that Pelagius found friends at
Rome and for a time appeared to dominate the Latin
church. In the long run he was doomed to failure not only
because of the superior controversial powers of his opponent but also because his theory was fundamentally democratic and Greek while the trend of the age was distinctly
autocratic and Latin. The *zeitgeist* had loaded the dice
against him, and it was inevitable that he should lose; nevertheless Rome always felt rather kindly toward him and
ultimately adopted semi-Pelagianism as its official attitude
toward the question of freedom. With the problems involved in this momentous discussion we shall have to deal
more fully in another section. Pelagius was condemned
and solemnly damned by the Council of Chalcedon in 451
A.D., and his name is still in much worse odor than his
doctrine. Religiously speaking, to call a man a Pelagian
is almost as bad as to dub him an Anarchist or a Bolshevist.

One of the interesting conflicts of Augustine was with his contemporary, Saint Jerome. The latter, after a personal experience during his youth somewhat similar to that of the Bishop of Hippo, likewise turned ascetic and founded a monastery at Bethlehem where he translated the Bible into Latin, lived on roots, and anathematized all species and varieties of heretics. Jerome wrote a commentary on the Epistle to the Galatians wherein he took the position, borrowed from Origen, that the celebrated row between Saint Peter and Saint Paul was primarily stage play and was got up for distinctly politico-theological purposes. Augustine read this commentary and, not knowing that he had all the Fathers against him, wrote a letter to Jerome in which he roundly denounced the ancient hermit for even suggesting that the founders of the church would condescend to anything approaching duplicity. He sent this letter by a personal messenger who promised to deliver it in Palestine, but when he got as far as Rome he lost his nerve, or his money ran out, or some other untoward circumstance intervened to prevent his farther travel. He showed the letter to some friends who speedily copied it and circulated it, with the result that it reached practically everybody else before it got to Jerome. When the latter discovered the situation it raised his temperature several degrees, but he did not quite explode at this time. He did protest against the undignified character of the transaction, and in due course of time his criticism reached the diocese of Hippo in North Africa. The learned Bishop was much distressed because of the circumstances and immediately wrote another epistle apologizing to Jerome but reiterating his original criticism. This letter he dispatched by a second friend who, strange to say, had precisely the same luck as his previous messenger. As a result this letter likewise obtained universal circulation in all the highways and byways of Palestine before it reached the convent of Jerome at Bethlehem. When it finally got there the lid blew off completely. Jerome said several things which tradition avers were not quite in the class of printable material, even at that early age. It appears that the air was blue around Bethlehem for several weeks, but the tumult finally subsided and in the end peace was established by a third letter which seems to have reached its destination. Saint Jerome is one of the picturesque characters in the pages of hagiology. All the painters liked to portray him when they were suffering from indigestion or had just returned from a quarrel with their lady loves. He is always disclosed to us as lean and lank and bony and bald and bearded, and the artist who could best intensify these characteristics was sure to take the prize in a Jerome competition. By common consent the leading picture in this class is the *Last Communion of Saint Jerome,* by Domenichino, which hangs in the Vatican gallery. Any one who has seen this picture will always remember it. It looks as though the painter had taken an actual skeleton for his model in drawing Saint Jerome. People who like really hideous things will get the worth of their money by crossing the ocean to look at this painting.

The life of Augustine came to a close amid stormy surroundings. The Vandals invaded Africa under the leadership of their chief, Genseric, and ravaged the country with such severity and with such exaggeration of the looting proclivity as to make their name a synonym for this particular vice. The Roman forces were driven into the city of Hippo toward the end of May or the beginning of June, 430. The siege continued throughout the summer. In early August the Bishop, then over threescore and ten years of age, contracted the fever. It soon became apparent that he could not recover. With characteristic abasement he ordered the penitential psalms to be written out and placed against the wall where he could see them as he lay in bed. As the old chronicle puts it, "These he looked at and read in the days of sickness, weeping frequently and profusely. And that he might not be restrained, about ten days before his death, he asked of us who were present that no one should come in, except at those hours at which the physicians came to see him or when refreshments were brought. And so it was done as he wished; and he had all that time free for prayer." We are also told that he was sound in limb and in his senses of hearing and seeing when he left this world.

IV

The doctrinal theories of Augustine revolve around two pivotal positions: the greatness of God and the littleness of man. In all the course of human history we find no defender of imperialism so thoroughgoing as the real founder of Latin theology. Not only does he advocate the idea that the Deity is a species of super-Emperor sitting above the clouds and possessing the power of the Cæsars magnified to an infinite degree, but he insists that the one outstanding sin of sins is to refuse the most unquestioning and slavish homage to the universal Ruler of the world. Adam and Eve, together with all of their innumerable descendants, richly deserve to burn alive forever in hell because they dared to disobey a single requirement of the great Monarch even under the stress of deceptive temptation. The slightest intimation of opposition in a case of this kind is, from Augustine's point of view, worthy of eternal damnation. He fairly grovels in the dust before the Almighty in page after page of his *Confessions*. The opening paragraph of the book, great and justly famous as it is from the standpoint of rhetoric, illustrates clearly this atti tude:

"Great art Thou, O Lord, and greatly to be praised; great is Thy power, and of Thy wisdom there is no end."

And Thee would man praise, who is only a particle of Thy creation; man, bearing about him his mortality, the witness of his sin, and the witness that "Thou resistest the proud"; yet would man praise Thee, although so insignificant a part of Thy creation. Thou movest us to delight in Thy praise; for Thou madest us for Thyself, and our hearts are restless until they rest in Thee. Grant me, Lord, to know and understand which is first, to call on Thee or to praise Thee? and whether it be first to know Thee or to call on Thee?

All this is very eloquent and reads well, even amid the democratic environment of our modern age. Augustine amplifies the thought over and over again in a thousand different forms. Take for example these words from the fourth section of the first book:

What art Thou, then, my God? What can I say, but the Lord God? "For who is Lord but the Lord? or who is God save our God?" O most high, most good, most powerful, most Almighty; most merciful, yet most just; most hidden, yet most near; most beautiful, yet most strong; stable, yet incomprehensible; unchangeable, yet changing all things; never new, and never old; renewing all things, and "making old the proud, and they know it not"; ever in action, yet ever at rest; still gathering, yet lacking nothing; supporting, filling, and overshadowing all things; creating, nourishing and ripening; seeking, yet having all things. Thou lovest, without passion; art jealous, without uneasiness; repentest, yet grievest not; art angry, yet always calm; changest Thy works, Thy purpose unchanged; recoverest what Thou findest, yet didst never lose; art never in need, and yet art gladdened by gains; never covetous, yet exacting usury.

And so it goes on, world without end, *ad infinitum et ad nauseam*. Such fulsome praise might well have become

wearisome to even the most august of Oriental monarchs.
The author of the *Confessions* seems to derive supreme
satisfaction from abasing himself in the Divine Presence.
No one can read his works with anything approaching the
scientific attitude and escape the conviction that we have to
do here with something that is distinctively abnormal and
pathological.

Two reasons have been assigned for the imperialistic
theology of Augustine. The first makes it a product of
historical environment. The Roman Empire was crumbling
to pieces and the glory of the past shed its last dazzling rays
in a sunset of golden splendor. Augustine himself reflected
the embodiment of the Latin spirit; the very genius of Rome
was incarnate within him. Now, the essence of the Roman
concept, at least of his day, was the dream of world empire
under a single and centralized authority. There had been
a time, it is true, when Rome was a republic, but those
ancient days had been buried forever under the magnificent
tread of the Cæsars. Rome and Empire had come to be
synonymous words. Just as the Jews after the Exile
dreamed of a greater Israel to be, so Augustine, amid the
collapse of the Western Empire, dreamed of a new Roman
imperialism with its Emperor in the heavens, and its vice-
gerent enthroned within the seven hilled city of the Tiber.

Those who have made a careful study of the psychology
of Augustine find some explanation of his extraordinary
tendency to magnify the Deity, and to take delight in pros-
trating himself before Him, in the presence of mental ab-
normality. Whether the author of the *Confessions* was a
Masochist or not may well be a subject for further investigation. Certainly he has the Masochistic attitude, not only in
his excessive groveling before the object of his worship but
also in the strange delight which he appears to take in
recounting the tortures of eternal damnation, to which we

shall have to make reference later. To assume a certain degree of mental perversion is perhaps the best explanation one can give for that strange juxtaposition of love and cruelty which one finds so constantly in the writings of the great theologian. Side by side with the most touching and beautiful ascriptions of praise to the divine love we find the most revolting and hideous gloating over the torture of unfortunate and, from any correct ethical standpoint, entirely innocent human beings. Making every allowance for the crude moral standards of the age it seems impossible to reconcile these conflicting attitudes without assuming something like a Masochistic tendency.

Whatever may be the explanation the fact remains. The one central conception of the Augustinian theology is the absolute sovereignty of God. Around this everything else revolves; to this everything else returns. Having postulated this great central fact as the keynote of his philosophy Augustine rigidly follows its implications to their logical conclusions. He never dodges nor evades the issue. It is this unerring logic which, as in the case of Calvin after him, constituted the chief source of his power and influence. Whether men liked his explanation or not they could scarcely deny the fact that it constituted a real interpretation of the universe. It did not simply muddy the waters or wander around in an aimless and beatific fog. It got somewhere, and got there with clearness and precision. The fact that the moral nature of the universe completely went to pot under the Augustinian system did not greatly disturb an age which was accustomed to every-day indulgence in cruelty, violence and the most callous disregard of human suffering. Men were not squeamish about the Deity torturing human beings endlessly for His private satisfaction when they did so much of it on a smaller scale for their own delectation. With this phase of the matter we need not concern ourselves

further. In many respects Augustine was doubtless no
worse than his age. It is not so much his cruelty that
astounds us as it is the strange admixture of tenderness and
severity, of romantic affection and of callous brutality which
clutters the pages of his works.

V

Next to the divine sovereignty in the Augustinian system
must be placed the insignificance of humanity. No pessimist
in all the history of thought ever had such a poor opinion of
man as Augustine. Again and again he magnifies his
weakness, his sinfulness, his incompetence, his ignorance, in
short, everything that others have found valuable in his
nature. The doctrine of total depravity as a result of the
fall of Adam is a central feature of his thought. All infants are born into the world under the doom of perdition,
and unless the sin of their first parents has been washed away
by the water of baptism they must spend eternity in the
realm of the inferno. Later on, when he formulated his un-
compromising doctrine of election, according to which certain of these infants were chosen from all eternity to be
saved and others to be lost, he did not fully explain what
baptism had to do with the matter. An unbaptized bene-
ficiary of predestination must surely be better off than one
not so fortunate in the matter of election who had nevertheless received the cleansing virtues of the sacrament.

Augustine wrestled for many years with the problem of
evil. As a mere lad he had been drawn to the Manichean
teaching by the idea that it furnished the easiest solution of
the difficulty. His restless desire for an imperial Deity
made it impossible for him to be content with dualism. Having decided that God must be omnipotent and supreme he
was faced with the age-long question why an omnipotent

and loving Deity could permit evil and suffer it to exist in the world. Throughout his life he returns to this question again and again. He never really settles it, although he reaches a tentative conclusion in harmony with his main thesis. That conclusion is expressed in the idea that since God is all-wise and all-good and all-powerful evil must be in reality nothing. This theory, which as we have observed was to be revived by Mrs. Eddy many centuries later, came the more naturally to Augustine because of his mistaken exegesis of the first chapter of Genesis. Like most theologians of his time he knew nothing whatever about Hebrew and therefore assumed that the account of creation involved the formation of the world out of nothing. Of course, the Hebrew text conveys no such meaning. Starting with the postulate which this erroneous exegesis supported it was easy to assume that if nothing is evil and the world is made out of nothing therefore it must be naturally very bad. Hence also arises the predilection for sin and all manner of meanness which Augustine discovers to be so universal among the children of Adam.

Strangely enough, no human being ever becomes absolutely bad. Even the devil must have some trace of good in him or else he would vanish into nothingness. There must be some good in hell because if it were totally bad it would cease to exist. Upon the Augustinian hypothesis there will always be a minute fragment of good in perdition since otherwise the devils would become completely evil, that is, become absolutely nothing and their punishment would be at an end. Therefore the Almighty allows them to possess just enough good to preserve their being in order that they may be tortured without any possibility of escape. Hell keeps getting worse all the time, with a perpetually increasing quantum of misery, but without the slightest chance that it will ever vanish into the total evil of annihilation.

Man being nothing more than a vile and disreputable pawn of the All Supreme has, of course, no real freedom or power of self-determination. The Augustinian doctrine of predestination, which is the characteristic most easily remembered in his theology, flows inevitably from his conception of divine sovereignty. If God is all-powerful and all-knowing He must will everything that happens. Moreover, everything must happen as He wills it. All sorts of ingenuous dodgings, such as the self-limitation of the divine power, are swept aside by the unerring logic of the Bishop of Hippo. It must be admitted that he is invariably consistent in his position upon this question. He never doubts for a moment that all the evil that ever has been or ever will be, from the seductive snare of the tempter in Eden to the betrayal kiss of Judas in Gethsemane, has been directly ordered and premeditated by the Sovereign of the Universe. The devil himself exists because the Lord wants him to exist. All the crass brutality of the ages, the sufferings of the innocent through myriads of years, the unpitying will of nature as expressed in disease, famine and death, are but embodiments of the eternal decrees of the Emperor of the Universe.

At times Augustine seems to rebel against his own conclusions. Evil appears so foreign to the grace and goodness of God that he can scarcely think of the two as related. It is when such considerations disturb him that he cries out, as he often does in his writings, *Unde malum? Unde malum?* [Whence evil? Whence evil?], and echo does nothing more than to hurl back the cry upon his own soul. Had he not been so helplessly and hopelessly imperialistic he might have found a rational solution of the difficulty. Obviously, a good God can have nothing to do with evil, and if evil exists it simply means that there are some things which even the good God can not eliminate or control. It seems strange that any one could repeat the Lord's Prayer as often as Augustine without ever discovering this underlying truth of its petitions.

We have referred already to the controversy with Pelagius. It arose out of the conviction of the British monk that morality is impossible without the possession of freedom. When men believe that they have no control over their actions they will inevitably follow the line of least resistance and the possession of moral character becomes impossible. The disastrous consequences of the fatalistic hypothesis from an ethical point of view had been observed by Pelagius among his parishioners, and he set out to oppose it by boldly declaring that every man is responsible for his own actions and is capable of determining them. This philosophy, which in one form or another is a truism of modern ethical thought, ran counter to the views of Augustine on election and irritated him to greater efforts in behalf of his hypothesis. Technically, the Roman theologian won but in actuality he lost. Catholics and Protestants alike are semi-Pelagians to-day with few exceptions, although they do not like to wear the name. Augustine's conception is not only impossible morally but is destructive of church organization and discipline. Why should any one belong to the church if the principle of fatalism rules the world? What will such membership avail if we are not of the elect, and if the reverse is true what difference does it make whether we are in or out of the church? It did not take the occupants of the papal chair long to discover the danger of such teaching, and from Gregory onward they soft-pedaled it, while doing the utmost homage externally to its author.

Aside from his views on election, which were destined later to wreck the church, Rome could well afford to do honor to the name of Augustine. He it was who laid the foundations of that glorious dream of world imperialism which found a partial expression in the Holy Roman Empire and which still agitates the bosoms of the faithful. The church, and the Bishop of Rome as its head, stands on earth for the Lord in heaven and therefore deserves and should receive the unquestioning homage of all. Augustine will not tolerate any disobedience or lack of respect for the authorities of the ecclesia. Their word, to him, is sacred and their will is law. No wonder that the masters of the Vatican, in spite of what the doctrine of election did for them later in the hands of John Calvin, have never been able to find it in their hearts to condemn Augustine. His autocratic zeal, his worship of centralized power, his slavish submission to authority, outweigh everything else. When the account is balanced the pendulum still swings in his favor. Thus he is, always has been, and doubtless always will be one of the four great doctors of the church.

VI

As the Bishop of Hippo grew older he became sterner and more morose. It is a common truism that the later works of his life are the harshest, the most pitiless and the most unbending of his writings. Calvin, unfortunately, modeled his system after the teaching of Augustine's concluding years. If one desires to discover what this doctrine is like all one needs to do is to turn to the seventeenth or next to the last book of *The City of God,* and read the chapter headings. Here are a few of them: "Whether an earthly body may possibly be incorruptible by fire; whether a fleshly body may possibly endure eternal pain; nature's testimony, that bodies may remain undiminished in the fire; of hell and the qualities of the eternal pains therein; whether the fire of hell, if it be corporeal, can take less effect on the incorporeal devils; whether it be not justice that the time of the pains should be proportioned to the time of the sins and crimes; the greatness of Adam's sin, inflicting eternal condemnation upon all that are out of the state of grace; against such as hold that the torments after the judgment shall be but the means whereby the souls shall be purified; against those who would prove all damnation frustrated by the prayers of the saints; against those who exclude both men and devils from pains eternal; of such that hold that heretics shall be saved in that they have partaken of the body of Christ"—and a multitude of others of similar tenor.

When one reads the pages contained in these chapters one is struck with the obvious desire of the author to remove even the slightest possibility of hope from the damned. Some of the propositions appear humorously grotesque in the light of modern standards, but we must remember that Augustine wrote with tremendous earnestness and that there is not the slightest touch of irony in his teaching. He fully believed that all who belonged to the class of the non-elect, all non-baptized infants, all heretics of every description, in short, everybody except a certain limited and exclusive group selected for no merit of their own but merely by the caprice of Omnipotence would burn forever in unending torture which, by a special interposition of the Divine Power, could not be terminated by dissolution or extinction. To the arguments of those who would show that no material body can suffer eternally Augustine comes back with the statement that everything is possible with God and that there are greater miracles than this now actually in existence. He cites some of them:

The Garamantæ have a fountain so cold in the day that it cannot be drunk of: so hot in the night that it cannot be touched. In Epirus is another, wherein if you quench a torch, you may light it again thereat. The Arcadian asbestos being once inflamed, will never be quenched. There is a kind of fig tree in Egypt whose wood sinks, and being thoroughly steeped (and the heavier, one would think), it rises again to the top of the water.

The apples of the country of Sodom are fair to the eye, but being touched, fall to dust and ashes. The Persian pyrites, pressed hard in the hand, burns it, whereupon it has the name. The selenites is another stone wherein the waxing and waning of the moon is ever visible. The mares in Cappadocia conceive with the wind, but their foals live but three years. The trees of Ceylon, an isle in India, never cast their leaves.

There appears to be some lurking doubt in his mind as to the certitude of all these phenomena, as he indicates clearly in the opening section of the next chapter, which starts out after this fashion; "Perhaps they will answer, Oh, these are lies, we believe them not, they are false relations," but he comes back strong with a vigorous impeachment of the false miracles of the heathen and an equally strenuous defense of the validity of true miracles. Even allowing, he says, that some of these things may be a trifle exaggerated, enough remains to prove conclusively the fact of miracle. If, therefore, miracles are always happening in the natural order of things why should any one doubt the possibility of people being burned alive in hell without being consumed?

It is not enough that the fact of eternal damnation should be proved but the justice of it must also be demonstrated. Augustine set about this task very earnestly and no doubt accomplished it entirely to his own satisfaction. From our modern view-point his reasons appear so trivial as to be humorous, but they no doubt carried great weight in an age which would have been hopelessly disconsolate without the worst possible hell which the human imagination could devise. Augustine fully and adequately met the demands of the times. Anything more lurid, cruel or diabolical than he has pictured in the seventeenth book of *The City of God* it is impossible to conceive. In this matter he set the pace for all succeeding generations.

It is just here that the baneful influence of this neurotic and Masochistic African has been most profoundly manifest. When we read the history of the Middle Ages, with its farrago of *autos da fé*, torture chambers, burnings at the stake, breaking on the wheel, and all the other hideous nightmares which nominally Christian peoples permitted to flourish in their midst we can understand that these things are only faint imitations on the part of human beings of the divine hell-fire of Augustine. What the Lord was forever doing to the great mass of created beings his servants conceived it necessary to practise on a limited scale themselves. Hence they tortured, burned, racked and destroyed with all the ingenuity of pain that they could devise the unfortunate beings with whom they chanced to disagree. The church itself took a leading hand in the matter through the Inquisition and other similar tribunals. Protestants were quite as cruel as Catholics because they were equally the spiritual descendants of Augustine. The state no less than the church was plunged in an abyss of atrocities. The horrible punishments inflicted by the medieval penal codes are scarcely conceivable at the present time. Nightmares are not profitable and we shall therefore go into this subject no further. Professor Workman puts the situation very mildly when he says that for a thousand years "the dark shadow of Augustine was cast across the church." Humanity has not yet emerged entirely from its spell, but the indications are not lacking that the dawn of a new day is at hand.

CHAPTER VIII

ANSELM

BETWEEN Augustine and Anselm no name of importance appears in the history of Christian thought. Humanity passed through a period of dreary waste with scarcely a single ray of light to illumine the darkness. The Vandals were besieging the city of Hippo when the founder of Latin theology breathed his last. The Roman Empire, as the author of *The City of God* fully recognized, was falling into hopeless ruin. The old cultures were passing away. The glory that was Greece and the grandeur that was Rome were being eclipsed forever. The magnificent architectural and sculptural products of the ancient civilizations were being cast down and buried beneath the débris of cities sacked and burned by their conquerors. Of the older literature scarcely a shred was left. The art of printing was not yet in existence, and it was an easy matter for a library to be destroyed. Copies of books were few and rare, and it was not difficult for editions to become exhausted. It was no wonder that in a few centuries something like a pall of universal night appeared to have settled over the world. Not without reason do we speak of this period in the life of collective humanity as the Dark Ages.

During the centuries which passed between the death of Augustine and the birth of Anselm the church was the one centralizing and dominant force in the Western World. Deprived of effective political leadership the peoples of Europe turned to the popes for stabilization and guidance. It is only fair to say that they did not turn in vain. One can not withhold a measure of admiration for the states-manlike qualities of many of the occupants of Saint Peter's chair during these dark and turbulent years. Some of the popes, it is true, were mediocre or worse, but after every discount has been made they stand out as the representatives of the best which the spirit of the times could afford.

Gregory the Great (590-604) is often said to have been the last of the Fathers and the first of the schoolmen. He was a theologian of only average ability, but he possessed a practical turn which was of the utmost importance in the development of the church. The first monk to become a pope, he introduced somewhat of the monastic discipline into the structure of the hierarchy. He laid the foundations of that dream of imperialism which the Vatican has never since ceased to cherish. He was honest, devout and capable and sincerely thought that the more power the church possessed the better it would be for the world. He did not believe very much in secular education. A letter has come down to us which he addressed to his friend, Desiderius of Vienne, when he heard that the latter was teaching grammar and the reading of the poets:

A report has reached us which we can not mention without a blush, that thou expoundest grammar to certain friends; whereat we are so offended and filled with scorn that our former opinion of thee is turned to mourning and sorrow. The same mouth singeth not the praises of Jove and Christ. . . . If, hereafter, it be clearly established that the rumor which we have heard of thee is false, and that thou art not applying thyself to the idle vanities of secular learning, we shall render thanks to God, who hath not delivered over thy heart to be defiled by the blasphemous praises of secular men.

The point of view contained in this epistle was characteristic of the Dark Ages. It only disappeared when the rediscovery of the ancient classics, and especially Plato and Aristotle, turned men's thought once more to the pursuit of rational knowledge. It was this changed attitude which marked the beginning of the Renaissance.

I

In the fourth decade of the ninth century two things of importance happened in the history of thought. In 844 Paschasius Radbert, a monk of New Corbie, brought out a pamphlet entitled *The Sacrament of the Body and Blood of Christ*. In this document the author boldly asserts what came to be known later as the doctrine of transubstantiation. The long and somewhat unwieldly word does not appear to have been used until the beginning of the twelfth century, but the doctrine is to be found substantially complete in the pages of Radbert. Two things entered into it: first, the medieval philosophy of substance, and second, the medieval fondness for miracle. By virtue of the former a philosophical basis was given to the idea, while the latter explains the motive for its exploitation. Throughout the Middle Ages men were obsessed with the idea of substance. All reality was placed in this underlying substratum while everything discernible by the senses was classed as merely appearance or accident. If asked to define this imperial Substance the philosopher had nothing to say. Substance, he could only tell you, is the essence of everything but by virtue of that fact we know nothing about it. By a stupendous and constantly recurring miracle the bread and wine, when consecrated by the priest, have their substance converted into the actual flesh and blood of Christ. The attributes, or accidents, of color, taste and sensual appearance in general, are not affected, but this amounts to nothing since the reality, the underlying Substance, is changed. If you asked again how we may know that the change has taken place the reply is that we know it through faith, just in the same way as the early Fathers knew that the Three are One and the One Three. As a matter of fact, the doctrine of transubstantiation can be rationalized more easily than the orthodox doctrine of the Trinity. Of course, both positions frankly make their appeal to the miraculous for their final justification.

The doctrine of transubstantiation was not accepted by the church without a struggle. It was opposed vigorously by Ratram during the lifetime of Radbert, and later by Berengar, the head of the cathedral school in Tours (1088). It was not until the Fourth Lateran Council, (1215) that the theory was formally made a dogma of the church. It was reaffirmed at the Council of Trent during the period of the Reformation and has ever since remained one of the central tenets of the Roman Catholic faith.

Somewhere about the year 847 John Scotus Erigena sailed from Ireland and settled at the court of Charles the Bald of France. John the Scot, as he was popularly styled, was the greatest scholar of his age—which was not saying much, for few monarchs of the time could write their own names. What little culture there was appears to have been centered in Ireland, which for nearly a century enjoyed the distinction never afterward possessed by the Emerald Isle of being the center of civilization for the world. At this time the Irish were called Scots, which accounts for the popular title worn by John. The latter was a real philosopher in his own way, and wrote a book on metaphysics which has survived to the modern age under the title *The Division of Nature*. The volume is Platonic and pantheistic in color and appears to be indebted for most of its ideas to the so-called works of Dionysius the Areopagite. John brought his book to Paris, where the French King surveyed it sagely from the outside and pronounced it a great production, as indeed any book whatever would have been to him.

The courtiers, not wishing to be outdone, vied with one another in lauding a volume which they could neither read nor understand. Thus did John become the hero of the court and bask serenely in the royal smile. He partook of the fat of the land and came near being canonized by the church. Unfortunately for his permanent reputation, a century or more after his death, when education had become more general, his book was dug up and was discovered to contain the most damnable heresies. It was condemned by the Council of Paris in 1209 and was suppressed by Pope Honorius III in 1225, as he tells us, because of its truly abominable teaching. Great indeed was the consternation and distress of the ecclesiastics when they reflected that they had been so tardy about discovering the iniquities of the Scot that they permitted him to die in the natural order instead of making a bonfire out of him as he deserved. The best they could do was to commit him to perdition and to hope that he was receiving the punishment in the inferno which circumstances had prevented him from experiencing in this life. Having burned his books and having properly condemned him to limbo the leaders of the church set about their other tasks with a reasonably clear conscience.

II

Anselm of Canterbury was born at Aosta, in Italy, in 1033 and died in 1109. He is famous in church history as the Archbishop of Canterbury who did more than any other man to popularize the Roman church in England. The facts concerning his life need not detain us long. He was an ecclesiastic born and bred, and his sole interest was in the affairs of the church. He strenuously maintained the clerical independence of his see and withstood all the pressure of the English crown to bring him into subjection. He has a place of importance in English secular history because of his struggles with the King, but he is of far greater significance by reason of his contributions to the history of thought. He wrote three books which were of epoch-making importance in their respective fields. These three works were entitled the *Proslogium*, or discourse on the existence of God, the *Monologium*, or treatise on the being of God, and the *Cur Deus Homo*, which is the most famous book on the subject of the atonement ever written. All three of these works taken together cover less than three hundred pages, and yet each of them has become of the utmost significance in the annals of speculation. In two respects especially has the author proved himself a pioneer. In the *Proslogium* he first set forth his famous ontological argument for the existence of God, while in the *Cur Deus Homo* he outlined for the first time what came to be for centuries the orthodox view of the atonement. It may be worth our while to probe a little more carefully into both of these contributions.

The ontological argument, as it is styled, is outlined in detail in the opening sections of the *Monologium*. Stated in the briefest form it asserts that we must believe in the possibility of a Perfect Being. Starting from this point, we are compelled by the force of our own logic to admit that if such a Being can be conceived He must exist, for if He did not exist He would not be absolutely perfect, since He would lack one element of perfection, that is to say, existence. But by virtue of our previous assumption He must be absolutely perfect; therefore, He must exist. This proof was regarded as unassailable for centuries, and is still found in some of the older text-books on apologetics. Although criticized rather vigorously at the time when it was put forth it was pretty generally accepted in the world of scholarship until the advent of Immanuel Kant. When the latter published his *Critique of Pure Reason,* in the second half of the eighteenth century, he devoted a considerable portion of the book to the refutation of the ontological argument for the existence of God. So effectually was his work accomplished that it has never needed revision. Anselm's thesis is more of a theological curiosity than anything else at the present time.

The Kantian argument is simple enough. It is based on the impossibility of passing over from the order of thought to the order of reality. Ideas are the copies of objects but are not objects in themselves. Moreover, the fact that I have an idea does not prove that an object exists corresponding to my concept. It may well be that no such entity can be found. There is a vast difference between the idea that I own a million dollars and actually having a million dollars in the bank. Of course, the idea might correspond to the fact, but again it might not. In any case, the mere presence of an idea has no bearing in itself on the actual existence of the object. All that the idea of a Perfect Being can claim is perfection in its own order, that is, in the order of thought. It can never skip across from thought to reality and assert existence because it happens to be an idea of perfection.

Of course, the followers of Anselm have tried to answer Kant by saying that an exception must be made in the case of the one Perfect Idea. The German philosopher is right, they say, in so far as concepts in general are concerned. It is only in the case of the one highest and all-perfect concept that an exception can be made. Reality may be predicated of this highest idea although it may well be denied to any other. Of course, this argument simply begs the question. There is no reason in the nature of the case why an exception should be made in the matter of the highest concept. By definition it is still an idea and has no more claim to reality than any other idea. Upon the basis of pure reason the Kantian thesis is still water-tight and is likely always to remain so.

Anselm, by formulating the ontological argument, started the schoolmen upon the engaging task of proving the existence of the Deity by appealing to logic alone. It was not long before other reasons were added to the onto-logical proof. Aristotle himself supplied the cosmological, or argument from a First Cause. The universe, it was asserted, is admittedly in existence. Being here it must have come from somewhere; in other words, it must have had a creator. All finite causes lead back to an infinite First Cause which comprehends and explains them. This First Cause must obviously be God. To the ontological and cosmological arguments the schoolmen speedily added a third, the teleological or argument from design. This has been elaborated in great detail in the later writings of Paley and Butler. Notwithstanding its dissection at the hands of Kant in the *Critique of Pure Reason* it persisted in theistic literature until the time of Darwin and the publication of the *Origin of Species*. A great deal of the opposition of the English clergy to the Darwinian hypothesis is said to have arisen because practically every preacher had at least one sermon which proved the existence of God by the argument from design. If natural selection represents a fact these sermons had to be thrown in the discard. Of late years there has been a tendency to restate the argument from design in evolutionary terms. Like the ontological argument it seems to represent something inherent in human thought even though it is inadmissible from a strictly logical point of view.

III

The *Cur Deus Homo (Why God Became Man)* sums up and makes incarnate the genius of Latin theology. All of the legalism, the imperialistic tendencies, the desire to strike balances, the disposition to interpret every feature of life in terms of a law court, may be found in this book. Christianity is adjusted to the juristic maxims of medieval law, and its philosophy is interpreted in such terms alone. Briefly stated, Anselm's argument is this: man, acting through Adam, had committed an infinite sin by disobeying the divine command. This infinite sin, according to medieval law, demands an infinite penalty. Man, being finite, can not pay such a debt. Moreover, being sinful by nature, he has more to do than he is able to accomplish in looking after his own personal sins without attempting to square the account of Adam. Hence, there was need for infinite compensation. This was furnished by God sending His own Son, that is, Himself, into the world to become man and by dying on the cross to furnish an infinite satisfaction for the infinite sin of humanity. This is why God became man. As man, He took the place of Adam and could therefore legitimately pay the debt. As God, His sacrifice was of infinite merit and therefore was adequate for its purpose. Anselm rejected completely the old idea advanced by Gregory of Nyssa, that the atonement represented a ransom to Satan. Instead of this he substituted the idea of a duality in the divine nature. God the Father, as the incarnation of justice, demands inflexibly the payment of a penalty which the sin of Adam has incurred. God the Son, as the incarnation of love, voluntarily pays the debt which justice demands. This solution gets rid of Satan as a sort of subsidiary deity and interprets the dogma in more distinctly monistic terms. Hence, it speedily became popular with churchmen of all classes. Some few of the schoolmen, notably Saint Bernard, held on to the older ransom-to-Satan theory, but it was not long before Anselm triumphed throughout the domain of theology. After the Reformation the leading Protestant theologians, practically without exception, accepted the satisfaction theory.

The *Cur Deus Homo* is written in the form of a dialogue, being apparently modeled after the writings of Plato with which Anselm was tolerably familiar. Only two people appear in the dialogue, Anselm himself and a lay figure named Boso, who plays the part of an echo throughout the production. A good example of the style and substance of the book is furnished in Chapter VIII of Part II, where it is discussed "how it behooved God to take a man of the race of Adam and born of woman":

Anselm. In four ways can God create man, viz., either of man and woman, in the common way; or neither of man nor woman, as he created Adam; or of man without woman, as he made Eve; or of woman without man, which thus far he has never done. Wherefore, in order to show that this last mode is also under his power, and was reserved for this very purpose, what more fitting than he should take that man whose origin we are seeking from a woman without a man? Now whether it be more worthy that he be born of a virgin, or one not a virgin, we need not discuss, but must affirm, beyond all doubt, that the God-man should be born of a virgin.

Boso. Your speech gratifies my heart.

Anselm. Does what we have said appear sound, or is it unsubstantial as a cloud, as you have said infidels declare?

Boso. Nothing can be more sound.

Anselm. Paint not, therefore, upon baseless emptiness, but upon solid truth, and tell how clearly fitting it is that, as man's sin and the cause of our condemnation sprung from a woman, so the cure of sin and the source of our salvation should also be found in a woman. And that women may not despair of attaining the inheritance of the blessed, because that so dire an evil arose from woman, it is proper that from woman also so great a blessing should arise, that their hopes may be revived. Take also this view. If it was a virgin which brought all evil upon the human race, it is much more appropriate that a virgin should be the occasion of all good. And this also. If woman, whom God made from man alone, was made of a virgin [*de virgine*], it is peculiarly fitting for that man also, who shall spring from a woman, to be born of a woman without man. Of the pictures which can be superadded to this, showing that the God-man ought to be born of a virgin, we will say nothing. These are sufficient.

Boso. They are certainly very beautiful and reasonable.

The above quotation is typical of the method and manner of medieval scholasticism. The idea that the Deity had tried every other possible way of producing human beings except the method of the virgin birth previous to the Incarnation, and that he had reserved this one particular means for the production of the God-man, is medieval to the core. No speculation can be too ingenuous, no hair-splitting too tenuous to displease or dissatisfy the scholastics. It was this characteristic which was most readily discerned by the common mass of humanity, and it is this feature which is usually uppermost in the average man's mind when the word "scholasticism" is pronounced in his hearing.

The satisfaction theory of Anselm, as it is usually styled, carried with it a number of implications. First of all, it established the idea of a treasury of merit which later proved of so much importance to the practical work of the church. Even though the sin of Adam was adjudged to be infinite yet the satisfaction furnished by the atonement, being likewise infinite, was held not only to balance the debt but to establish a credit of goodness for the use of the church which could be drawn on whenever needed. In this way the doctrine of indulgences grew up through the control by the clergy of the infinite treasury of merit created by the death of Jesus on the cross. It was natural, also, that the treasury should be enlarged to include the surplus merit of the saints who passed out of this life with a comfortable balance in their bank-account with heaven. In an age when practically all thinking was done in purely juristic and mechanical concepts the ideas of merit and satisfaction, as they were introduced by Anselm, proved tremendously popular. They squared with current views of punishment and penology, and they were easily comprehended by the most illiterate hearers. Moreover, they were highly satisfactory to the authorities of the church for they invested the custodian of Saint Peter's keys with ever increasing power and revenue. It was no wonder that Anselm was made a saint. The only surprising thing is that he had to wait so long for his canonization. It was more than three centuries after his death, in the year 1494, that the most corrupt, venal and sensual of even the Borgia line of popes, Alexander VI, conferred upon the author of the *Cur Deus Homo* the distinction of sainthood. From the standpoints of personal character, administrative ability and intellectual insight the choice was never more worthily made.

As for the substitutionary theory of the atonement it still holds sway over a large portion of the nominally Christian world. Roman Catholicism accepts it in somewhat guarded fashion, and Protestant fundamentalism does the same thing. A distinguished free-church theologian of the last generation is on record as having said that the *Cur Deus Homo* remains the greatest book on the atonement ever written. The idea of satisfaction, of weighing exactly transgression and penalty against each other in the balances seems primitive, no doubt, but it is still entertained by a large portion of the human race. Although it has passed out of the philosophy of modern jurisprudence it nevertheless enters into the thinking of the average juryman and is of decisive importance in helping him to reach a verdict. The substitution idea in its baldest form would probably be rejected to-day by the majority of Christians,

and certainly would have no standing in our courts of law.
No matter how many good people might volunteer to go to
the electric chair or to the gallows in the place of an actual
murderer no modern court would permit such a substitution.
There is, indeed, a story to the effect that some time during
the last century a wealthy Chinaman who had killed another person in Shanghai and had been tried and sentenced
to death by the English court attempted to escape the
penalty by substituting a poverty-stricken representative of
his own race whom he had secured to take his place. The
English court, of course, refused to accept the substitution.
In fairness to Saint Anselm it should be said that he thought
of the sacrifice of Jesus as a meritorious atonement because
he completely identified the God-man with the human race.
In this way it was possible for Christ to pay the debt without involving the idea of mechanical substitution. By becoming man Christ actually identified Himself with Adam
and therefore took upon Himself the punishment of the
latter. It required the nicest kind of Middle-Age hair-
splitting to explain how He could do this without really
involving Himself in sin, but Anselm is equal to the task.
Like all other theologians when pushed to the wall he falls
back upon the Mystery explanation. In Chapter XVI of
Part II of the *Cur Deus Homo* he says:

Boso. As, therefore, you have disclosed the reason of
those things mentioned above, I beg you will also explain
what I am now about to ask. First, then, how does God,
from a sinful substance, that is, of human species, which was
wholly tainted by sin, take a man without sin, as an un-
leavened lump from that which is leavened? For, though
the conception of this man be pure, and free from the sin of
fleshly gratification, yet the virgin herself, from whom he
sprang, was conceived in iniquity, and in sin did her mother
bear her, since she herself sinned in Adam, in whom all
men sinned.

Anselm. Since it is fitting for that man to be God, and also the restorer of sinners, we doubt not that he is wholly without sin; yet will this avail nothing, unless he be taken without sin and yet of a sinful substance. But if we cannot comprehend in what manner the wisdom of God effects this, we should be surprised, but with reverence should allow of a thing of so great magnitude to remain hidden from us. For the restoring of human nature by God is more wonderful than its creation; for either was equally easy for God; but before man was made he had not sinned, so that he ought not be denied existence. But after man was made he deserved, by his sin, to lose his existence together with its design; though he never has wholly lost this, viz., that he should be one capable of being punished, or of receiving God's compassion. For neither of these things could take effect if he were annihilated. Therefore God's restoring man is more wonderful than his creating him, inasmuch as it is done for the sinner contrary to his deserts; while the act of creation was not for the sinner and was not in opposition to man's deserts.—Who, then, will dare to think that the human mind can discover how wisely, how wonderfully, so incomprehensible a work has been accomplished?

Boso encores him at this point, and we need not pursue the investigation further. To do Anselm justice, he only resorted to the Mystery explanation when everything else had failed. He had the philosophical intuition, and he loved reason for its own sake. He is a real logician, and once you grant his premises there is no escape from the conclusions which he reaches.

IV

Anselm was the first of the great realists of the Middle Ages. The controversy between realism and nominalism colored the whole course of human thinking for many centuries. The most famous statement of the questions at issue is contained in the words of the *Isagoge* of Porphyry, which Professor Workman declares "played a greater part in the history of thought than any outside the Bible":

Next concerning genera and species, the question indeed whether they have a substantial existence, or whether they exist in bare intellectual concepts only, or whether if they have a substantial existence they are corporeal or incorporeal, and whether they are separated from the insensible properties of the things, or are only in those properties and subsisting about them, I shall forbear to determine. For a question of this kind is very deep, and needs fuller investigation.

At bottom the protagonists in the struggle were no other than Plato and Aristotle. The realists were followers of the former and the nominalists of the latter. To Plato the only ultimate reality appertained to the eternal ideas which preceded all material creation and of which every material object is but an imperfect copy. These ideas were obviously universal and abstract, and therefore lacked any sort of concrete individuality. Aristotle, on the other hand, held to the idea that the individual is the only reality and that abstract or universal ideas are simply mental concepts which we use for purposes of thinking but which have no other reality. We must not regard this apparently pedantic controversy as either meaningless or trivial. As a matter of fact, there is scarcely an important problem of our present-day civilization which has not sprung out of it. In philosophy the line of descent from medieval realism to Hegel and post-Hegelian idealism is clear and distinct, while on the other hand the conclusions of nominalism are revealed in their extreme form in the skepticism of David Hume and in the radical empiricism of many other philosophers. As we shall see later, the tendency of the more brilliant thinkers of the Middle Ages was to make a

synthesis of the opposing views and find the truth somewhere between the two extremes. This middle-ground position was styled conceptualism and was first promulgated
by Abelard. It asserted that the universal was real, but its
reality was expressed only through the individual. We can
not pause at this point to discuss the question further. It
received greater amplification in the thought of Saint
Thomas and his chief rival, the Franciscan Duns Scotus.
One interesting fact about the controversy was the peculiar
and somewhat contradictory terminology involved in it.
Realism, for example, in the medieval sense, meant the most
thoroughgoing idealism according to the ordinary usage of
language. Hence, a modern realist believes almost the exact opposite of what the medieval realist so stoutly asserted.
The present-day usage is therefore almost exactly the reverse of the nomenclature of the Middle Ages. This is one
of the reasons why the average man becomes confused when
he attempts for the first time to read the history of
philosophy.

There is one feature of the *Monologium* which deserves
especial attention. It is Anselm's identification of the Third
Person of the Trinity with the Eternal Spirit of Love or
Harmony in the world. The Second Person he identifies
with the spirit of intelligence or truth whose divine wisdom
created all things. The Holy Spirit, on the contrary, involves the idea of that eternal and universal good-will which
has been the source of all solidarity in the human race and
which has been responsible for all real social progress. Just
as the Divine Logos embodies that conception of the common reason or intelligence of the universe which binds men
together when they think correctly and rightly, so the Holy
Spirit represents that attitude of fraternal cooperation and
good-will which alone can serve to weld humanity into a
universal brotherhood. These ideas may seem fantastic

to our modern age, but the signs are not wanting that they will some day receive their just recognition. After all, what has our modern emphasis upon individualism given us except strife, warfare, greed and the hatred of one class for another? Saint Anselm may have been a trifle idealistic in his conception of the Trinity, but for our own part we can see no better solution than his for the perplexing problems of our age. To become incorporated with the Eternal Intelligence which is embodied in the thought of the Logos, or with the Eternal Love which is embodied in the thought of the Holy Spirit, remains the best way and indeed the only way out of the tangled maze of our modern materialism.

The schoolmen have been accused, not without some reason, of being impractical and visionary. No one who is acquainted with their works will deny the justice of this impeachment. Nevertheless, with all their idealism they touched practical realities to a far greater extent than a majority of their critics appreciate. For one thing, they were genuine thinkers and lived in an age when there were fewer external distractions than exist to-day. They had, it is true, only a limited intellectual and cultural background compared with the enormous mass of literary and scientific data which is available to us, but it must be remembered that they had Plato and Aristotle, and having these they needed little else to serve as a basis for vigorous and independent speculation. How many of our modern writers have added anything to the intellectual reaches of the two masters of ancient thought? The Middle-Age theologians knew their Plato and knew their Aristotle, and knowing them could not fail to think with accuracy and precision. Here, at least, they deserve the imitation of our casual and sophisticated modern age.

Anselm was a realist because he knew more about Plato

than he did about his great successor. Aristotle was not genuinely appreciated for nearly a century later, but when his works became thoroughly known he speedily forged ahead of his rival. When we come to discuss the climax of scholasticism in the writings of Saint Thomas Aquinas we shall have a great deal to say about the Stagirite. When Anselm lived the works of Aristotle were scarcely known to Western Europe. Plato had received a partial introduction through the somewhat mystical idealism of Dionysius the Areopagite. John the Scot had popularized the former's works to a considerable extent among the intelligentsia. Nevertheless, John, by passing over into a sort of vague pantheistic philosophy, had tended to bring discredit upon the Platonic teaching. Anselm showed that it was possible to interpret the most fruitful conceptions of the great Athenian in terms of orthodox Christian theology. There was nothing heretical about the successor·to Lanfranc. He was an ecclesiastic to the core and his one supreme allegiance was to the church. Orthodoxy never had a stouter champion or a more worthy one. We may shrink from some of his conclusions as we do from those of Augustine; we may criticize his legalism and his mechanical ideas of justice; we may feel amused at some of his hair-splitting dialectic; but when we have done our worst we come away with the impression that we have had to do with a real thinker and scholar, and one who has, moreover, a message that is not entirely worn out. The ontological argument may not help us much in our modern struggle against atheism, and the satisfaction theory as elaborated in the *Cur Deus Homo* scarcely seems to belong to our age, but the conception of an Eternal Wisdom into which we must somehow enter if we are to find rationality and peace and of an Eternal Love which we must make our own if we would achieve universal brotherhood are still fruitful ideas. Modern individualism is rapidly going to seed and holds no promise for the future. Narrow nationalism, tribal jealousy, individual monopoly and greed, must give way to the true corporate life of the world. Here it is that Saint Anselm points the way out. We can afford to forget the greater portion of his theology. In fact, the things for which his name usually stands possess nowadays only an historical interest. It is the larger realities which he half unconsciously proclaims that possess eternal value. For this reason there is a sense in which it may be said that the future belongs to him. It may well be that the precise form in which he expressed his views may prove ephemeral, but the ideas themselves are sure to live. When the Golden Age arrives there will be a niche in the temple of thought for Anselm. He will have many companions, it is true, but there will be none of them more worthy or more appreciated than their master.

CHAPTER IX

ABELARD

ABELARD was the most brilliant theologian of the Middle Ages. He was the forerunner of humanism and the real founder of modern education. He was the greatest teacher of his age and, with one exception, possibly the greatest instructor of all ages. Students thronged from every part of the world to attend his lectures, and no one ever went away disappointed. Keen and penetrating in his thought, he possessed the most remarkable talent for expression, and the physical charm of his personality added to the impressiveness of his words. He came of noble blood and he tells us in his letter to Philintus that his father took especial occasion to train him in the polite learning of his age. Voluntarily, when a mere youth, he cast aside his inheritance in order to give himself wholly to study. To quote his own language, "To my brothers I leave the glory of battles and the pomp of triumphs; nay, more, I yielded them up my birthright and patrimony. I knew necessity was the great spur to study, and was afraid I should not merit the title of learned if I distinguished myself from others by nothing but a more plentiful fortune." Perhaps nowhere in the literature of biography will you find a better statement of the true ideal of the scholar than is contained in these words. They embody the keynote of their author's life. From first to last he was a student, loving knowledge for its own sake and loyal to truth without thought of reward. He would have spurned our modern conception of making education a profitable thing for its possessor. The word "profit" was not in his vocabulary. He had the medieval contempt for money combined with the Renaissance passion for knowledge. No wonder that he will always rank among the half-dozen supreme scholars of the world!

I

Strange it seems that a man of such intellectual proclivities should have become the hero of one of the world's most famous romances. Few people in Paris know anything about the philosophy of Abelard, but even the gamins on the street are familiar with the adorable idyl of Heloise. Anybody who visits the city for more than a day can not escape paying proper homage to the tomb of the two lovers, just as one never visits Verona without pausing for a moment beside the grave of Juliet. It is well that this should be done. The great romances of the world are not too numerous. Hero and Leander, Paris and Helen, Antony and Cleopatra, Paolo and Francesca, Dante and Beatrice, Petrarch and Laura, Romeo and Juliet, and, last but not least, Abelard and Heloise. The mere recital of these titles stirs up memories of tragedies unique and unparalleled in the pages of history. Of all these thrilling stories perhaps the most luridly dramatic may be found in the fateful experience of Abelard. We read the personal confessions of the philosopher with a touch of critical sympathy. Obviously, he had no slight opinion of himself, and as he is ready enough to acknowledge, his thoughtlessness and vanity were largely responsible for his misfortunes. His attitude toward his teachers, William of Champeaux and Anselm of Laon, was anything but gracious. The latter, especially, seems to have merited better treatment at his hands. Champeaux, in all probability, deserved Abelard's charges of jealousy and persecution, but even in his case it would have been better for his pupil not to have made use of so sharp a tongue.

The story of Abelard's life may be told in a few words. He left his father's home and went to Paris, where he studied under the best known scholar of his day, William of Champeaux, usually reputed to be the founder of realism. Abelard's criticism of his character seems to possess at least a tinge of prejudice. He was, he tells us, "a professor who had acquired the character of the most skilful philosopher of his age, but by negative excellencies only as being the least ignorant. He received me with great demonstrations of kindness, but I was not so happy as to please him long; for I was too knowing in the subjects he discoursed upon, and I often confuted his notions. Frequently in our disputations I pushed a good argument so home that all his subtlety was not able to elude its force. It was impossible he should see himself surpassed by his scholar without resentment. It is sometimes dangerous to have too much merit."

One can readily imagine that the author of the above lines made a rather difficult pupil. It was no wonder that in a short time he ceased to attend the lectures of his master and decided to start out as a teacher on his own score. He sought and found a position at Melun, where he tells us that he was pursued by the jealous cunning of Champeaux but that he easily triumphed over all opposition. If we may accept his own statement as correct his lectures were always crowded and in a short time he entirely obscured the renown of his master. In spite of his triumphs, for some reason which he does not divulge he decided to change his location from Melun to Corbeil. The fatigue of traveling brought on a severe illness and his physicians advised him to return to his native province in order to regain his health. His comment upon their decision that they were perhaps in league with Champeaux seems wholly unmerited. One would like also to forget his childish boast, "I leave you to imagine whether my absence was not regretted by the better sort." It helped him to regain his health when he heard that his old teacher had become a monk. This holy decision received no encomium from the critical pen of his biographer. The motive, Abelard tells us, "was not penitence for having persecuted me but on the contrary was ambition to achieve some church dignity." In this William succeeded, for he was speedily appointed to a bishopric, but much to the disgust of his pupil and rival he did not quit Paris and the care of his schools. He went to his diocese to gather in his revenues but returned and passed the rest of his time in giving lectures. We suspect that he must have possessed more merit than we would gather from a casual perusal of the memoirs of Abelard. In any event, the latter confesses that he often engaged in forensic battles with him and could truthfully use concerning their outcome the language of Ajax to the Greeks:

> If you demand the fortune of that day
> When stak'd on this right hand your honours lay,
> If I did not oblige the foe to yield,
> Yet did I never basely quit the field.

About this time news came to Paris that Berenger, the father of Abelard, had retired to a cloister at the age of sixty. His son's somewhat ironical comment is expressed in the words, "He offered up to heaven the languid remains of a life he could make no further use of." Shortly afterward the wife of Berenger took the same resolution. Apparently the monastic career in those days was not altogether irksome. Abelard tells us that his mother did not entirely abandon the satisfactions of life when she made her profession. Her friends were continually at the grate and

hence her son writes, "the monastery, when one has the inclination to make it so, is exceedingly charming and pleas-
ant." Obviously the religious life afforded the better-class
people of the day relief from the responsibility of managing
their estates without depriving them of the simpler and more
quiet pleasures.

The example of his parents appears to have determined
Abelard to turn his thoughts toward the church. He decided to study divinity and, inquiring for a director, was
recommended to Anselm who, he tells us, was regarded as
the very oracle of his time but who, in his own opinion, was
more venerable for his age and his wrinkles than for his
genius or learning. The only effect of consulting him on
any difficulty was to be made much more uncertain on the
point at issue. Those who saw him at a distance admired
him, but closer acquaintance was certain to bring dis-
illusionment. From Abelard's point of view, "he was a
great master of words and talked much, but meant nothing.
His discourse was a fire which instead of enlightening, obscured everything with its smoke; a tree beautified with a
variety of leaves and branches but barren of fruit." Here
again one suspects that the picture is overdrawn. Obviously,
the instructor who had Abelard for a pupil was scarcely to
be envied.

It was not long before he discovered that the Master of
Laon could teach him nothing. He therefore left school
again and launched out upon his studies on his own score.
In a short time he made such progress that he secured, to
use his own language, "an incredible number of students"
and received gratuities from them proportionate in value
to the reputation which he had acquired. Apparently in
these days tuition was a voluntary matter depending primarily upon the inclination and means of the student.

II

Abelard was now at the zenith of his career. He was the most popular teacher of his day and was envied by all his competitors and adored by his admirers and friends. His position seemed secure, and so it might have remained had he not met Heloise. As a philosopher he explains what follows in terse but withal rather evasive fashion. "All men, I believe, are under a necessity of paying tribute at some time or other to Love, and it is vain to strive to avoid it." He tells us that he had always held aloof from dissolute pleasures, considering them as beneath his dignity and position. It was only when he found the niece of Fulbert, a Canon of Paris, who surpassed all her companions in beauty, attractiveness and wit, that he surrendered his heart. His description of his romance should be read in his own letters and in the companion epistles which were addressed to him by Heloise. He acknowledges that he deceived Fulbert and by adroit trickery gained access to his house where he remained as a tutor of Heloise in order that he might the more effectively apply his suit. In the end he succeeded, was discovered and was forced to leave. He secured a lodging near his former residence and found means for clandestine interviews with his inamorata. He tried to engage her servant, Agaton, in his interest but only succeeded in making her an enemy because of her jealousy. In the end he eloped with Heloise, who was about to become a mother, and over her protests made her his wife. She objected to assuming this honorable status because she felt that it might stand in the way of preferment for Abelard. It is creditable to him that he would not accept her sacrifice. They were married, but their happiness did not prove of long duration.

Fulbert, the Canon, was beside himself with rage when he learned what had happened. Abelard characterizes his

attitude by saying that the elopement "filled him with the
deepest concern and had liked to have deprived him of the
small share of wits which heaven had allowed him." He
adds a bit of unworthy slander which his respect for Heloise
should have made impossible. The revenge of Fulbert was
tragic in the extreme. He hired a ruffian to assault Abelard
by night and to mutilate him before he could protect himself. The consequences of this tragedy are written in detail
in the confessions which have come down to us, and constitute one of the classics of romance. Distraught by
jealousy and remorse, Abelard retired to a monastery and
obliged his wife to enter the nunnery of Argenteuil. Later
on he built a chapel for her and left her in charge of it for
the remainder of her days. As for himself, he wandered
from pillar to post seeking rest everywhere but finding
none. He became the greatest theologian of his age, but
his sarcastic tongue made him many enemies and he was
constantly subject to ecclesiastical persecution. His books
were condemned by a council and burned, a circumstance
which he characterizes as a "cutting sorrow" and so entirely overwhelming that "the former calamity I suffered
by the cruelty of Fulbert was nothing in comparison to
this." He retired into a waste place to escape from his
enemies, but was pursued by his students who followed him
even into the desert in order to receive his instruction. At
last the Duke of Brittany made him Abbot of St. Gildas,
where he remained during his later days. He had no control over his inferiors, and all his surroundings were of the
most melancholy character. It may be well to quote a few
more words from his letter to Philintus: "I live in a barbarous country, the language of which I do not understand;
I have no conversation but with the rudest people. My
walks are on the inaccessible shore of a sea which is always
stormy. My monks are known only for their dissoluteness,

and live without any rule or order. . . . Sometimes they surround me and load me with infinite abuses; sometimes they abandon me and I am left alone to my own tormenting thoughts." Worst of all, he is unable to give up his unhappy passion for Heloise. In vain he appeals to heaven for comfort and peace. Again, to use his own language, "in the midst of my retirement I sigh, I weep, I pine, I speak the dear name of Heloise, and delight to hear the sound. . . . I am thoroughly wretched; I have not yet torn from my heart the deep roots which vice has planted in it. For if my conversion were sincere how could I take pleasure in relating my past faults?" And he tells his friend Philintus, who likewise had suffered great misfortunes, that they should both "receive without murmuring what comes from the hand of God and not oppose our will to His. Adieu; I give you advice which, could I myself follow, I should be happy."

Concerning the quarrel of Abelard with Bernard we shall have to speak later. Here we need only remark that the Abbot of Clairvaux constituted one of the special thorns in the side of his great rival. Abelard was condemned and was compelled to burn his own books in public and to renounce the views which he had expressed in them. He appealed to the Pope, but his appeal was not allowed. On all sides he met only opposition, criticism, contumely and contempt. The most brilliant intellect of his day, he was at least metaphorically trodden under foot by dull and muddy-minded ecclesiastics who were not worthy to touch the hem of his garment. Having lost everything which this world can give, he turned to eternity as the sole hope of satisfaction. He was always a true son of the church, and bitter as it must have been for him to eat his own words, he never refused to recant when his ecclesiastical superiors demanded it. Like Erasmus after him, he was not born to be a martyr.

He could think with extraordinary penetration and he had a capacity for expression which few men have ever equaled, but the hand of fortune was heavy upon him and he was denied even the peace of an ascetic like Bernard.

Broken in health and discouraged in spirit, he left his post at St. Gildas and became a wanderer once more. He fell ill at the famous Abbey of Cluny while on his way to Rome. The Abbot treated him kindly, sympathizing with his misfortunes, but it was impossible to prolong his life. He died in the spring of 1142, while the April flowers were just bursting into bloom. He had reached the age of sixty-three. Twenty-two years afterward Heloise passed away, and was buried beside him. In 1817, over six centuries later, the celebrated tomb was erected over their bones in the cemetery of Père La-Chaise.

III

So prosaic and philosophical a writer as Henry Hallam tells us that the love-letters of Abelard and Heloise constitute the one work of real interest written during the six hundred years which elapsed after the death of Boethius. Even to-day the volume possesses attractive features and may be found in editions of various kinds in practically all of our better-class bookstores. There are six letters in the collection. The first was addressed by Abelard to his friend Philintus. The second is from Heloise to Abelard, the third from Abelard to Heloise, the fourth and fifth from Heloise to Abelard, and the sixth and last from Abelard to Heloise. All of the letters were originally written in Latin, somewhere about the years 1128 or 1129. The collection remained in manuscript for nearly five centuries, and was first printed in Paris the year that William Shakespeare died, that is, in 1616.

It is quite impossible to summarize or condense these immortal documents. After eight centuries they seem as lifelike and human as they must have appeared to the few who read them when they were written. Take for example the inscription of the first letter of Heloise:

To her Lord, her Father, her Husband, her Brother; his Servant, his Child, his Wife, his Sister, and to express all that is humble, respectful, and loving to her Abelard, Heloise writes this.

She then proceeds to state the circumstances which induced her to write. The letter of Abelard to Philintus, usually published as the first of the collection, by chance fell into her hands. She acknowledges that her familiarity with the writing induced her to read what was not intended for her eyes. Her curiosity, by her own confession, cost her dear, for the letter contained a most pathetic statement of the romance which she was endeavoring in vain to forget. As a result she felt impelled to write again, and with this apology she begins her communication.

There are passages of deep insight in this memorable document which help us to understand both the character of the author and the inner nature of the man to whom she is not simply speaking the language of prejudiced devotion when she says:

Let me always meditate on your calamities, let me publish them to all the world, if possible to shame an age that has not known how to value you.

Doubtless, when these lines were written she did not dream that they had in them the spirit of prophecy. This very letter is quite sufficient to rehabilitate the name and fame of Abelard and to make them immortal.

She asks for the privilege of corresponding. Her appeal is pathetic in the extreme. "Letters," she says, "were

first invented for consoling such solitary wretches as myself."
She does not want him to go to any special trouble in order
to write to her. "Write always to me carelessly and without
study. I had rather read the dictates of the heart than of
the brain." She appeals to him to give some thought to the
encouragement and spiritual upbuilding of her own life
and of those in the convent with her. Augustine, Tertullian,
Jerome, she says, did this and were not criticized for it.
Moreover, she is really his wife, and even the church could
not condemn such a correspondence. She recalls vividly the
circumstances of her self-immolation. "I have hated myself that I might love you," she says. "I came hither to
ruin myself in a perpetual imprisonment that I might make
you live quietly and at ease." Then follow the memorable
words, "Riches and pomp are not the charm of love. True
tenderness makes us separate the lover from all that is
external to him and, setting aside his position, fortune or
employments, consider him merely as himself."

At the close of the letter she frankly acknowledges that
she finds no satisfaction in her religious devotions. She
entered the convent not through any spiritual emotion or
by reason of any inclination of her own, but solely because
of her desire to please her husband. She is not irreligious,
but she has not yet learned to substitute religion for love.
After recapitulating her devotion in a sea of stormy words
she apologizes for her apparent although in no sense real
self-praise by saying, "I ought to speak less to you of your
misfortunes and of my sufferings. We tarnish the luster of
our most beautiful actions when we applaud them ourselves." Her final appeal is contained in the lines which
have become classic:

A heart which has loved as mine can not soon be in-
different. We fluctuate long between love and hatred before we can arrive at tranquillity, and we always flatter

ourselves with some forlorn hope that we shall not utterly be forgotten.

There is nothing finer than those words in the literature of romance. When they were written Heloise was thirty-two and Abelard fifty. Ten years had elapsed since their misfortunes had separated them. They were never again to be united until their bones were placed in one grave in the old cemetery of Père La-Chaise. This first letter of Heloise is the gem of the collection. Abelard replies to her, but he writes less in the spirit of the lover than of the votary to religion. There is the note of hopelessness in every line and the evident effort to forget the joys and tragedies of the past. It is obvious that the author is trying to conform to the discipline of the church and to crush completely every dictate of natural affection. From the standpoint of the cloister the old romance had been a guilty thing. Having lost all else Abelard does not wish to surrender heaven by clinging, even in memory, to his sin. He tells Heloise that there are some whom God saves by suffering. "Let my salvation be the fruit of your prayer. Let me owe it to your tears and to your exemplary holiness." Of course, he refuses to continue the correspondence. To comply with her request could bring no real happiness to either of them and could only endanger their eternal salvation. There is one place alone where they may be united. And here too Abelard closes his letter with a prophecy which has passed into fulfillment. "I hope you will be willing when you have finished this mortal life, to be buried near me. Your cold ashes need then fear nothing, and my tomb shall be the more rich and renowned."

In spite of his refusal to prolong the correspondence Heloise wrote two more letters. Their superscriptions indicate the varying character of their contents. The first is addressed:

To Abelard her well-beloved in Christ Jesus, from He-loise his well-beloved in the same Christ Jesus.

and the second begins simply:

Dear Abelard.

It is clear that the author is proceeding well with the process of sublimation. She encourages her husband to aspire to greater things. She still believes that everything is possible to his genius, only he must not surrender. No man ever needed encouragement more than the one to whom she was writing. It was his final misfortune that he could not receive from her the courage which she would have given him.

The last letter of the collection, the final communication of Abelard in response to the two which he had previously received begins like a dirge. "Write no more to me, Heloise, write no more to me; 'tis time to end communications which make our penances of naught avail." The rest of the letter is in the same strain. It is filled with the note of remorse, the stings of conscience and the ever-present fear of hell. Even these gloomy reflections can not entirely extinguish the memories of the past. It is this fact which fills him with the greatest apprehension. Fame, fortune and love have all left him. He has suffered from the malice of his foes and from the envy of his friends. Broken in body and spirit, only the hope of heaven is left him, and he is not sure of that. One can not help regretting that William Shakespeare died before these letters became the property of the public. What might not the author of *Hamlet* and the *Sonnets* have done for such a figure? And yet the letters do not need any further touch of genuis to secure their immortality. They speak for themselves and their simplicity and truthfulness constitute the highest form of art. Like the *Letters of a Portuguese*

Nun and the *Sonnets from the Portuguese,* which may have
drawn their inspiration from them, the brief correspondence
of these lovers of the twelfth century will never lose its
charm.   Alexander Pope made the story of Abelard the
subject of a poem but added nothing to his reputation by
doing so.   It was impossible for the author of *The Rape
of the Lock* to enter into the spirit of such a romance.   One
couplet will suffice to show the distance between artificial
and real sentiment:

> In vain lost Eloisa weeps and prays.
> Her heart still dictates and her hand obeys.

IV

As a theologian Abelard ranks with the great rationalists of the ages.   He is in the direct line of succession
from Theodore to Erasmus.   No man ever reasoned more
clearly, more fearlessly, or more successfully than he.
There was scarcely a touch of the mystic about him.   He
never allowed his emotions to interfere with his intellect.
In every respect he was in advance of his age.   He is the
most modern of all the schoolmen.   The current supersti-
tions of the times were unthinkable to him.   If in his later
years he bowed in slavish submission to the dogmas of the
church it was only because he wanted to close his shattered
life in peace and with the benediction of his superiors.   In
the controversies which centered around him he never com-
promised the truth.   With unerring directness his mind
proceeded straight to the point involved.   It is a tribute to
his intellect that most of his contemporaries ascribed the
bitter attacks upon him to jealousy.   No other teacher was
in his class, and there were many who essayed to teach in his
day.   Out of circumstances such as these arose many of his
misfortunes.

Against the satisfaction theory of the atonement,

as promulgated by Anselm of Canterbury, Abelard urged what has come to be known as the moral interpretation of the doctrine in question. The legalistic view of Anselm was utterly impossible to so clear thinking an intelligence as his. In its place he urged the idea that Jesus suffered as a perfect example of goodness and that we are morally transformed by following in His footsteps and by taking up His cross after Him. The atonement thus becomes a thoroughly rational and ethical doctrine, although it must be conceded that it loses something of the driving dynamic of the older view. Nevertheless, the standpoint of Abelard remains of immense significance in the history of thought. Liberals throughout the ages have owned their allegiance to him, and the moral theory is perhaps more popular than any other in the religious world to-day. Henry Ward Beecher accepted it and preached it with persuasive eloquence. Whatever judgment we may pass upon it, no one can deny that it has gained in appeal since it was first promulgated.

It was when he attempted to rationalize the doctrine of the Trinity that Abelard became involved in the most serious difficulty. Since the days of Nicæa the Trinity has always been a sore spot for orthodoxy. Nearly five centuries after Abelard's day Calvin had no hesitancy about burning Servetus at the stake because the latter had doubts concerning the sacred Mystery of the Three who are One and the One who is Three. The irrational contradictions involved in the current orthodox statements were impossible to Abelard, as they must always be to any one who attempts to think clearly on the subject. As an honest and sincere son of the church he sought to remedy this defect. His interpretation, while not in any sense hostile to the doctrine itself made it more appealing to the rational inquirer. Moderate as were his emendations they could not escape the fury of his detractors. On all sides he was accused of being a Sabellian, an epithet which had been little used since the days of Arius. He denied the charge and argued his case with precision and power, but envy, superstition and ignorance constituted a trinity which he could not overcome. The majority of people felt convinced that a man who could make abstruse doctrines so clear and simple must surely be in league with the devil, and therefore had no further use for him. He was condemned and was compelled to burn his books, as already stated, with his own hands. When we think of the fact that this was in the twelfth century we may well believe that he was fortunate in not himself constituting the bonfire. The church was too thoroughly committed to the worship of Mysteries to countenance a rationalist like Abelard. Hence his Trinitarian views were placed on the index and are still regarded as heretical by Catholics and Protestants alike.

It was obvious that so clear-sighted a theologian would find little to admire in the major tenets of Augustine. His points of affinity were rather with Pelagius, although in the matter of free will he did little more than follow the orthodox semi-Pelagianism of the church. The ideas of total depravity, original sin and irresistible grace were unthinkable to him. Again, like Erasmus, while fully conscious of the evils and vices of the church he would have shrunk from the cold calculating fatalism of many of the reformers. He was always scientific in his turn and temper. One of his best known works is entitled the *Sic et Non (Yes and No)* which consists of over one hundred and sixty theological propositions culled from the Fathers, with an affirmative and a negative answer to each of them likewise culled from the same sources. The purpose of such a book is obviously to show that every proposition has two sides and that the search for truth demands fairness and the attitude of impartiality. A type of mind like this is farthest from the partizan and prejudiced temper of the vast majority of theologians. It appeals to those who seek for truth but not to those who worship authority. Both types of mind are to be found in abundance, but only the most unbridled optimism would declare that the former outnumber the latter.

V

No sketch of Abelard would be even partly adequate without some reference to his controversy with Bernard of Clairvaux. The latter was in many respects the most powerful ecclesiastic of his day, making popes pretty much at his will although never caring to become one himself, and setting all Europe by the ears through his fiery proclamation of the gospel of the Crusades. Bernard was some twelve years younger than Abelard, and was of an altogether different type of mind. He was the prize fundamentalist of his day, and reaction was his middle name. Anything went with him provided it could be proved that it was old, that it was mysterious, and that somebody associated with the church had at some time or other approved it. He believed thoroughly in the old Gregorian doctrine that Christ paid a ransom to the devil through his atonement, and for this reason he looked with eyes of suspicion even upon Anselm, whose satisfaction theory had already begun to play havoc with the older view. As for the Trinity, Bernard was of course more orthodox than orthodoxy itself. If he could have added anything to the current hypothesis which would have made it more irrational or intellectually impossible he would have done so, but the task had been essayed and completed too many times previously for anything to be left open in that field. All that he could do was to take it as he found it, and this he did with enthusiasm and dispatch. As for transubstantiation, he swallowed it whole and, like Oliver Twist, asked for more. Miracles were his steady diet, and he never had too many of them. The only point where he came near the border-line of heresy was in his disposition to advocate ten sacraments instead of the sacred seven. This over-enthusiasm was not altogether contrary to authority because the question was still regarded as partly unsettled.

In his personal nature and bearing Bernard was a thoroughgoing ascetic. He regarded all romance as sinful and was scandalized by the love-affair of Abelard. He was himself a model of celibate virtue, suppressing, we are told, any temptation to concupiscence by plunging into an icy pond which was located conveniently near the monastery. That he had succeeded in completely sublimating all lower desires is clearly indicated by his allegorical treatment of the Song of Solomon, to which we have referred in an earlier chapter. No one can read the headings of the traditional divisions of this Oriental idyl as Bernard has written them without realizing that the man who could discover only hidden spiritual meanings in the erotic imagery of the words must have possessed a peculiar type of mind. These chapter ascriptions are still preserved in the King James text but have been discreetly eliminated by all translators who have functioned during the last hundred years.

Bernard was a mystic, and wrote a few of the really great hymns of the church. He was dull, pious and moral according to his lights. As is not unusual with this mental equipment he possessed unbounded enthusiasm and emotional eloquence capable of setting on fire the populace who hung upon his words. Although he considered any lapse from celibacy or any failure to accept any portion of the orthodox creed as the most damnable sins, he had no hesitancy about inciting men to leave their families and to take swords in their hands in order to cut to pieces the Mohammedans simply because the latter had the Holy Sepulchre in their possession. It is, of course, useless to expatiate upon ethical contradictions in any individual, but Bernard certainly had his full share of them. In all probability he was little if any worse than his age. Certainly it can not be claimed that he rose above the general thought level of his day.

It was quite inevitable that a crusader of the type embodied in Bernard should come into conflict with an intellectualist like Abelard. Obviously, any one who glorified doubt, who dared to criticize the Fathers, who questioned the infallibility of the Old Testament at all points, who said that the gospel and not the words of the text was what counted, was too dangerous a man to be allowed to roam at large. Bernard went after him with hammer and tongs and succeeded in securing his condemnation. The scandal involved in his enemy's private life only spurred him to greater indignation. There were no scandals at Clairvaux. Moreover, Abelard had no interest in the Crusades. Quite clearly, the man needed watching, and Bernard was the heaven-sent messenger to do the work. Abelard recanted and saved his life but was left with a crushed and broken spirit. Bernard triumphed and carried the applause of the world with him. It is fortunate that verdicts of this kind must ultimately appear before the cold, clear and critical bar of history. That tribunal has long since reversed the twelfth-century judgment. Aside from his hymns Bernard is practically forgotten. Even the most conservative theologians would not think of accepting his dogmas. On every point involved in his controversy with Abelard the judgment has gone against him. With his antagonist fate has dealt more kindly. Both as a philosopher and a lover Abelard ranks among the immortals. Men still quote his words, and his thought is fresh and vital in our modern age. The eternal years belong to him and his name will never be forgotten.

CHAPTER X

AQUINAS

THOMAS AQUINAS is the central figure in medieval theology. In him we find scholasticism at its best, and his influence remains potent in our modern world. Orthodox Roman Catholicism still takes its cue from his writings and his works are yet regarded as authoritative in the seminaries of the church. It is no slight tribute to his genius that this situation exists. The Church of Rome is always ready to adopt a new system of thought provided it will serve its purposes better than the old. Seven centuries have passed since the birth of Saint Thomas and no more satisfactory interpreter of theology has been found. As far as we can see to-day the great Dominican is likely to remain the cherished idol of the Vatican.

Thomas Aquinas was born in 1227, of a noble family in Italy, and from his earliest childhood was committed to the service of the church. At the age of seventeen he entered the Dominican order, and possessing a zeal for learning, he went to Paris where Albertus Magnus, who was called the Universal Doctor, lived and taught. We do not know much about Albertus to-day, but in his own time he possessed a reputation that extended from one end of Europe to the other. Aquinas was his most celebrated pupil and in a few years was destined to surpass his master. At the age of twenty-one the young Italian began his theological career. For twenty-six years he studied and taught and wrote, and at the age of forty-seven he died. His foremost work, and one of the half-dozen greatest productions of its kind in literature, is his *Summa Theologiæ,* or *Comprehensive System of Theology,* which included within itself the entire thought of the Middle Ages. Aquinas had many imitators and copyists but no real rival. His chief antagonist, the Franciscan, Duns Scotus, possessed a different type of mind and in no sense challenged the comprehensive synthesis of Saint Thomas. When one has read the *Summa* he has not only become acquainted with the zenith and flowering of scholastic speculation, but he has also penetrated the heart of the education and artistic culture of the Middle Ages.

I

The background of the Thomistic theology is to be found in the writings of Aristotle. By the time Saint Thomas appeared on the scene the works of the two great Greek philosophers, Plato and Aristotle, had become known throughout Europe. Plato had exerted a primary influence during the eleventh century, but with the wide-spread diffusion of the teachings of Aristotle during the twelfth and early thirteenth centuries the latter took the lead. Saint Thomas was an Aristotelian primarily, but he did not refuse proper respect to Plato. The fact is that his extraordinary capacity for synthesis led him to include both thinkers in his scheme of knowledge and to subject them both to the universal authority of the church. This was indeed the heart and core of the whole Thomistic philosophy. To fit everything that there is into an orderly scheme, to throw nothing aside as useless, to find a place for even the most bizarre and apparently absurd realities, above all to place religion at the capstone of the arch and the pope at the capstone of religion—these were the matters which gave him his chief concern. An ambition like this was sufficiently lofty to stir the enthusiasm of a lad of twenty-one. If he did not succeed completely in his exalted purpose it must at least be said of him that he came nearer to the goal than any one before him or after him. What Harnack describes as the definition of theological science during the thirteenth century may well be regarded as an epitome of the work of Saint Thomas:

. . . the submitting to dialectic-systematic revision of ecclesiastical dogma and ecclesiastical practice, with the view of unfolding them in a system having unity and comprehending all that in the highest sense is worthy of being known, with the view of proving them, and so of reducing to the service of the Church all the forces of the understanding and the whole product of science.

The comprehensive quality of his genius may be understood when we remember that his two great idols were Aristotle and Augustine. Any attempt to reconcile the speculations of these two opposing thinkers would drive the ordinary philosopher to despair. Not so with Aquinas. Each was equally significant to him, and he found a way to incorporate the thought of both into his *Summa*. If he occasionally warps Augustine we may readily believe that his actions were motivated only by that stern necessity before which gods and men must bow.

It is no wonder that the church venerates such a master. Every dogma which the ecclesiastical organization has formulated, the Nicene symbol, the Chalcedonian pronouncements, the mystery of transubstantiation, the sacramental teachings of the councils, the conceptions of original sin and total depravity, purgatory and indulgences, everlasting heaven and eternal hell, in short, the whole mass of doctrine which had accumulated for ten centuries is included under his elaborate scheme. Nothing is left out in the cold. He has tender feeling for even the waifs of doctrine which had once, as it were, clung to the shadow of the church. Nor did he stop with merely theological matters. It is perhaps his greatest contribution to later thought that he opened the way for scientific investigation in the name of the church. By bringing all knowledge under one centralized conception he made it possible for science to find a place within the pale of orthodoxy. If it be said that the reconciliation is achieved by the simple process of the lion swallowing the lamb it should at least be remembered that Jonah lived for three days inside the fish and the lamb of Catholic science has lived for many centuries within the church. What this has meant for the lamb we need not for the present inquire. It is the fact alone which concerns us here. No one can question that the *Summa* gave an immense impetus to science and art alike. Just what this influence meant in both fields we shall try to make clear a little later.

II

How was it that Saint Thomas went about his colossal task of reconciling all the different fields of thought? The key to his method may be found in his conception of the reciprocal relations of reason and revelation. In a general way, the universe is like a pyramid with the Deity at the apex. The first section of the figure, that is, the portion nearest the top, belongs to the supernatural and supersensual world and can be apprehended only through the dogmas of the church. The lowest part of the pyramid belongs to the field of reason, and here science and other purely humanistic disciplines have their sway. The passage from the lower to the upper realm is through the sacraments, and especially the initiatory rite of baptism. The church has to do primarily with the upper part of the pyramid, but inasmuch as this is built upon the lower and inasmuch as the whole structure is in reality one it is quite impossible to separate the secular from the divine.

It is patent that the above scheme of things is so contrived as to enable practically everything to fit into it. Any dogma which appears contrary to reason, as for example the orthodox view of the Trinity or the doctrine of transubstantiation, is immediately referred to the higher realm of revelation and is thus eliminated from the field of reason. On the other hand, any matter which can be resolved by intellectual processes without running counter to the authority of the church may be safely left to the scientists and humanists who inhabit only the lower quarters of the pyramid. In this way the church opens the door to science while at the same time retaining complete and absolute control over the field of dogma. Saint Thomas never drew an exact line between the two realms. Certain questions he found quite difficult to allocate. For example, the proofs of the divine existence might well be referred to revelation and to the authoritative dogma of the church. Saint Thomas, however, felt that with the new ontological proof of Anselm and with the cosmological argument of Aristotle to buttress the other evidence it was safe to leave the question in the lower half of the pyramid. Since the negative arguments of Kant have come into play there is a disposition in some circles to save the day by removing the whole question to the realm of revelation. Perhaps they think that Saint Thomas was over-adventurous in taking it from thence in the first place. In any event, so long as the Thomistic system endures there will always be room for it in the upper part of the pyramid.

It must be clear also that the *Summa* is an exceedingly satisfying volume from the standpoint of ecclesiastical authority. It gives the last word to the church in every case, and while it finds a place for science that place is always in submission to theology. It is true that the churchmen contend that no conflict is possible between reason and revelation since they occupy different positions in the general scheme of things. No conflict is indeed possible if science is willing to take orders from the church at every turn of the road, to investigate only such fields as are allotted to her, to go only as far in her investigations as dogmatic edict permits, in short, to be satisfied with forever reasoning in a circle and upon the express condition that the circumference of the circle is on no account to be overpassed. It is true that some investigators can play the game according to these rules, but in the main scientists find it impossible to conform to them. In order to achieve real progress thought must be free and the search for truth must be the only goal of endeavor. To put barriers around the experimenter, to hedge him about with authoritative dogmas, to tie his hands with ecclesiastical pronouncements is, in the long run, to prevent him from achievement. We can not refuse a measure of admiration for the synthetic genius of Thomas Aquinas. Like all great absolutisms it has the element of grandeur about it. Like all of them, too, it has within it the seeds of decay. Life is not after all so simple that it can be tidied up after this fashion. There are more things in heaven and earth than are dreamed of in the philosophy of Saint Thomas. Nevertheless, it represents a real achievement of the human intellect, and he would be an ungracious churl who would leave it without at least a note of respect.

It is quite needless to say that no romantic indiscretions attached to the name or fame of Saint Thomas. He was theology incarnate, and the monastic discipline sufficed for all the needs of his life. Here too he became an object worthy of supreme beatification by the ecclesiastical authorities. An irreproachable celibate, a man who reduced all knowledge beneath the overlordship of the church, who put everybody and everything in subjection to the pope, what other than sainthood could be reserved for such an individual? Saint indeed he was made, and that in comparatively short order. Anselm waited for some centuries, but there was no need of delay in the case of one so patently beatified as the author of the *Summa*. So sovereign a champion of orthodoxy assuredly deserved all the honors which the church could give. Abelard never became a saint, nor Theodore, nor Origen, but fame has canonized them nevertheless. Let us not begrudge the tinsel trappings which ecclesiastical favor bestows upon its devotees.

III

To be acquainted with the *Summa Theologiæ* is to possess the key to the understanding of the Middle Ages. Not only is this true in philosophy and theology but it is also true in the fields of letters and art. The supreme literary figure between Virgil and Shakespeare was undoubtedly Dante Alighieri, and Dante was the poetical incarnation of Saint Thomas. One of the best-known commentators of the great poet says that a knowledge of the works of Aquinas is an indispensable requirement for the proper understanding of the *Divine Comedy*. On the other hand, it is equally true that the student who is familiar with the theology of the Florentine poet needs no further introduction to the thought of Saint Thomas. It may be worth our while to indicate in the merest outline the significance of the above statement.

In the month of May, 1265 A.D., Dante was born at Florence. Thomas Aquinas was still alive at this time and did not die until the poet was nine years of age. That year, 1274, was memorable to Dante because it was the date when he first saw Beatrice, who afterward played such a significant part in his life. The thirteenth century was replete with events of historical significance. The year after Dante was born Roger Bacon sent a copy of his *Opus Majus* to Pope Clement IV. From that moment we may date the first faint beginnings of modern science. The French Kings were interfering in Italy, and all Europe was in more or less turmoil. Dante was five years old when Louis IX of France, the only king who ever officially became a saint, died before Tunis in Africa. He was eleven years of age when Giotto, the real founder of Renaissance painting in Italy, was born. Four years later, in 1280, William of Occam, the last of the schoolmen, first saw the light. It was about this time that Dante studied at the Universities of Padua and Bologna, the two oldest and most famous of the Italian schools. How long he remained a student we do not know, but nine years later, in 1289, he took part in the battle of Campaldino, where the Florentines defeated the people of Arezzo.

The year 1290 was an epoch-making one for the poet. It was the date of the death of Beatrice and is touchingly memorialized in the thirty-second canto of the "Purgatorio." In this year the poet served in the war waged by the Florentines against the inhabitants of Pisa and was present at the surrender of Caprona, in the same autumn. The next spring when he was twenty-six years of age, he married Gemma Donati. This lady unfortunately failed to measure up to the standard of Beatrice, and as a consequence the union was not happy. Nevertheless, six children, five sons and a daughter, were born in the family. In 1294, Dante wrote his *Vita Nuova,* and the next year Marco Polo, the celebrated traveler, returned from the East to Venice where he delighted the populace with marvelous stories concerning the Orientals, most of which were accepted unanimously by his contemporaries, rejected with the same unanimity by their successors, and under the searching criticism of modern investigation proved to have been at least half correct. The English and the Scots were at war about this time, and William Wallace, one of the foremost of the northern heroes, was leading the cause of freedom. In the year 1300, the date which he himself had chosen as the time when he saw the vision of his *Divine Comedy,* Dante was made Chief Magistrate of Florence. He was in office only a few months, and a little over a year later he was tried and banished from the city. This sentence was later changed to one of death at the stake if he could be apprehended. Two years afterward he joined with other exiles in an unsuccessful attack upon Florence. That same year, in May, the bridge over the Arno broke down during a representation of the infernal torments which were being exhibited on the river. Dante describes this happening in the twenty-sixth canto of the "Inferno." On July twentieth of the same year Petrarch, whose father had been exiled from Florence at the same time when Dante was banished, was born at Arezzo. Four years later Duns Scotus, the great scholastic rival of Thomas Aquinas, if tradition be correct, was buried alive through an error of his physicians. In 1312 the order of the Knight Templars was abolished and its leading representatives executed under circumstances of the most revolting cruelty. In 1313 Boccaccio was born, the third of the great triumvirate of Italian authors, and Dante took refuge at Ravenna, which became his home from that time forth. In September, 1321, not many years before the birth of Chaucer, Dante died at Ravenna of a complaint which the chroniclers tell us was brought on by disappointment at his failure in a negotiation which he had been conducting for the Venetians in behalf of his patron, the ruler of Ravenna.

One can not understand the spirit of Dante, which is the spirit of the Middle Ages, without some acquaintance with the history of the time. When we read the lurid pictures of cruelty and torture in the pages of the "Inferno" they seem fantastic and impossible to us, but the fact is that there is not a single species of torment recorded in Dante which was not literally extracted from the history of his own age. Schopenhauer told the truth long afterward when he said that Dante made the "Inferno" quite a dramatic and interesting book because he wrote it from real life, while the "Purgatorio" and "Paradisio" lacked dramatic quality because they had no such realistic background.

Filling in the theological skeleton of Saint Thomas with the dramatic horrors of every-day life, Dante succeeded in producing a work of surpassing artistic merit. From the standpoint of esthetics it will doubtless always take rank as one of the half-dozen supreme achievements of poetical genius. The fact that it is quite impossible for the average reader to take its theology seriously is sufficient proof that we have traveled a long way from the formulations of Saint Thomas. Few Roman Catholics, we opine, believe very ardently nowadays in the reality of Dante's vision of hell, and yet that vision is quite identical with the teaching of the *Summa* and with the general thought of the Middle Ages and of the Reformation period as well.

What is the eschatology which Dante elaborates in the one hundred cantos of his great poem? Stated in the simplest possible form it is this: there are three divisions of the future world, the abyss of hell where the wicked are tortured forever, the mountains of purgatory, where those who are part good are punished until the dross is burned out of their natures, and the celestial heights of paradise, where the beatified of all ages live in everlasting bliss. It is noteworthy that the "Inferno" is not only the first, most interesting and most realistic of the three poems but that it is also the longest. Dante is obviously more at home here than anywhere else. It is worth noting the classes of people who are assigned to the nine circles of perdition. The first includes unbaptized infants and the souls of virtuous people who for one reason or another failed to be baptized. Included in this number are of course the great philosophers and worthies of the ancient world. A little farther on, in the second circle, which is given over to never-ending gales and storms of wind, Dante locates the distinguished figures who have loved not wisely but too well throughout the ages. Here we find the immortal story of Paolo and Francesca, which is doubtless the best-known incident in the writings of Dante. Later on we meet the punishment of the gluttons, the covetous, the hypocrites and, last of all, the traitors. In every instance the principle upon which Dante constructs his scheme of punishments is purely and solely the Levitical maxim of "an eye for an eye and a tooth for a tooth." The gluttons grovel in the mire, the hypocrites are loaded with heavy cloaks of gilded lead and burned alive, a punishment which, by the way, is said to have been meted out quite frequently by the Emperor Frederick II of this period. Murderers are plunged into rivers of boiling blood, schismatics are cloven asunder, and envious people have their eyelids sewn together. As illustrating the characteristic difference between the Latin and the Saxon types of mind it is worth noting that at the very bottom of hell, in the frozen heart of the ninth circle, along with Judas Iscariot Dante puts Brutus and Cassius, the liberators of Rome from the tyranny of Cæsar. Shakespeare, the incarnation of the northern genius, on the contrary idealizes Brutus as the one faultless hero of his dramas and the embodiment of ethical perfection.

The picture contained in the "Purgatorio" is less lifelike than the lurid silhouettes of the "Inferno," but is quite in keeping with the fundamental dogmas of the church. In the seven terraces which rise higher and higher on the mountain are to be found many souls of mixed quality and sinful life who nevertheless have been able to avail themselves of the good offices of the church and therefore have a chance to climb upward to paradise. The difference between the souls in purgatory and the souls in hell, as Dante has pictured them, appears to be primarily that in the one case they rejoice in their sufferings because they understand their purgatorial value, while in the other case they curse and denounce the pains which they are obliged to endure.

In the "Paradisio," under the guidance of Beatrice, we are taken from planet to planet and from star to star and are given highly idealized pictures of the abodes of the blessed. It must be confessed that they are decidedly tame in comparison with the lurid reality of the "Inferno." Moreover, a great deal of space is taken up with purely theological discussions and compliments to ecclesiastical dignitaries. Saint Thomas himself figures quite prominently and very politely makes a long speech in praise of the virtues of Saint Francis, the founder of the rival order of Franciscans. On the principle that one good turn deserves another, Bonaventura, the General of the Franciscan order, delivers an elaborate panegyric on Saint Dominic, the founder of the Dominicans. Solomon is dragged in to describe what the appearance of the blessed will be like after the resurrection of the body. It must be confessed that, considering his wisdom, he does not throw great light upon the question. In Canto 24, Dante has apparently about run out of copy. He has Saint Peter conduct an examination upon the subject of faith which does rather slight credit to the pedagogical qualifications of the immortal fisherman. In Canto 26, Saint John continues the examination upon the subject of charity and in Canto 27 Saint Peter comes back with some hot shot concerning the covetous behavior of his successors in the papal chair. Evidently there were a few popes with whom Dante wished to square accounts.

Thomas Aquinas died before he reached the age of fifty. He had already attained a great reputation, and tradition ascribed his early demise to poison. Dante has embalmed the legend in the twentieth canto of the "Purgatorio," where he says:

> To Italy came Charles; and for amends,
> Young Conradine, an innocent victim, slew;
> And sent the angelic teacher back to heaven,
> Still for amends.

The story may be correct but it is not necessary to assume its accuracy. The average span of life during the Middle Ages was much shorter than it is to-day. Medical science was yet in its infancy and the best treatment which most people possessed, if disease overtook them, was to pray to the particular saint who had that special malady in charge and to let the matter rest at that point. Under such circumstances Aquinas did pretty well in passing beyond his fortieth birthday. As was true in the case of Saint Francis, who also died comparatively young, the world lost heavily when the great Dominican passed into the beyond.

IV

Not only in literature but also in the fields of art and education Saint Thomas was the supreme inspirer of his day. Those who have read John Ruskin's *Mornings in*

Florence will recall his illuminating description of one of the Spanish chapel frescoes in the old church of Santa Maria Novella. This picture, more than any other in existence, sums up the entire pedagogical conception of the Middle Ages. Not only does it furnish us with a complete copy of the university curriculum, it also gives us a clear insight concerning the dominant ideal which pervaded the educational theory and practise of the period. Perhaps few people who visit Florence appreciate its significance in spite of Ruskin's splendid tribute, but it is nevertheless true that a thorough study of this one painting will furnish more real information to the average student than a cursory inspection of all the treasures in the Pitti Gallery.

Let us turn for a moment to the picture and its interpretation. It is in the comparatively small Spanish chapel which is just beyond the old courtyard that tradition credits with being the birthplace of the Renaissance. Here we are told Boccaccio and his friends used to assemble and tell stories, and here too were gathered many other of the brightest lights of those early days of culture. The picture itself contains as its centerpiece a noble portrait of Saint Thomas, who is thus characterized as the guardian of all education, both sacred and profane. At the top of the painting, in the very point of the arch, are the three supreme virtues, Faith, Hope and Love, with Love at the summit of the three. All are pictured as winged figures, with Faith bearing a cross. Underneath the three superior virtues are the four subsidiary ones, Temperance, Prudence, Justice and Fortitude. Temperance is in the act of bridling a black fish upon which she stands. Prudence has a book in her hand, Justice wears a crown, and Fortitude, as usual, is represented with a tower in one hand and a sword in the other. These seven symbolic figures are ranged immediately above the great throne of state upon which

Saint Thomas sits with an open book in his hands and an expression of inane satisfaction upon his face. On both sides of the throne are placed sundry of the more important prophets and evangelists, who are represented as basking with supreme appreciation in the sunlight of the great Dominican scholar. Ruskin identifies the figures on the left as David, Saint Paul, Saint Mark and Saint John, leaving the farthest one over undeciphered. On the right he locates Saint Matthew, Saint Luke, Moses, Isaiah and Solomon. Certainly no doubt can be expressed concerning the picture of Moses for the conspicuous horns springing from his brow make the identification absolute. Curiously enough, all of the Middle-Age artists represent Moses with horns. The error arose from an erroneous translation of the Hebrew text in the Pentateuch and persisted throughout the early period of the Renaissance. Solomon, too, is definitely located by the crown upon his head. Immediately crouching beneath the feet of Saint Thomas are three figures whose foreign costume and appearance clearly mark them out as the trinity of great Arabian philosophers, Avicenna, Averroes and Maimonides, who were thus brought into proper penitential attitudes toward the foremost genius of the church.

The real significance of the picture is to be found in the figures which occupy the lower portion of the work. Here we have in vivid and graphic form a complete synopsis of medieval education. In this section, as everywhere else, the magical number seven holds sway. As there are seven sacraments in the church so there are seven theological sciences corresponding to that great realm of revelation which Saint Thomas had committed to the special guardianship of the church. Next to this higher seven we have another heptad which includes the natural sciences appertaining to the lower realm of reason in the universal pyramid of Aquinas. The theological sciences, in the order in which they occur in the picture, are civil law, canon law, practical theology, contemplative theology, dogmatic theology and polemic theology. These various disciplines are all pictured by female forms which embody in some respect or other the peculiar characteristics of each science. Underneath these symbolic figures are the portraits of the men who have been chosen by the artist as especially representative of the various studies under which they are placed. Under civil law, for example, we have the Emperor Justinian, who still remains one of the supreme figures in legal lore. Under canon law we have Pope Clement V, who likewise occupies a position of outstanding importance in the history of ecclesiastical jurisprudence. Under practical theology we have Peter Lombard, whose text-books of maxims long served as the practical homiletical guide of the church. Contemplative theology is depicted by a portrait of Dionysius the Areopagite, to whom we referred in detail in earlier chapters of this book. Dogmatic theology is represented by Boethius, the most eminent theologian in that sterile period of the Dark Ages between Augustine and Anselm. Mystic theology is represented by Saint John Damascene, the last name in Greek speculation, with whom also we have had to deal in an earlier section. Polemic theology, which properly and naturally follows all the others, is interpreted by Saint Augustine, who is thus given a position of honorable subordination to Saint Thomas Aquinas. Above all of these figures are small medallions containing symbolic representations of the sciences with which they are associated. Ruskin has dug out the meaning of these medallions with infinite patience, and probably with accurate results.

The natural sciences are more interesting to readers of this modern age than are their theological counterparts.

At the time this picture was painted the reverse was doubtless true. When we remember that this was nearly three centuries before Galileo and Bacon we can understand that science, in the true sense, was not yet born. The seven studies which constituted the entire liberal arts curriculum of this olden time were arithmetic, geometry, astronomy, music, logic, rhetoric and grammar. Arithmetic was placed above the figure of Pythagoras who had come to be known even in that day as the father of number. Geometry was of course represented by Euclid, who will doubtless always remain the first geometrician of the world. Astronomy, by strange misapprehension, was referred to Zoroaster who did, indeed, have high regard for the sun but could scarcely be called a patron of astronomy. Music is depicted by a savage-looking figure pounding vigorously upon an anvil. Ruskin, no doubt correctly, identifies him as Tubal-Cain, who is described in the book of Genesis as substantially the first blacksmith. The English critic reasons to the effect that strokes upon the anvil gave the first inklings of harmony to the human race. Logic is naturally enough entrusted to Aristotle, and rhetoric to Cicero. Grammar falls to Priscian, a name practically forgotten but potent during the Middle-Age period.

Thus it is that we have in this little out-of-the-way chapel in Florence a living and imperishable monument of the educational progress of the Middle Ages. Nothing could more completely embody the spirit of scholasticism at its best than this system of intellectual disciplines so completely controlled by the authorities of the church. All education centers around and is subordinate to religion. Moreover, the interpreter of religion is Saint Thomas, and it was the supreme ideal of the latter always to be subject to the pope. It is no wonder that the church is loath to give up the *Summa* as its authoritative text-book. Where else would it be possible to find such complete and thorough subjugation of the kingdoms of this world to the overlordship of Saint Peter's Chair? Not without reason do interpreters like Mr. Chesterton and Mr. Belloc long for the return of the Middle Ages.

V

The medieval church, despite its external unity, was rent by constant factional disorders. Chief among these tendencies to schism was the rivalry of the two great monastic orders, the Franciscans and the Dominicans. The latter gained tremendous prestige through the acknowledged skill of Thomas Aquinas, and this fact roused the Franciscans to redoubled efforts. Bonaventura, the head of the order, who was a contemporary of Dante, achieved a great reputation for his dialectical skill, but even his fondest admirers could scarcely claim that he equaled Aquinas.

The real rival of Saint Thomas arose in the person of Duns Scotus, the acute and brilliant thinker of the north who possessed, with the sole exception of Abelard, the most penetrating intellect of the medieval period. Throughout his life the great Scot was unfortunate. Luck always seemed to be against him, and his evil genius pursued him to the end, for as we have already indicated tradition avers that he was buried alive through an error of his attendants. Subtle and discriminating to the last degree, he was persistently misunderstood by those who listened to his words. At Oxford he was ridiculed, and our English word "dunce" arose from the derisive use of his surname as an epithet. The Dominicans were jealous of him and could not brook the idea of any one rivaling the glory of Saint Thomas. Scotus himself appears to have lacked tact and certainly possessed few of the graces of style which gave such charm to the discourses of Abelard. In philosophy he antedated the modern emphasis upon the will which has taken such hold upon present-day thought. Just as Aquinas, with his deification of reason and intellect, anticipated Hegel and modern rationalism in general, so Scotus, with his stress upon the will, preceded Schopenhauer and much of modern empiricism. In the long run the great Franciscan asserted that reason is helpless to explain any of the more important facts of life and religion. Hence we must fall back upon the will of God as the only solution of the really difficult equations which we have to solve in life. If we are asked to explain the nature of original sin or predestination or the Real Presence or any of the other knotty and disturbing questions which are propounded by the skeptics our only answer must be that God willed it so, and beyond that we can not go. The arbitrary will of God thus becomes the foundation of all morality as well as of all religion. In many respects the system of Scotus would seem to be better adapted to the practical needs of Catholicism than the more moderate intellectualism of Aquinas. By making everything depend upon the arbitrary will of supreme authority a sure foundation is laid for unquestioning obedience. It is not without reason that the Jesuit order has always favored the philosophy of Scotus. Should the intellectual foundations of Thomism crumble completely beneath the fierce glare of modern criticism, the Vatican may well turn for refuge to the unfortunate Duns with his unassailable bulwark of irrationality expressing itself in the inscrutable will of God.

The thought of Scotus was carried farther by his disciple, William of Occam, who brought nominalism to its final form. Only the individual is real, from William's point of view, and in his thought we are at the farthest pole from the Platonic realism of Saint Anselm. The reformers were accustomed to making sport of William and the schoolmen of his day, but as a matter of fact much that is in modern Protestantism is embodied in their teaching. The doctrine of individual freedom, the idea of independence, the disposition to revolt and to set up one's standard for one's self, are all foreshadowed in the thought of nominalism. Moreover, the skepticism of David Hume and a great deal that came to be embodied in the later Association School of Psychology may be traced to Occam. There is, in fact, very little in the modern age which does not derive its basic inspiration from at least some suggestion of the schoolmen.

The fourteenth century witnessed the greatest architectural development in Europe and the beginnings of the great fresco painting of the Italian Renaissance. The fifteenth century marked the starting-point of that period of discovery which was destined to revolutionize the life of the world. In 1453 Mohammed II captured Constantinople and put an end to the Eastern Empire. Less than forty years later Columbus planted the flag of Spain on the islands of the Western Hemisphere. The Borgias were ruling in the Vatican and Savonarola was thundering against the vices of the age in the great Duomo of Florence. In 1495, three years after the discovery of America, Gabriel Biel, the disciple of Occam and the thinker who is usually styled the last of the schoolmen, passed out of existence. It was time for him to die. The old order had changed, giving place to the new. The Renaissance was in full swing and the ominous foreshadowings of the great Protestant Reformation could already be detected. The world was breaking up, and no one could prognosticate the future. The good old days of monasticism were at an end. The supremacy of the church was being challenged on all sides and the unquestioning loyalty of medieval scholasticism struck a discordant note in the thought of the times. What was left of the old faith still held to Saint Thomas, but half of the world deserted him. Moreover this half counted among its supporters the aggressive nations of the modern world, the Germans, the Dutch, and above all, the Anglo Saxons who were destined to dominate the mighty realms beyond the seas. To most of these iconoclasts the name of Saint Thomas possesses a faint and far-away sort of coloring which reminds them of musty clothing stored away in old out-of-the-way chests of drawers. He is an antique and nothing more. They may occasionally look up his name in the encyclopedia, but he has no living interest for them.

And yet there are those who have kept the memory of Saint Thomas green. His philosophy is still the accredited basis of Roman Catholic education and there are millions of students who reverence his name. It may well be that his influence is at its zenith, and that he will soon be superseded by some one who can serve the church of the twentieth century as he served the church of the twelfth. Should this turn out to be true it ought not to be esteemed anything to his discredit. Assuredly eight centuries constitute a sufficient length of time for one man's thought to preserve its influence unabated. Whatever criticism we may pass upon the substance of his philosophy we can not dispute the fact that he will forever remain one of the great synthetic geniuses of the world.

CHAPTER XI

ERASMUS was perhaps the foremost scholar of all time. In him were united the characteristics which go to make up the perfect student: acuteness of intellect, indefatigable industry and mental poise. We know very little about his ancestry and what information we possess is mainly derived from his own rather casual statements. His father's name was Gerrard; his mother, Margaret, was the daughter of a physician. Tradition avers that Erasmus was born out of wedlock, although there is no indisputable proof of this assertion. What seems perfectly certain is that he was left an orphan at a very early age and that both his mother and his father died before the lad was fourteen. Erasmus tells us that his parents would have left an estate large enough to have given him the university education which he so greatly desired had it not been for the knavery of his guardians. These were two in number, a banker and a schoolmaster. Originally there had been a third, a burgher, but he soon died of plague so that his associates were left solely responsible for the care of their ward. The latter, in one of his most scorching epistles, indicts them for criminal negligence and corruption. He never forgave them because they took the cheap and easy way of educating him by sending him to a monastery and practically converting him to monkery perforce. It was the bad impression of the monastic life gained during these early years which was largely responsible for his later antipathy to all religious orders. It was his satirical wit which lashed the

monks to fury and which paved the way for the open revolt
of Luther. If this little sickly Dutch child had been treated
more considerately the history of the world might have been
different. Erasmus laid the egg and Luther hatched it, the
monks were accustomed to say, but the egg might never have
been laid if two muddle-headed and stingy old bourgeois
had paid a little more attention to their business.

I

Desiderius Erasmus was born at Rotterdam, Holland, in
1467. William Caxton was just beginning to set up his
printing press in England and Christopher Columbus was
scurrying around over the seas making trips to Iceland,
looking up the records concerning the adventurous Norse
voyages to Vinland four centuries earlier, and keeping the
knowledge gained to himself. Edward IV was King of
England, Louis XI, of whom every child knows through
Quentin Durward and *The Hunchback of Notre Dame,*
was King of France. Charles the Bold was Duke of Bur-
gundy and was the immediate liege lord of Erasmus. The
Renaissance was beginning to blossom to fruition and the
Reformation was less than half a century off. It was a time
of stirring activity and ferment. Next to Venice the Low
Countries, as our modern Holland and Belgium were
styled at that time, constituted the commercial center of
the world. Ghent, Brussels, Amsterdam, Bruges, and other
cities were great manufacturing towns and were populated
by craftsmen whose class-consciousness was thoroughly developed. Erasmus grew up among these surroundings and
unquestionably derived much from them. Even when a
child his chief passion was the desire for learning. His
parents encouraged his ambition as long as they lived, and
after their death the boy pursued his studies for himself. A

mind like his required no special tutelage. It was never necessary to urge him to study. In the interest of a rather fragile physical constitution it became far more essential to restrain his habits of application.

The convent experience of the little Dutch lad was always painful to his memory. He never refers to it in his letters except with indications of scorn and displeasure. It remained a sore spot throughout his life. Altogether he must have spent a dozen or more years in this semi-imprisonment, but whatever its inconveniences may have been it certainly did not prevent him from acquiring that perfect scholarship which was the despair of his rivals and the unceasing admiration of his friends. Even Cicero himself could not write Latin as could Erasmus. In his hands the language of Tully became infused with life and originality. He knew Greek too, though not so perfectly as he understood Latin, and he was apparently the master of whatever else there was to be learned during his day. He wrote books with great rapidity, his *Praise of Folly*, one of the foremost satires ever produced, occupying him less than a fortnight in its actual composition. He composed at odd hours and sandwiched his literary efforts in between the multitudinous incidents of an extraordinarily busy career. He constantly suffered from ill health and was often obliged to give up work on this account. His disposition was free and easy-going, and it was impossible for him to say no to a friend. Hence, people of all sorts imposed on his time and were never refused audience.

This penniless orphan, put out as a foundling upon the charity of the church, became the associate on equal terms of popes and emperors and noble lords and ladies, in short, of the greatest and most exclusive scions of his time. He was bosom friend of Henry VIII when the latter was still Prince of Wales and, like Nero in his early years, gave every

promise of becoming the most humane and enlightened
monarch of his day. Sir Thomas More, who wrote *Utopia*
and who later had his head cut off by this same Henry,
constituted the third of the trio who sent one another
affectionate letters and were boon companions in the higher
intellectual circles of London. Erasmus liked England and
stayed there a good part of his time after he was freed from
his monastic vows by the special dispensation of the Pope.
He was essentially a wanderer, however, and he went to
Paris, to Rome, to Freiburg, finally to Basel, where he died
on July 12, 1536. The news of the execution of Anne
Boleyn by her royal husband and lover must have reached
him just before he passed away. He had known Henry
when such an action on his part would have been unthinkable. The Catholics had definitely turned down
Melanchthon's pacific Augsburg proposals of 1530. The
Pope was ready to flatter the greatest scholar of his time
by granting him ecclesiastical preferment if he would come
out boldly against the Lutherans. This was precisely what
Erasmus did not want to do. During his lifetime, especially
when he was young, the thought of death filled him with
horror and aversion. When the end actually came he met
it with peace and tranquillity. Perhaps it seemed a relief.
Notwithstanding his heretical affiliations and the damage
which he had done to the church he was accorded a magnificent funeral and was buried in state in the cathedral. To
this day neither Protestants nor Catholics know exactly
where to place him. No satisfactory biography of him has
thus far appeared. Froude's *Life and Letters* remains the
best in English, but it is not really a biography. Perhaps
when a few more centuries have elapsed some one capable
of understanding him will tell the story of his life. Until
then he can afford to wait.

II

The publication of the Greek New Testament with its Latin translation by Erasmus was the immediate precursor of the Reformation. Not only the text itself but the singularly illuminating and interpretative notes which were appended shook the foundations of the established church. Intelligent people were able to read the teachings of Jesus and the simple story of the building of His Kingdom for themselves, and they were not slow to compare what they read with what they saw on the banks of the Tiber and elsewhere throughout the ecclesiastical world. Erasmus published his book with the idea of inviting this comparison, and it was this fact which enraged the clergy against him. He always stood in with the popes and many of the higher officials, primarily because they loved culture and no one else in the world had as much as he, and perhaps incidentally because they recognized the truthfulness of much of his criticism. Taine may be stretching matters a little when he avers that Leo X was substantially an atheist, but there can be no doubt that the Borgia and Medici popes who ruled at this time were far more interested in art and luxury than they were in religion. They liked the courtly grace of Erasmus, and he enjoyed their intellectual and artistic companionship. Moreover, it was a time when people were not squeamish about their treatment of heretics. The courtly and gracious King Francis I made a special point of roasting in chains above a fire those who disagreed with him religiously and was accustomed to grace these executions with his own royal presence. In Italy and England and Spain things were not much better. Erasmus had said enough about the church to have burned a hundred wretches of lesser significance. The monks longed to make him the center of an *auto da fé*. He was too much an intellectualist, too self-poised and rational to enjoy being

made a martyr. Martyrs, after all, must almost necessarily
be fanatics, and Erasmus was the farthest removed from
such a type of mind. He did not relish the idea of sharing
the fate of Huss or Servetus. His one guarantee of safety
was his friendship with the Pope, and it was no wonder
that he did not want to sacrifice it.

Up until the time when Luther broke openly with the
church and proceeded to destroy its unity completely,
Erasmus was counted among the reformers. His attacks
upon the corruption within the organization and upon its
abuses were even more vigorous though less coarse and
vituperative than were those of Luther himself. The monks
hated him, as we have seen, and he was denounced on all
sides as a heretic. Nevertheless, when Luther set in motion
his open rebellion Erasmus recoiled from the consequences
of the schism which he saw impending. After four centuries
of sectarian rivalries and divisions we are coming to recognize the acute foresight of the great humanist. Erasmus
wanted reform, he wanted to return to the ideals and
practise of the New Testament, he wanted to restore the
simplicity of the Apostolic church, but he also wanted to preserve its unity. Most of the reformers, including Luther,
Calvin and Zwingli, could not foresee the consequences of
schism. Erasmus alone had the breadth of comprehension
which enabled him to look down the centuries and recognize
the evils that would inevitably follow in the wake of the
Reformation.

On another vital point he differed from Luther and his
companions. The latter, as we shall see later, were Augustinian to the core in their theology. They believed in
original sin, total depravity and unconditional predestination. These conceptions were unthinkable to so keen a
mind as that of the author of *The Praise of Folly,* and he
had no sympathy whatever with them. When the Catholics

goaded him into writing something against Luther he quite properly selected the freedom of the will as his topic. Luther replied with his usual invectives and restated his case in Augustinian terms.) It must be confessed that Erasmus lost his temper also during this controversy, but in the main his equable disposition saved him from the grosser forms of expression. It was an age when there was no disposition to mince words. Everybody was serious, dreadfully, terribly serious—everybody except Erasmus, whose keen incisive intellect could not help seeing the comic side of what was going on. There was a touch of Voltaire about him, though only a touch. The great French satirist was entirely lacking in what may be styled the religious instinct, while Erasmus was essentially and sincerely devout. Nevertheless, he wanted his religion to be reasonable, ethically sound, and worthy of sincere devotion and respect. He never had any religious convolutions like Luther, and the gloomy austerity of Calvin was totally foreign to him. He was a humanist, a scholar *par excellence,* and withal a man who did not think it necessary to make an inferno out of this world in order to enjoy paradise in the next.

III

It is customary for the biographers of Erasmus to style him a trimmer, sometimes even a coward. This too, in spite of the fact that he spoke out in the most severely critical terms concerning ecclesiastical abuses long before Luther nailed his theses to the door of the church at Wittenberg. The truth is that Erasmus could see no utility in the iconoclasm of most of the reformers. He recognized that Luther's crude Augustinianism was impossible from an ethical point of view and that the world would some day have to discard it even though the period might be long

postponed. The crassness and coarseness of many of the
Protestants were disgusting to him, and yet he had perhaps
less use for the monks. His penetrating intellect could see
the weak spots in both sides, and hence found it impossible
whole-heartedly to support either. His attitude is clearly
expressed in a notable letter written to Pope Adrian VI in
the month of February, 1523. The Pope had appealed to
him to give him counsel concerning the best measures for
opposing the heretics. In particular his Holiness wished
for Erasmus to come to Rome in order that he might receive the benefit of his personal counsel. Erasmus, then
living at Basel, replies in part as follows:

Your Holiness requires my advice, and you wish to see
me. I would go to you with pleasure if my health allowed.
But the road over the Alps is long. The lodgings on the
way are dirty and inconvenient. The smell from the stoves
is intolerable. The wine is sour and disagrees with me.
For all that I would like well to speak with your Holiness,
if it can be made possible. Meanwhile you shall have my
honest heart in writing. Your eyes and mine will alone see
my letter. If you like it—well. If not, let it be regarded
as unwritten. As to writing against Luther, I have not
learning enough. You think my words will have authority.
Alas, my popularity, such as I had, is turned to hatred.
Once I was Prince of Letters, Star of Germany, Sun of
Studies, High Priest of Learning, Champion of a Purer
Theology. The note is altered now. One party says I
agree with Luther because I do not oppose him. The other
finds fault with me because I do oppose him. I did what
I could. I advised him to be moderate, and I only made his
friends my enemies. At Rome and in Brabant I am called
heretic, heresiarch, schismatic. I entirely disagree with
Luther. They quote this and that to show we are alike. I
could find a hundred passages where Saint Paul seems to
teach the doctrines which they condemn in Luther. I did
not anticipate what a time was coming. I did, I admit,
help to bring it on, but I was always willing to submit what
I wrote to the church. I asked my friends to point out

anything which they thought wrong. They found nothing. They encouraged me to persevere; and now they find a scorpion under every stone, and would drive me to rebellion, as they drove Arius and Tertullian.

This letter was, of course, addressed to the Pope and was intended to be strictly confidential. He advises his Holiness not to persecute the heretics but to seek the causes of their dissatisfaction and by removing these to disarm opposition. Adrian might possibly have taken this counsel, but he was helpless in the hands of his ecclesiastical advisers. Worn out by worries and vexations he died and left the papacy to Clement VII, who believed in sterner measures and was determined to crush out Lutheranism by force. Erasmus persistently refused to second the violent methods of the Vatican. He did not like Luther, and he considered his theology reactionary and crude, but he nevertheless sympathized with his indignation against the moral evils of the church and with his desire for reformation. The popes were incensed at him because he would not violently attack the heretics, while Luther and his companions hurled epithets against him because of what they considered his cowardice and poltroonery. The truth is that he was thoroughly sincere, but he was too keen-minded and unbiased in his reasoning to permit himself to wear a factional collar. Hence he was denounced by all parties and understood by none. Even after four hundred years men still misunderstand him and write biased books about him because they are hopelessly beneath his intellectual range.

There is nothing easier than to take sides and to become a partizan. Such a procedure involves no particular exercise of the intellect because the leader of your party insists upon doing your thinking for you. All he wants is obedience and support. If you are willing to give these you will be rewarded with political or ecclesiastical plums, as the case may be. Partizanship is therefore not only easier but it also pays better than to assume an attitude of impartiality. Independent thinking and unbiased judgment are exceedingly rare. Strangely enough, when they are found the partizans of all groups unite in condemning them. Such thinkers, we are told, are compromisers, mollycoddles, jellyfish, and a variety of other opprobrious things: this because they have been strong enough and fair enough to examine both sides of the question at issue and to refuse to find truth entirely in the possession of either of the contestants.

No man in history illustrates this principle more clearly than Erasmus. He was a reformer to the core, but he did not wish to destroy the old order without putting something better in its place. With many things advocated by Luther and his associates he had the warmest sympathy, but he saw clearly that it would cost a fearful price to purify the church by the methods which these men advocated. Not only would it involve the perpetual jealousies and schisms of warring sects, but it would turn the clock backward from the milder conclusions of Aquinas and the schoolmen to the harsh and terrible conceptions of the latter days of Augustine. He had no stomach for these things, and most of us who are fair-minded Protestants to-day will concede that there was much sanity in his forebodings. He was willing and anxious to return to the New Testament, but he had no desire to help in the construction of a church built upon the morbid and gloomy tenets of the Bishop of Hippo. The reformers did not go back far enough for Erasmus. They wanted to stop at Constantinople, at Chalcedon, at any rate at Nicæa. He wished to return to Jerusalem and to Antioch. Failing in this he could see no advantage in substituting the unending hell of Augustine for the milder purgatory of Saint Thomas, or the semi-Pelagianism of the popes for the rigid predestination of the author of the *Confessions*. He thought that all the ends of the Reformation could be gained by peaceful and rational means, and he could see no ultimate good in resorting to force and violence. As he was the first advocate of Christian union among the reformers so was he likewise one of the earliest devotees of world peace and the international mind. Like Plato and Aristotle, in all things he thought far ahead of his age. He paid the price for the clearness of his penetration and he is not yet through paying it.

Naturally, when we once come to understand Erasmus we can not help asking the question as to what might have happened if his counsels had prevailed. Of course, the Reformation would have assumed a different form. The church would have preserved its unity and have regained its apostolicity and holiness. Christianity would not have been split into multitudes of warring sects each more intent upon outdoing its neighbor than upon building the Kingdom of God. Political and ecclesiastical functions would have been separated once and for all, and the simplicity of the early Christian gospel would again have made its unique appeal to the hearts of men. Perhaps war would have been abolished and the era of world peace have been ushered in. All these and many more things might have happened if Erasmus could have directed the course of events. Nothing is, however, more futile than to indulge in such speculations. The men of the Reformation period being what they were, that is to say, bigoted, partizan, and incapable of thorough rationality, could not and would not follow such a leader. They were fit only for partizanship, for schisms, for broils and battles and destruction. They could neither see the right way nor follow those who were more clear-visioned than themselves. Catholics and Protestants alike were obsessed by the demons of intolerance, irrationality and hatred. Wars in the name of religion became the general

order of the day. Selfish individualism developed as the
prime motive to action in Protestant communities, while
the Catholic nations sank into a stupor of superstition and
decay. Erasmus might well have agreed with the dramatist
that "it is a mad world, my masters." Assuredly, the world
was mad, and desired no dealings with men of sanity and
discretion. What it wanted was zealots, partizans, poli-
ticians and warriors. It got what it wanted, and to a large
extent it still has it.

IV

On January 28, 1521, Erasmus was at Louvain in
Belgium, at the old university which has since been immortalized during the World War. Cardinal Campeggio had
come to see him in order to consult with him about how to
deal with Luther. In a letter written about this time the
great humanist gives the key to his life. He says, "My
work has been to restore a buried literature and recall
divines from their hair-splittings to a knowledge of the
New Testament. I have never been a dogmatist. I think
the church has defined many points which might have been
left open without hurt to the faith. I know not how popes
came to their authority. I suppose it was as the bishops
came to theirs. Each presbytry chose one of its members
as president to prevent divisions. Bishops similarly found
it expedient to have a chief bishop to check rivalries and
defend the church against the secular power. . . . If
Luther's books are in your people's hands let them do as
I do; take the good in them and leave the bad."

It is quite obvious from the above statement that its
author had no real faith in the doctrine of Apostolic Succession, or in the orthodox Catholic theory of Saint Peter's
Chair. Instead of these he accepts the prevailing modern
conception of the origin of the episcopate and does so with-

out apology. In spite of statements like these the popes consulted him and flattered him. Only a short time before his death Paul III offered to make him a cardinal in order that he might take part in the proposed general council which was to solve the problems of the church. Erasmus refused because of ill health, and his death a short time afterward proved that he was sincere in his declination. On the other hand, up until the close of his life he was a warm friend of Melanchthon and was on good terms with many other Protestants. If the Council of Trent had been held ten years earlier, and if Erasmus and Melanchthon could have been present at its sessions the whole history of the modern world might have been different. Erasmus knew this and did his best to save the day for peace and unity. Unfortunately, there was not enough sanity in the world to make it possible for him to succeed. Everywhere men wanted to rebel, to fight, to kill, to upset everything and to listen to no word of moderation. Even the peasants caught the fever, as was indicated by the wild and ill-omened uprising of the Anabaptists. Under such circumstances Erasmus was like a feather blown before the wind. All that was left to him was to write down his protestations and leave them for the judgment of the future.

Although Erasmus was a loyal Catholic throughout his career, and died in full communion with the church, he will live in the history of thought as preeminently the founder of Christian humanism. The truth is that he was essentially neither Catholic nor Protestant in his theological views. He was Protestant in the sense that he looked upon the New Testament as the one essential authority in religion, but he was Catholic in his adherence to the unity of the church and in his desire to avoid open and outward schism. Above everything else he was an intellectualist, a believer in the supreme authority of reason, and an advocate of humanistic culture as essentially harmonious with religion. His spiritual descendants are to be found with neither of the two older religious groups of the Western World, but with two other lines of succession, widely separated it is true, and yet springing in a large measure from a common source.

V

The first of the movements to which we refer is what is usually known as Socinianism, the precursor of modern Unitarianism and of liberal Christianity in general. Lælius and Faustus Socinus were Italian noblemen who had imbibed the tenets of the new learning and who sought to take them over in the field of religion. Faustus, the nephew of Lælius, was the more energetic and the more important of the two reformers. A distinguished American theologian has expressed the difference between the humanism of this new movement and the reformation principles of Luther in the epigrammatic statement, "Faustus Socinus was a gentleman in search of a religion; Martin Luther was a sinner seeking salvation." Undoubtedly, there is much truth in this statement, and yet it possesses a touch of exaggeration. The Socinians did not define salvation as did Luther, and yet they were not entirely ignorant of its meaning. They thought of it in terms of character building and moral fiber rather than in the arbitrary conception of Augustinian grace, but it was salvation in any case.

The Socinii were preeminently intellectualists. Like Erasmus, and like the Protestants in general, they accepted the New Testament as their ultimate standard of authority. Unlike most of their Unitarian successors, they believed in the miracles and especially in the virgin birth and the resurrection. They insisted upon interpreting the New Testament teaching in a strictly rational way. They believed in free will and broke at this point with all the orthodox Protestant groups. They rejected the mysticism of Luther as embodied in his teaching concerning justification by faith, and insisted, on the contrary, that a man is justified solely by the moral character which he develops. While they did not entirely eliminate the idea of supernaturalism their conception of religion was primarily scientific and humanistic. In all these things they followed Erasmus.

Faustus Socinus went to Poland and built up a considerable following in that kingdom. In the end he and his associates were persecuted as heretics and were driven out of the country. They were scattered throughout the Western World and started liberal movements wherever they went. In England they became the precursors of the Broad Church party, and in America their influence may be detected in the thought of Channing and Parker. The rejection of the orthodox doctrine of the Trinity brought them into the greatest disrepute with the older religious groups. In their attempts to rationalize the dogmas of the church it was, of course, impossible to avoid such a conflict. Socinianism lacks the driving power and dynamic of the more mystical interpretations of Christianity, but it has always possessed a strong appeal to cultured and scholarly minds, and the future historian of the church will have to reckon with it in ever-increasing measure.

VI

The Socinians were upper-class people, scholars, gentlemen, nobles, and their converts came, for the most part, from the higher ranks of society. It was natural that the influence of Erasmus should be felt in such a group. At almost the identically opposite pole must be placed the religious insurrectionists made up of those pariahs and untouchables of the Reformation world, usually known as the Anabaptists.

It has been only recently that we have been able to get at even an approach to an understanding of these unfortunate people. Protestants and Catholics alike were bitterly hostile to them and suppressed their literature and all authentic history pertaining to them with the same ferocious rigor which was exercised toward the Gnostic writings by the ancient orthodoxy. For centuries the worst epithet which could be hurled against an individual was to style him an Anabaptist. The term atheist was respectable by comparison. People in all countries were made to believe that the Anabaptists were guilty of every crime which the mind of man could conceive, and there was indeed nothing too bad to attribute to them. Nowadays we know that these impressions were sheer propagandist falsehoods, aimed not so much against heretical teaching as against its social implications. We know now that the enormities attributed to the peasant revolts in Germany were very much like the atrocities attributed to the Germans during the late war. In both cases there were no doubt some grains of fact mingled with the most distorted and malicious exaggeration. Nevertheless, the propaganda was successful. Not only were the Anabaptists suppressed but their name was blackened for at least four centuries, and it is probable that the exact facts concerning their history never will be known.

The Anabaptists were in many respects the oldest Protestants. They represented the undercrust movement toward freedom of the Reformation period. Their doctrines were circulated almost exclusively among the peasants and the serfs, who constituted at that time such a large proportion of the population of Europe. Occasionally some scholar or noble sympathized with their views and threw in his lot with them, but to do this meant certain martyrdom for these outcasts had no state protection like that which was afforded Luther and the more respectable reformers.

Luther, Calvin and Zwingli, if not nobles, were at least bourgeois and were on the most friendly terms with the upper classes. The Anabaptists, on the contrary, were hunted down like wild beasts by their oppressors and were tortured with a cruel ferocity which finds no parallel in the history of ancient or modern times. The leader in their ill-advised rebellion, John Bockhold, was done to death with such fiendish barbarity that the Roman Catholic Bishop who was officially obliged to witness the execution died of sheer horror the next day. George Bernard Shaw says that nothing quite so fiendish is to be found anywhere else in history. Later researches are disclosing that John was not at all the monster he has been painted, but that on the contrary he was a man of very considerable intelligence, sympathy and courage. Balthasar Hubmaier, who became the intellectual leader of the Anabaptist movement, possessed his doctorate in philosophy and was in some respects the superior of Luther or Calvin. By throwing in his lot with the down-trodden masses of his day he lost caste and was rewarded for his folly by being burned at the stake in Vienna. Luther and Calvin, as well as Zwingli, saved their followers and themselves by denouncing the Anabaptists in the most un-measured terms. Luther was especially vehement in his attacks upon the poor wretches and encouraged the nobles in the wanton cruelty with which they suppressed the re-bellion. Calvin, as we shall see later, wrote his famous *Institutes* not so much against the Catholics as against the Anabaptists, with whom he desired to make it clear he possessed no points of contact. Zwingli denounced Hub-maier and helped to drive him out of Switzerland after he had been put to rout in public debate with the Anabaptist scholar.

What did the Anabaptists believe that made them the objects of such universal execration? As their name in-

dicates, they practised adult baptism only and rejected christening. This meant, of course, that they repudiated the
conception of infant damnation which orthodox Protestants
and Catholics alike accepted. Moreover, Luther and his
associates were committed to the state church idea and
recognized fully the fact that without putting all the children
into the fold when they were born a state church is impossible. Like Erasmus and the Socinians, the Anabaptists believed in free will and were thus marked off sharply from
Calvin, Luther and Zwingli. In the main, they were orthodox upon the questions of the Trinity and the person of
Christ. Many of them were premillenarians and practically
all of them accepted what came to be known later as the
congregational conception of the church.

More significant than their theological teaching was
their conception of Christian ethics. Accepting the teaching
of Jesus with a greater degree of realism than their neigh-
bors, they opposed war and usury and demanded something
approaching a fair share of the economic goods which they
produced. Some of them attempted to set up more or less
fantastic communal systems, modeled after their conception
of the Jerusalem church. Inasmuch as their adherents were
mostly of the poor and uneducated classes in some instances
these experiments were doubtless attended by excesses of
various kinds. The worst that can be said of them, however, will not stand comparison with the inhuman barbarity
which their overlords exercised in crushing their subjects'
attempts to secure a greater measure of freedom. The story
of the Anabaptists constitutes one of the darkest pages both
in human history and in the annals of religious persecution.

The spiritual descendants of these heretics are to be
found in the Free Church groups which were especially
numerous in England and America but which are now
scattered throughout the world. Among these may be

reckoned the modern Congregationalists, Friends, Baptists, Disciples and Mennonites. All of these communions are derived in one way or another, at least to a very large extent, from the Anabaptists. Standing for freedom in religion, for an emphasis upon ethical Christianity and for the separation of church and state, these minority groups have played no slight part in the evolution of modern democracy. In many respects they have reflected the spirit of Erasmus more than the Socinians. His desire for the simplicity of the New Testament, his insistence upon ethical Christianity, his passion for human freedom, to speak of no other features, were all reflected in the later history of the Anabaptists.

Erasmus died before the general council which he had so long advocated could be assembled. When it finally arrived it was too late for anything to be done except to deepen the chasm between the old church and the reformers. Roman Catholicism, which looked hopeless ten years after Luther started the Reformation, pulled itself together with remarkable vitality. In 1540 a Spaniard named Ignatius Loyola founded the Society of Jesus and thus furnished the church with a powerful weapon against the heretics. Contarini and Melanchthon failed to agree at Regensburg in 1541, and from this time on no further negotiations were attempted. In 1563 the Council of Trent adjourned, after anathematizing all Protestants and Protestant doctrines and throwing down the gauntlet to any and all comers who might refuse to prostrate themselves before the pope. Erasmus had been dead over a quarter of a century—dead, as we ordinarily define the word. Like all great men his spirit still lives and will some day lead the followers of his Master into that perfect unity which embodies freedom and that perfect freedom which finds complete expression only in union.

CHAPTER XII

LUTHER

DENYING one Christian truth after another, and falling under the ban of the Church, he joined her enemies, and ridiculed, by speech and writing, in the most opprobious terms, the teachings of Catholic faith, its moral precepts and ancient practices; till finally, in 1525, he trampled under foot his solemn vows of religion, and married Catharine Bora, herself an ex-nun. With consummate cunning, Luther had recourse to the aid of princes, governments, and the nobility, whose attention he called to the wealth locked up in monasteries, to the episcopal revenues, etc. At the same time he preached the doctrine: the one hundredth part of the present wealth of the Church is sufficient for its support. This artful policy of the man who once, at the altar, had vowed undying fidelity to his Church, accomplished its purpose. Many princes and governments joined him, took possession of the Church property, and forced their subjects into the new religion. Luther died in February, 1546, complaining that, to his own personal knowledge and observation, the German people had become, since the beginning of the new religion, more immoral, wicked, and unprincipled than they had formerly been.

Thus writes the Reverend Father Businger, in his *Church History for the Use of Catholic Schools,* translated into English by the Reverend Richard Brennan, LL.D., and bearing the imprimatur of John Cardinal McCloskey, Archbishop of New York. Cardinal Gibbons also adds these words of approval: "This book, in my judgment, is well adapted for the use of schools and is calculated to impress upon youthful minds a knowledge of the salient points of Ecclesiastical History." Other bishops and holy men of divers descriptions contribute similaɪ testimonials of praise. Evidently, therefore, the view of Luther entertained by large numbers of young people who have received their education in the parochial schools is fairly represented by the quotation from Father Businger.

On the other hand, perhaps larger numbers of young people, especially in America, who do not attend the parochial schools, receive quite a different impression of the most prominent figure in the Protestant Reformation. In a brief life of Martin Luther intended for school use and written by Doctor William Rein, Seminary Director at Eisenach in Germany, we find the following statement:

The history of mankind presents us with many great names, but with few great men. And even among those that are called great men, few there are whose records will bear a close scrutiny. In most cases the character of the private man is distinct from the influence of his public career.

Among the immortal names that have honored their kind and glorified their God, stands pre-eminently the name of Martin Luther. Yet not in name alone does his greatness shine forth in splendor after the lapse of four centuries, but in word and deed, in character and influence. His private life and public career are a unit, for both were the manifestations of a sincere soul, a generous heart, a true man.

This is, of course, a Protestant opinion. It is only fair to say, however, that praise of Luther may be found outside the ranks of the orthodox reformers. No one, for example, will accuse Heine of being ultra-orthodox, and yet he says of Luther, "He created the German language. He was not only the greatest but also the most German man of our history. In his character all the faults and all the virtues of the Germans are combined on the largest scale. He was a complete man, I would say an absolute man, one in whom matter and spirit were not divided." Similarly, Thomas Carlyle, who likewise was not plagued with orthodoxy, writes:

I will call this Luther a true great man, great in intellect, in courage, affection, and integrity, one of our most lovable and precious men. Great not as a hewn obelisk, but as an Alpine mountain, so simple, honest, spontaneous, not setting up to be great at all; there for quite another purpose than being great! Ah, yes, unsubduable granite, piercing far and wide into the heavens; yet in the clefts of it fountains, green beautiful valleys with flowers! A right spiritual Hero and Prophet; once more a true son of Nature and Fact, for whom these centuries and many that are to come yet will be thankful to heaven.

Perhaps the most brilliant and imposing panegyric of all is that of Krauth. It is too lengthy for quotation, but a few sentences are typical of what precedes and follows:

He made a world rich forevermore, and, stripping himself in perpetual charities, died in poverty. He knew how to command, for he had learned how to obey. Had he been less courageous, he would have attempted nothing; had he been less cautious, he would have ruined all; the torrent was resistless, but the banks were deep. He tore up the mightiest evils by the root, but shielded with his own life the tenderest bud of good; he combined the aggressiveness of a just radicalism with the moral resistance—which seemed to the fanatic the passive weakness—of a true conservatism. Faith-inspired, he was faith-inspiring. Great in act he was great in thought, proving himself fire with fire, "inferior eyes grew great by his example, and put on the dauntless spirit of resolution."

I

What manner of man could inspire such contradictory opinions? Is it possible to attain sufficient detachment from inherited or party prejudice to be able to see Luther as he actually was? The task is not easy because the source materials for his biography are all colored with bias and tinctured with partizanship. Nevertheless, the main events of his life are for the most part undisputed. Let us take a glance at these facts before we attempt to interpret or appraise them.

Martin Luther was the son of Hans Luther, or Ludher as the word was originally written. The family name of Luther's mother was Ziegler. Martin was born on the tenth of November, 1483, in the little town of Eisleben. His mother remembered very distinctly the exact hour and day of his birth, but after he grew up she was not certain of the year. From other evidence, however, there can be no doubt that the correct date was 1483.

Hans Luther was a miner and had moved to Eisleben in order that he might work in the copper deposits which were plentiful at that time in this part of Germany. There was an old tradition industriously circulated by Luther's enemies that Hans had been obliged to leave his former home at Mohra because he had killed a peasant who had pastured his horses without permission on the meadows of the Luther farm. This legend appears to have been without other foundation than the violent temper and impulsive disposition which were characteristic of the family. Luther's parents did not remain long at Eisleben but moved to Mansfeld, a few miles distant, where the family grew up. Later on the reformer said of his early life, "My father was a poor miner; my mother gathered wood and carried it home on her back in order that her children might be educated." This could not have been for many years, for it is on record that Hans Luther succeeded in purchasing a house on the main street of the city of Mansfeld and also in becoming the proprietor of two smelting furnaces. So prosperous, indeed, was he that he attained that highest dignity in the gift of lesser municipalities, a seat on the town council. Meanwhile his family had multiplied in real German fashion. We read of six children besides Martin, and this may not exhaust the list. The Luther paterfamilias was not what might be called a mollycoddle. He believed in corporal punishment and was not slow to put his philosophy into practise. Martin tells us that his father flogged him so severely that he ran away from home and was embittered against him for a long time. Nor was the good *hausfrau* much behind her husband in the matter of discipline. Again her son tells us that "because of a mere nut she whipped me so hard that the blood flowed. Her severe and earnest treatment of me led me to enter a cloister and become a monk." How much of Luther's later melancholy and persistent dread of hell-fire arose from the constant fear of punishment at the hands of his parents it would be hard to say. Perhaps Mr. Bertrand Russell would infer a great deal, and others may agree with him. Luther himself says that his parents meant well in their hearts, their mistake being in their lack of knowledge of scientific pedagogy.

At Mansfeld he received his first instruction in reading and writing and in the rudiments of Latin. If he thought to escape from severity at home by entering the schoolroom his dreams were doomed to a rude awakening. To use his own language, "the schoolmasters in my days were tyrants and executioners; the schools were jails and hell! And in spite of fear and misery, floggings and trembling, nothing was learned. Time was wasted over many useless things and thus many an able mind was ruined." By way of illustration of his thesis he recounts the fact that he was lashed fifteen times in the course of a single morning because he did not know what had not been taught him. The religious instruction which he received was calculated to scare the wits out of him. There was much talk of damnation and judgment, with Jesus Christ as the Supreme Arbiter. Later on Luther felt poignant regret because for years he had been so trained that he grew pale and trembled when the name of Christ was mentioned, since he had been taught to look upon Him in no other way than as a severe and angry judge.

Six years after Columbus discovered America, when a mere boy of fifteen Martin Luther entered the city of Eisenach as a student. He had been at Magdeburg for a year previously but had left for no very well assigned reason. Probably his expenses were more than his father felt could be afforded. At least one of the reasons assigned for sending the lad to Eisenach was the fact that the Luther family had numerous relatives living in or near that city whom the sagacious Hans calculated might be of assistance in helping Martin through school. This was a miscalculation, for again the latter tells us that he had to beg his bread from house to house while he was studying at Eisenach. At length, largely by virtue of his fine tenor voice, he won the favor of Ursula Cotta, the wife of Conrad Cotta, one of the foremost citizens of the place. Thanks to her help, Luther managed to get through school and to acquire enough proficiency in his studies to enable him at the age of eighteen to enter the University of Erfurt. By this time Hans had absorbed more substance and felt able to furnish sufficient support to permit his son to take his university course. The latter studied Greek and Latin and made himself especially proficient in music. He took his Bachelor of Philosophy in 1502, and two years later he acquired his master's degree, which was probably about equivalent to a modern doctorate. His father wanted him to become a jurist, and he actually began to attend lectures in law. Then something happened which not only changed his life but the life of the entire world.

II

On the sixteenth of July, 1505, Martin Luther held a farewell reception for a few of his friends in the city of Erfurt. Contrary to his father's wishes, he was to become a monk the next day. Old Hans was violently opposed to monasteries and to any sort of ecclesiastical vocation. He wanted his son to study law in order to acquire competence and perhaps to make fame for himself and the family. It seems clear that Luther received no encouragement in his purpose to enter the cloister. Why, then, did he take the step? The answer is simple: he was in mortal fear of hellfire. He had been sick for some weeks while in school and thought himself on the verge of eternity. After he recovered he went home to visit his parents at Easter. While on the road he accidentally cut an artery in his leg and again feared that he would die. In great distress of mind he prayed for help to the Virgin Mary and apparently received it for the wound stopped bleeding, and when it broke forth again that night he was able to quench the flow of blood by a similar invocation. Not long after this circumstance he tells us that he had a friend who was suddenly murdered, a fact which caused him much worry and foreboding. Melancholy settled upon him and he wandered about in aimless fashion with the pit of hell ever yawning a short distance in front of him. While in this frame of mind he was returning to Erfurt from his home when a furious thunder-storm burst over him and he fell half dead to the earth, crying out, "Deliver me, Saint Ann, and I will become a monk." Saint Ann was the special patron of all miners and was doubtless revered in the Luther home on that account. It was this final vow which decided the question of his life calling. He felt that the case against him was so severe already that if he dared to break his vow he would certainly be precipitated into perdition upon the occasion of the next thunder-storm which might happen to sweep over his home. Moreover, thunder-storms then as now were rather plentiful in that part of Germany. Hence, there was nothing left for him but to become a monk.

The Augustinians constituted one of the less significant orders of the medieval church. In England they were popularly known as Blackfriars, from the color of their robes. They pretended to derive directly from Saint Augustine, although the line of succession appears somewhat dubious. They entertained the greatest reverence for the somber writings of the Bishop of Hippo, and Luther was early instructed in the iron-clad theories of predestination which Augustine has immortalized. The more he read of the great Doctor's writings the more terrified he became. Obviously, he must belong either to the ranks of the elect or the damned. The important question was, Which? He went to the Prior to find out. All that the good Father could tell him was that he should fast, pray and observe the rules and trust the rest to the Lord. He obeyed the instructions with downright German thoroughness. Afterward he said of his experience at this time, "I was a pious monk, and so strictly did I keep the vows of my order that I may say that if ever a monk has entered heaven through monkery then I also could have entered . . . and if I had continued much longer I would have tortured myself to death with vigils and prayers, reading and other work, and I exerted myself to the utmost to obey the church precepts and to punish and castigate my body with fasts and vigils, prayers and other exercises more than all those who are my bitterest enemies and persecutors. Hence I now teach that such fool works can never justify anyone in the sight of God." The "fool works" to which he refers did not, in fact, bring any peace to his mind. The more he fasted the more the devil beset him. His ecclesiastical superiors tried to comfort him in various ways, but could give him no assurance of salvation. For many centuries the church had made it a rule not to grant any such assurance. The practical significance of this policy is readily apparent. Once a man is given definite certainty of salvation he may grow less zealous in his devotion to the organization. Hence it is wiser to keep him more or less uneasy as to the future. It is true that the communicant was generally informed that as a true son of the church purgatory was the worst that could happen to him. This not being a hopeless situation was calculated to ease the minds of most people who thought about the subject. Luther, unfortunately, had been reading Augustine's writings, where the future is divided into two sections only and purgatory is left out of account. The doctrine of election is always dual. Nobody ever heard of a person being predestined to purgatory. Therefore, the orthodox consolations helped Luther not at all. He felt sure that he was foreordained either to heaven or hell, and he was greatly afraid it might be the latter. It must always be remembered that the flames of perdition were much more real in these medieval days because they were so often duplicated in the execution of criminals. Burning at the stake was a common punishment, and even more hideous tortures were every-day occurrences in the legal records of most communities. As we have already remarked, there is nothing in Dante's "Inferno" which is not a replica of some actual incident in the history of his own time. It was quite easy to anticipate hell in the future when there was so much of it all around one in the present. Luther believed in it and was nearly driven insane by his fears of torment.

At length he found relief. While he was reading that same Epistle to the Romans which produced the conversion of his great forebear Augustine the light suddenly dawned on him. He read the words, "Therefore being justified by faith, we have peace with God through our Lord Jesus Christ," and a great load was lifted from his soul. A Voice seemed to say to him that he need have no fears. He belonged to the chosen of God and nothing could harm him here or hereafter. In the same way that Augustine turned his back upon heathendom and became a loyal son of the church Luther turned his back on the church of Augustine and became a joyous and exuberant heretic. Externally the results were different, but in substance they were identical. Both men found peace and found it by the same process, albeit with not exactly the same external trappings. It is interesting to observe, in this connection, that three centuries after Luther a distinguished Protestant named John Henry Newman left the Anglican faith and became a Catholic for identically the same reason which made Luther leave the Catholic faith and become a Protestant. Luther wanted certainty and definite assurance of salvation. Newman wanted the same thing. Both got what they wanted by opposite processes. If Luther could have taken Newman's place and Newman could have taken Luther's the history of the world might have been very different.

III

In the little town of Pirna, in Saxony, lived a goldsmith named John Dietz. John begat a son who acquired the name of Dietzel, or Little Dietz. In process of time this was shortened to Tetzel. The lad grew up and attended the University of Leipsic, where he attained his degree in philosophy. He entered the Dominican order and became a preaching friar. It was about this time that Pope Leo X found it expedient to raise some money in order to complete Saint Peter's Cathedral. When we recall the fact that this edifice cost at least fifty millions of dollars it must be admitted that it required considerable business acumen to finance its construction. There were various ways of raising money open to the ecclesiastical authorities, but the method of indulgences proved by far the most remunerative. Orders went out from the Vatican to push the sale of such certificates throughout the Catholic world. It was necessary to find good agents for handling the trade, and Little Dietz soon had a job waiting for him. He started out by selling "milk and butter letters." These were documents which granted permission, during the Lenten season, to the faithful to partake of victuals prepared with butter and milk, contrary to the ordinary laws of the church. Finding that he was a good salesman, the Bishop who had charge of the matter for that part of Germany speedily sent out Tetzel wherever he could be used. The Lutheran historians, at any rate, give sufficiently graphic accounts of his methods of procedure. To begin with, he had a big voice and unparalleled audacity. In order to sell his wares he no doubt exaggerated the papal instructions. He rode in a magnificent wagon surrounded by a large retinue. At every city he entered he was preceded by the ringing of bells, the singing of church choirs and the burning of torches. Leading the procession was the papal bull borne upon a velvet cushion and carried with great state into the church. Here, beneath a red cross to which the papal banner was affixed, Tetzel mounted the pulpit and harangued the huge audiences which his parade had attracted with a discourse not unlike those used by the old-time venders of patent medicine in the days of frontier America. The women were advised to sell their veils and to purchase indulgences. It was currently reported that upon the treasury of Tetzel was inscribed the motto, "Soon as the coin in the box doth ring, the soul can into heaven spring." For nine ducats one might get away with church robbery and perjury. Murder came a little less, being rated at eight, and adultery was listed at six. Lesser offenses were, of course, cheaper. Even the poorest rogues could afford to buy a few indulgences, and everybody was sure to need some at one time or another. It was good business and in spite of the fact that times were hard and money scarce Leo did very well with his collection.

Luther, having found peace for his soul entirely independent of the regular church procedure, might have remained quietly in his monastery during the remainder of his days had it not been for Tetzel. Having lost all confidence in the ordinary method of securing salvation proclaimed by the church through the sacraments, Luther had no patience at all with the gross mountebank proceedings of the papal agent. Perhaps he did not sympathize with the idea of his simple country people being fleeced of their hard-earned savings for the benefit of an Italian cathedral. Perhaps, also, as an Augustinian he had not too much use for the rival order of Dominicans. In any event, his indignation waxed so warm that on the thirty-first of October, 1517, he nailed his famous ninety-five theses to the door of the Wittenberg church and by that action started the Protestant Reformation. It was not in itself a very spectacular performance. It was quite customary to affix such notices to the church door and few people stopped to look at Luther's when he tacked them up. Later on they were read and things began to happen. They are not through happening yet. This apparently trivial action of an unknown Saxon monk by some peculiar fatality became one of the most important events in the history of the world.

IV

Luther's theses blew the lid off and Germany was almost immediately transformed into a seething religious and political caldron. It became obvious every day that the old church was tottering, and only a miracle could save it from ruin. The Pope issued a bull of excommunication, and Luther promptly burned the bull at nine o'clock in the morning on the twelfth of December, 1520. It was only three years after he had started things going by nailing his theses to the church door, but those three years had sufficed to shake the papacy to its foundations. So serious had the situation become that the Emperor Charles summoned the reformer to appear before an Imperial Diet held at the city of Worms in the spring of 1521. Luther went and contrary to expectation came away alive. Upon being pressed he had said at the Diet that neither the Pope nor the councils could contravene Holy Scripture. This was not especially pleasing to the representatives of the Vatican who were present. Undoubtedly they would have enjoyed making a bonfire of the uncouth Saxon monk, but the Elector of the most powerful German principality was his protector and it was not safe to repeat the technique which had served so well in the case of John Huss. The opposition to the heretic was nevertheless so powerful that the Elector was constrained to abduct him and hide him in the old castle of Wartburg where he remained for some months. It was during this time that he accomplished his monumental task of translating the Bible into the German vernacular, and it was also during this period that he had his famous interview with the devil resulting in the evil one being driven off by a blow from Luther's ink bottle. The reformer's account of the incident is characteristic:

It was in the year 1521 that I was in Patmos on the Wartburg, alone in my little room, no one being permitted to come to me save two pages of honor who brought me food and drink. They had bought me a bag of hazelnuts, of which I ate from time to time, and which I locked up in a chest. One evening on retiring, I heard some one at the hazelnuts, cracking one after another with force against the rafters; then the noise approached my bed, but I cared little for that. After I had fallen asleep there began such a tumult on the stairway, as if threescore barrels were being thrown down. I arose, went to the stairs, and cried out, "Art thou here? (meaning the Evil One). So be it." I then commended my soul to the Lord Jesus Christ, of whom it is said (Psalm viii 6), "Thou hast put all things under His feet," and retired to rest. For this is the best method to expel him (the Devil): despising him and calling upon Christ. That he cannot endure.

But finally, when Satan exceeded all bounds, as the legend records, Luther threw his ink-stand at him, and he never returned again! It was not the first nor the last time in the history of the world when the devil was put to flight with a pot of ink.

We need not recount Luther's later history in detail. It is, of course, the story of the Protestant Reformation. One incident ought perhaps to be chronicled in addition to what we have written. On the thirteenth of June, 1525, when he was forty-one years of age, he married Catharine von Bora. She was fifteen years younger than her husband and had been a nun until she escaped from her convent two years before her marriage. Catharine belonged to an old and noble family and whatever attacks have been made upon Luther there can be no doubt that his domestic life was happy and honorable. Of course, his enemies assailed him more bitterly than ever, but this had ceased to disturb him. The sound common sense of his German associates supported his action and he set the precedent for the abolition of celibacy throughout Protestantism. Moreover, he abolished the ground distinction between clergy and laity which lay at the heart of the Roman Catholic system. The dual standard of morality for priest and layman was

smashed to atoms. Here, as elsewhere, Luther was fight-
ing the battle of democracy.

V

Three principles stand out as basic in the teaching of
Luther. The first was his insistence on the Bible as the only
authority in religion; the second was the doctrine of justification by faith; and the third was his emphasis upon the
right of private judgment in matters of religion. These
three considerations became the corner-stone of Protestantism and have remained so for the most part down to the
present time. It may be well to consider what Luther
meant by each of them.

In asserting that the Scriptures and the Scriptures alone
constitute the ultimate authority in religion Luther did not
especially contradict the substance of Catholic theology.
Generally speaking, the church had always held that everything done by the councils and the pope was implicit in the
Scriptures. It was true that tradition was considered as
authoritative along with the text and that the church had
the last word in any case, but nevertheless the authority of
the Bible itself was never impeached. Luther took this
old doctrine and with his characteristic German bluntness
insisted that it should not be obscured but that it should
count for exactly what it was worth. If the Bible really
represented the supreme and final authority the voice of
tradition and, above all, the decrees and formulations of
popes and councils were only so much rubbish which needed
to be cleared away. Nobody disputed the authority of the
Bible; therefore it could be regarded as certain. On the
other hand, every one conceded that it was sufficient for
salvation; therefore there was no need to supplement it by
later and doubtful additions. In taking this position Luther
set the pace for the whole body of Protestants. One and

all they have consistently rejected the voice of tradition and
the dicta of ecclesiastical organizations as possessing any
real or ultimate authority. William Chillingworth, the
Oxford reformer of the seventeenth century, put the matter
tersely in his treatise entitled *The Religion of Protestants, a
Safe Way to Salvation,* when he said, "The Bible and the
Bible alone is the religion of Protestants."

The doctrine of justification by faith is a central feature
of Luther's theology. As we have already indicated, it
grew directly out of his personal experience. The Roman
Catholic church based its conception of salvation on the
sacraments as means of grace and asserted that only through
these channels could future happiness be achieved. Luther
had tried this system and had found that it did not give
definite or complete assurance. Therefore he boldly announced that only by immediate and direct communication
of the soul with God could peace be secured. Of course,
it is fair to say that Luther, like Calvin and Zwingli, was a
firm believer in predestination. In the last analysis, therefore, salvation depended on the divine election and nothing
which the sinner himself might do could affect the situation.
It was for this reason that the Roman Catholic sacramental
system was of no avail. Only God Himself knew who
belonged to the elect and since only the elect could be saved
the church's ceremonial rites were not of the slightest consequence. The one thing that counted was for the Deity
himself to speak directly and immediately to the soul of the
person whom He had chosen for salvation and furnish the
glad information to him. This is what Luther meant by
justification by faith. It was an immediate, personal revelation of the divine election and hence could be depended on
with absolute confidence. If one were really predestined
to be saved one need never fear being lost, and if one had
the direct and immediate assurance from the Deity that

one was thus predestined one need not worry over anything else. We shall have to deal with the tremendous dynamic wrapped up in this doctrine of election a little later when we discuss Calvin, but it was a presupposition of Luther's thinking as well. Faith, as Luther understood it, involved no element of will whatever. It was absolutely and entirely the gift of God. It was a very joyous and confident feeling and Luther expatiates upon it with much enthusiasm in his sermons and writings, but it was nothing for which the sinner himself was in the slightest degree responsible. Salvation in the first place was the gift of God through election, and faith, which was nothing more than the assurance of election, was likewise the fruit of the divine benevolence. Man himself was only a hopeless and helpless sinner, capable of receiving the divine blessing but absolutely unable to do anything for himself. Luther's theology here was simply the morbid fanaticism of Augustine revamped but scarcely revised.

It was in his conception of individual liberty involved in the doctrine of the right of private judgment that Luther struck his truest note. Roman Catholicism had built up a system of autocratic clericalism which left but little freedom to the individual. The church was made up of the clergy and the laity had nothing whatever to do with its real constitution. In fact, if all the laity had been wiped out of existence the church would have gone on as intact as before. As a result of this cleavage the right of private judgment was entirely eliminated. The layman had no power to determine any religious question for himself. He must look to the clergy for authoritative information. Hence, all matters pertaining to his spiritual and eternal interest were handed over to his ecclesiastical superiors. As a result the church kept the consciences of its parishioners in its own possession, and independent thinking upon religious matters was quite out of the question. Luther struck all this to the ground at a single blow. He abolished the distinction between clergy and laity and he demanded the right for every man to think freely upon all questions of ultimate importance to his destiny. It is not too much to say that this iconoclastic attitude was the foundation of modern democracy. Both in England and America this principle has found expression in religion and politics alike. It is questionable whether it would ever have achieved any place in the latter realm if it had not first found embodiment in the former. Martin Luther rather than Oliver Cromwell or George Washington was the author of modern political freedom.

VI

Many of Luther's views partook of the spirit of his age. While an advocate of freedom and a violent enemy of the autocracy of Rome, he was a staunch defender of the Saxon State and the upper classes in general. He was merciless in his condemnation of the Anabaptists, and he could scarcely find language strong enough with which to denounce the peasants who rose against their overlords in the early days of the Reformation. It is easy to say that security demanded his taking the course which he actually followed, but any one who has entered into the real spirit of Luther knows that such an answer is inadequate. He may have been a fanatic, but he was never a time-server or a politician. He opposed the Anabaptists on principle and not from motives of policy. While he came from the ranks of the working classes he never really had any sympathy with them. He was a bourgeois, and as was also true of Calvin and Zwingli, the Reformation in his hands represented a revolt of the lower aristocracy against the higher. He was ready to rebel against the Pope and the Emperor, but he always remained loyal to the Elector of Saxony and to the governing aristocracy of his own state. In this attitude he was unquestionably conscientious, and his action helped to lay the foundations for the great state churches which speedily became established in the name of Protestantism.

Not only in the field of politics but in other disciplines Luther was essentially and thoroughly conservative. He had small sympathy with any sort of philosophical speculation, and such glimmerings of science as existed during his day were entirely unknown to him. He disliked culture for its own sake and mistrusted Erasmus and the other humanists. His theology was antiquated, inasmuch as it meant really simply a return to Augustine with renewed and greater emphasis upon mystical experience than the old Bishop of Hippo had suggested. In substituting justification by faith for the Catholic system of salvation through the church and the sacraments Luther went back to a more primitive conception of religion, but certainly not to a more universal one. Immediate mystical experience is the simplest but scarcely the most highly developed form of religion. Moreover, it is essentially individualistic and anarchical. Luther tried to remedy this defect by giving a place to the sacraments and to the church in his system, but he found it impossible entirely to exorcise the demon of schism. During his own day Protestantism broke up into all kinds of warring fragments and has continued the process more or less ever since.

In his eschatology Luther was likewise Augustinian and primitive. There are just two compartments in the future world, heaven and hell, and every individual is destined for one or the other of them. Essentially, he has nothing to do with where he is going, and yet it is an exceedingly vital matter that he should know what is coming to him. He

secures this knowledge through justification by faith, provided he, of course, belongs to the elect. Luther uses the
word "justification" in a somewhat peculiar way. Its meaning with him is always purely forensic or legal and never
ethical. What is involved is the securing of a free pardon
which remits the penalty of damnation, but does not necessarily in any respect involve the moral cleansing of the
sinner. Here Luther broke with the Pelagians, the Socinians, the humanists and all the other fry who taught salvation by character instead of by grace. At best, man's
righteousness is nothing more than filthy rags. Steeped in
original sin, he is inevitably a wretched and miserable out-
cast and there is no health in him. For some reason known
only to the Deity Himself the latter extends him pardon and
graciously snatches him from the very jaws of hell which
had otherwise engulfed him forever. As we have already
stated, the belief in hell and the fear of it were very acute
with Luther. What he wanted above everything else was
to escape the flames. As a result of his early training he
had a thoroughgoing terror of the divine judgment. This
was the concern of his waking moments up until the time
of his conversion. Through the mystical experience which
he called justification by faith he knew that he was
pardoned, and rejoiced accordingly.

In his conception of the sacraments Luther was also
primitive and Augustinian. Baptism was to be administered
to the infant, although this scarcely seemed to fit in with
the idea that no one should have a place in the church until
he had secured the assurance of justification by faith.
Luther himself found the nut a hard one to crack. He
finally fell back upon the explanation that infants in some
miraculous way might be given faith before they reached the
period when they could be said to be conscious of the gift.
Inasmuch as faith to the reformer was always a mystical

conception the idea was, after all, not so preposterous as it might otherwise appear. Perhaps subconsciously Luther's essential conservatism and his recognition of the value of infant baptism in the establishment of any state religion may have played some part in his decision. Moreover, the Anabaptists were the one party which opposed christening, and they were made up of the lower classes and peasants, the very offscouring of the earth. Luther was intensely hostile to them and the very word Anabaptist was anathema to him. This consideration alone might well have turned the tide in favor of the ancient custom.

In his teaching concerning the Lord's Supper Luther almost went over to Roman Catholicism. He denied the material side of transubstantiation but undoubtedly wished to retain its spiritual connotation. Hence he stoutly asserted the doctrine of the Real Presence in his dispute with Zwingli at Marburg in 1529, and he was always unyielding upon this point. His theological position became known as "Consubstantiation" and was given a central place in later Lutheran theology. It is somewhat difficult to say just what Luther intended to express by the term, but he certainly had in mind a view much closer to the medieval conception of the subject than is to be found in any other Protestant interpretation.

VII

Luther passed away quite peacefully, between three and four o'clock in the morning, the eighteenth of February, 1546. After his death his followers continued his work. He had set in motion forces which could not be restrained. All Germany was in a tumult and the Counter-Reformation was beginning to gather strength. Protestantism was already crystallizing into fixed symbols and confessions, and the Council of Trent was beginning to formulate its immovable anathemas against the heretics of Germany. The medieval world was over; for good or ill the modern world had begun. Strangely enough, the cleavage between the old and the new assumed racial as well as political and religious lines of demarcation. The Saxon north was pitted against the Latin south. Here and there the lines crossed, but the general configuration remained and still remains.

With the later ramifications of Lutheran theology it does not seem necessary to deal. In the hands of Melanchthon and his successors a species of Protestant scholasticism gradually developed which outclassed the medieval type in the technicality and barrenness of its doctrinal discussions. Crypto-Calvinism, Majorism and Osiandrianism represent only a few of the countless *isms* which speedily arose to afflict people who had troubles enough without them. For the days of the Thirty Years' War were not far distant, and blood and rapine, famine and carnage were soon to set their seal once more upon the divisions of Christendom. In the name of Jesus men were to slay one another by the thousands, and to rejoice in doing it. In the meantime the theologians kept on spinning out more theories about justification and sanctification and all the rest while the people were killing one another in the wars or starving for lack of bread. In the end the Lutherans triumphed, and modern Germany emerged from the ashes. It was quite appropriate that a statue of Luther should stand first in the great Berlin cathedral of modern Protestantism. Elsewhere throughout the world the name of the Saxon reformer is likewise cherished and honored. The Great War prevented the world-wide celebration of the quadricentennial of the beginning of the Reformation. Perhaps in another hundred years a warless world may unite in doing justice to such an anniversary.

CHAPTER XIII

CALVIN

TO THE aged and beloved John Higginson:
There be now at sea a shippe (for our good friend
Elias Holcroft of London did advise me by the
packet) called the Welcome, which has aboard it a hundred
or more of the heretics called Quakers, with William Penn,
the scamp, at the head of them. The General has accordingly given orders to Master Malachi Haxsett of the brig
Porpoise to waylay said Welcome as near the end of the
Cod as may be and make prisoners of Penn and his ungodly
crew, so that the Lord may be glorified and not mocked on
the soil of this new country with the heathen worship of
these people. Much spoil may be made by selling the whole
to Barbedoes, where slaves fetch good prices in rumme and
sugar; and we shall not only do the Lord great service by
punishing the wicked but shall make great gayne for his
ministers and people.
Yours in the bonds of Christ,
COTTON MATHER*

John Calvin was the supreme theologian of the Reformation. Not that he possessed intellectual ability superior
to many others but that he had a genius for organizing his
thought and formulating it in a system which was clear and
distinct and could be understood by all. Like Luther, he
possessed little originality, and like Luther too his undisputed master was Augustine. As a matter of fact, Calvin
did little more than systematize the Augustinian doctrine of

---

*This letter is to be found in the archives of the Massachusetts
Historical Society in Boston.

election and apply it rigorously and logically to every department of theology. Augustine himself was never thoroughly
consistent in his views. His writings are filled with contradictions and it is possible to derive entirely opposing theories
from his works. Calvin surpassed him in whole-hearted
application of the principle which he had made central in
his thought and in unhesitating devotion to that conception.
Hence, Calvinism possesses a simplicity and logical com-
pleteness which can be affirmed of no other rival system in
the history of theology. Devotion to logic is, indeed, the
very heart of the Geneva reformer's method. Luther undoubtedly wabbles, and there are many inconsistencies between his theoretical formulations and his practical preaching. There is, for example, little doubt that he accepted
the teaching of Augustine concerning election, just as Calvin
did, but while Calvin carried the doctrine out to its most
complete and thoroughgoing consequences Luther was
prone to shrink from its implications in his sermons, and in
some of the greatest of them he seems frankly to disavow
it. When he discoursed upon his favorite theme, the freedom of a Christian man, he talked in terms which are thrilling and inspired and to which the best that is in our modern
age responds. Luther was primarily a mystic; Calvin was
primarily a rationalist. The one gave great place to feeling
in his life; the other was coldly intellectual. Luther passed
through a conversion crisis like his master, Augustine. No
such experience is recorded in the life of Calvin. While
these points of difference are clear and notable it should
also be remembered that the two reformers had much in
common. Both were essentially Augustinian in their thinking, both were Protestant to the core in their conception of
the church and in their allegiance to Christian freedom,
both were vigorously opposed to the Roman Catholic system and to all of its works.

I

While Calvin is generally regarded as the formulator of the Reformed theology it must be conceded that Zwingli was its original founder. The latter, along with Luther, was one of the pioneers of the Reformation. He began preaching his radical views in Switzerland about the same time that the Saxon reformer was turning the world upside down in Germany. His townspeople heard him gladly and speedily proceeded to wipe out all they could of the old faith. Switzerland, then as now, was made up of different cantons and there was considerable dissimilarity among the inhabitants of these petty geographical divisions. Some of the neighboring sections to Zurich, where Zwingli lived, remained true to the old religion, and war speedily broke out between the two opposing groups. The Swiss reformer himself fell in battle in defense of his views, thus attaining a distinction enjoyed, as far as we know, by no other theologian.

Zwingli, like Luther and Calvin, was a devoted follower of Augustine. In certain respects he pushed the doctrine of election farther than either of his contemporaries. He was wont to assert that Socrates, Plato and the other great figures in the classical world were saved although they lived before Christ, simply through the power of the divine election. Zwingli was a scholar, and in many respects a humanist. He repudiated the doctrine of transubstantiation in its entirety and thus came in conflict with Luther, who held on tenaciously to the substance of the old belief while discarding its grosser material implications. The Supper, to Zwingli, was nothing more than a historical memorial with no magical significance whatever. At Marburg, in 1529, he argued this matter with Luther for three days and presented many points in favor of his position. Luther met them all by constantly repeating, "This is my body," occa-

sionally punctuating his exclamations by blows upon the
Bible with his huge Saxon fist. Naturally enough, the disputants got nowhere and separated without reaching any
basis of agreement. As a consequence, the first two Protestant groups came into existence. Denominationalism was
born at Marburg and grew apace with the passing years.
Upon nearly every other point the Swiss and German reformers were agreed, but the dissension concerning the
eucharist was sufficient to cause irremediable schism between
them and their followers even down to the present generation.

The Reformed theology, of which Zwingli was the
originator, differed from the Lutheran in two essential respects. First, it gave greater prominence to the doctrine
of election, and second, it interpreted the sacraments and
especially the eucharist in a less mystical and more distinctly
rationalistic fashion. Luther made much of justification by
faith and was especially emphatic in his preaching of the
love of Christ. Zwingli and Calvin after him had more to
say about the sovereignty of God and the supremacy of
predestination. One distinction between Zwingli and Calvin is worthy of especial note. The Swiss reformer was
less ascetic in his temper than any other of his co-laborers
and far less than was Calvin. The fact is that there was
considerable of the humanistic touch about Zwingli. He
was inclined to revert to the old Greek Fathers rather than
to the Latin, and in certain respects he reminds one of
Clement of Alexandria or Origen. The essential difference
was, of course, that the Greeks believed in free will while
the Protestant theologian was an extreme advocate of predestination. Nevertheless, they had many points in common. The divine immanence rather than the transcendent
view of Augustine made an especial appeal to Zwingli.
The rationalistic bias of Erasmus was also characteristic of

the teacher of Zurich. It was no wonder that he could not understand or appreciate Luther. The sheer mysticism of the latter was entirely beyond his horizon. Left to himself Zwingli would never have divided the Reformation forces. It required the mystical fanaticism of the Saxon leader to take the step. Doubtless Luther was conscientious in his action, and no doubt he felt more keenly than Zwingli the obligation of unswerving loyalty to his deepest convictions. Nor could he be expected to see where the demon of schism would lead Protestantism once it got fully under way.

II

John Calvin was born at Noyon, in Picardy, France, July 10, 1509. This was eight years before Luther nailed his theses to the door of the Wittenberg church and twenty-two years before the Reformed movement lost its leader when Zwingli was killed in the battle of Kappel. The father of John, Gerard Calvin, or Cauvin, as it was written at that time, held a position of importance in the diocese of Noyon. There were six children born to the elder Calvin, four sons and two daughters. Only three of the sons survived to manhood, all of whom entered the service of the church. John Calvin received an appointment which enabled him to draw revenue from the cathedral church at Noyon sufficient to provide for his early education. There is nothing to show that the pinched circumstances which surrounded the youthful careers of both Erasmus and Luther found any place in the experience of the French reformer.

Calvin was educated at Paris, where he attained distinction in his classes. He seems to have hesitated about his choice of a profession. His father wanted him to study law and later sent him to the University of Orléans, where he received his forensic training. Throughout his university career the lad was noted for great mental activity and for exceptional severity of temper. Illustrative of this latter characteristic is the surname which he received from his associates. He was known commonly by the title of "The Accusative." At Orléans he would spend half the night in study and then arise early in the morning in order to meditate on what he had learned the night before. His incessant labor while in school undoubtedly laid the foundations for the prolonged ill health which marked the greater part of his career. It was at Orléans, while studying law, that The Accusative had his interest awakened in theology. One of his relatives was engaged in a translation of the Scriptures, and Calvin's attention in this way was called to the sacred books. He read them with interest and undertook the study of Greek in order that he might understand them the better. He mastered the language as he did everything else he essayed, and with his new knowledge came a new determination in religion. As we have previously observed, there was no emotional crisis in his life which in any respect parallels the experience of Luther. He passed by such slow and imperceptible stages from Catholicism to Protestantism that he probably did not know himself the exact moment when the transition was made.

Calvin's father died in 1531, and this fact left his son free to follow his own inclinations in religion. He went to Paris, and along with his friend, Nicholas Cop, who had been elected Rector of the University, he started an agitation for a reformation in the church. The King was much enraged when he heard of the effrontery of the two young theologues and ordered them to be arrested. Calvin fled for his life, and there is a tradition to the effect that like the Apostle Paul before him he was let down out of a window and succeeded in escaping from the city in disguise.

From this time on he became a wanderer, drifting around through France and Switzerland and finally winding up at Basel, where he published the first edition of his famous *Institutes of the Christian Religion* in the year 1536. The preface is addressed to King Francis I, and is one of the most powerful apologetics in the history of Christianity. The *Institutes* as a book probably takes first place among the theological writings which have been produced since the days of the Apostles. No other treatise has been so influential or has produced such far-reaching results. This is the more remarkable because Calvin was not yet thirty years of age when he wrote this epoch-making volume. It is only fair to say that the work possesses but slight claims to originality. It is a simple and well-arranged exposition of the chief data of the Christian religion interpreted in Augustinian terms. The significance of the treatment consisted in its simplicity and its orderly and logical arrangement. These characteristics made it an ideal textbook, and it soon became the authoritative religious manual for the majority of Protestants.

As a result of what appeared to be a chance circumstance Calvin passed through Geneva in July, 1536. His friend, Farel, was engaged in a life-and-death struggle to extend the reformation in the city. He appealed to Calvin to stop and join him in his great undertaking. The author of the *Institutes* had no desire to engage in such a task. His disposition was studious and retired rather than forensic or active. He refused Farel's request. Then ensued a dramatic incident. In the spirit of ancient prophecy the man about to be deserted turned to his companion and in the severest language laid the curse of God upon his head. Calvin was moved to reconsider his decision. Later on he wrote that in that moment it appeared to him as if God had seized him "by his awful hand from heaven." When one recalls what his conception of the Deity was like it was no wonder that he yielded.

Calvin stayed at Geneva the greater part of his life. Along with Farel he was banished in 1538 because the stern discipline which he imposed was more than the citizens could bear. Nevertheless, there was something so appealing about the order which he introduced into the community life that three years later, on September 13, 1541, he made his second entry into the city. The story of his conflicts with his enemies need not concern us here. After two years of physical torture from disease he died in Geneva on May 27, 1564, eleven years after he had given his consent to the death of Servetus. The story of the latter is worthy of separate attention, inasmuch as fate has linked it forever with the biography of Calvin.

III

Michael Servetus was born at Tudela, in Navarre, about the year 1511, being thus slightly the junior of Calvin. He studied the liberal arts at Saragossa and law at Toulouse. Like Calvin, he became interested in theology and speedily espoused the Reformed views. Contrary to the other leaders of the new movement, he attacked the doctrine of the Trinity and aroused the animosity of Bucer, one of the most moderate of them, to such an extent that he referred to Servetus as "a wicked and cursed Spaniard." This did not change the heretic's views, and he appealed to the public through two books which set forth in altogether too glaring fashion the contradictions in the orthodox view of the Three in One and the One in Three. In 1534 he went to Lyons, where he published an edition of Ptolemy's geography. Later on he received his degree as Doctor of Medicine from the University of Paris and proceeded to signalize his distinction by attacking Galen and the standard medical authorities in a work of astonishing vigor and originality. He appears to have been a physician of rather extraordinary ability, and there is some ground for believing that he, rather than Harvey, originally discovered the circulation of the blood.

In 1541 he passed on to Vienna, where he published another work entitled *The Restitution of Christianity* which caused him to be arrested and tried for heresy. On June 17, 1553, he was sentenced to be burned at the stake, but perhaps through some collusion with the authorities he was enabled to escape and fled toward Italy. On his way thither he attempted to pass through Geneva. While in the city he ventured to attend church and was recognized and apprehended by the order of Calvin.

The historical record of his trial, which lasted for over two months, is full of interest. Servetus defended himself in language which was of the most virulent, and by the standards of the time, blasphemous type. Calvin's replies are equally vituperative and coarse. In the end the judgment which had been passed upon the heretic by the Catholics was reimposed by the Protestants of Geneva. To Calvin's credit it appears that he sought to have the sentence changed to death by decapitation. Whether serious in this effort or not, it proved unavailing. Under circumstances of unequaled barbarity for even that callous age the wretched man was put to death on October 27, 1553. Attached to the funeral stake were the condemned books of the author and the manuscript which he had previously sent to Calvin for his criticism and approval. That the reformer of Geneva was primarily responsible for the persecution and death of Servetus appears to us to be unquestioned. Various attempts have been made to whitewash Calvin, but the record as it stands will not fairly admit of such an interpretation.

It is possible that at the last he repented his share in the ghastly transaction, but that fact, if it be a fact, does not in the slightest degree disprove his previous part in the apprehension and condemnation of the man whom he had come to regard as the enemy of the faith.

Calvin was married in 1539 to Idelette de Bure, the widow of an Anabaptist whom he had converted and who had died six months earlier. His wife lived eleven years and during that time bore him one child, a son who was born prematurely and lived only a short time. Within the limitations indicated by the above facts the marriage appears to have been a happy one. Calvin's stern and gloomy temper did not permit him to think much of the joys of life. He was a model of austerity and was impeccable to the last degree. He did not object to burning heretics if he thought such action conduced to the glory of God, but he was honest to the last penny in every monetary transaction, and in his private relations his word was ever as good as his bond.

IV

In order to understand Calvin's theological position we need only remember that he took the doctrine of Augustine, systematized and popularized it, and carried it to the limit of ecclesiastical formulation. The central thought with Augustine was the absolute sovereignty of God. Directly deduced from this basic position was the doctrine of predestination or election. Nothing could be clearer than the fact that the divine sovereignty carries predestination with it as a corollary. Equally clear must be the conclusion that salvation depends in the last analysis upon election and that the church therefore has nothing to do with it. The Catholic authorities recognized this tendency in the teaching of Augustine and speedily soft-pedaled it. As we have seen previously, the church adopted a semi-Pelagian position and penalized severely men like Gottschalk, Wyclif and Huss, who insisted upon taking Augustine too seriously. As a matter of fact, it was the great Bishop who still holds a foremost place in the pantheon of the church who was primarily responsible for the debacle of the Reformation. Had there been no Augustine in all likelihood there would have been no Luther and no Calvin. Only the Anabaptists and the humanists set the mighty Aurelius at naught, and of themselves they could never have broken the power of the papacy.

The doctrine of predestination put iron in the blood of the reformers. It reduced kings, princes, nobles, cardinals and popes to comparative nothingness in the presence of the elect. It destroyed the divine right of kings, negated the sanctions of social custom, and enabled a peasant with due solemnity to pass sentence of death upon the monarch of the realm. Fearing God intensely, the disciples of Calvin feared naught else on earth. Dignitaries possessed no terror for them nor were they stampeded in the presence of superior forces or material power of any kind. Being sure of their election nothing else in the universe mattered or could matter to them. When we think of the tremendous odds which the reformers faced in their rebellion against the established authorities in church and state we can see that nothing short of Calvin's rigorous teaching could have saved the day for his followers. The fact is that the doctrine of predestination was primarily responsible for the Reformation. Without it, so far as we can see, there would have been no Luther, no Oliver Cromwell, no *Mayflower* and no modern democracy. Autocratic in the extreme, as it was, it destroyed the lesser autocracies of earth and cleared the way for the rule of the people. Had it not been for John Calvin it is extremely unlikely that there would have been any Declaration of Independence or Constitution of the United States of America.

Having made the above statements it remains to say that predestination possesses its somber aspects as well as its brighter hues. It was, as Calvin himself once remarked, a horrible doctrine. The idea that from all eternity the Divine Sovereign doomed uncounted millions of conscious beings to everlasting torment just in order to manifest His own dignity and power seems so grotesquely inhuman as to make it inconceivable to our present generation. No wonder the men who believed this doctrine could be stern, intolerant and cruel if occasion demanded. Nothing more hideously immoral from the standpoint of social ethics can be imagined than the doctrine of election in its crasser form. It was a compound of unutterable inhumanity, injustice and Oriental despotism unequaled elsewhere in the annals of human thinking. Nothing more cruel than the idea of burning innocent people eternally can be imagined, nor can there be anything more unjust or more typical of the worst and most irresponsible types of despotic authority. Both Calvin and Augustine whom he followed fortunately ascribed other qualities to the Deity along with the prerogative of election, and in this way helped to neutralize its singularly immoral implications. Had this not been true one shudders to think of what might have happened to the world.

What actually happened was bad enough. Roman Catholicism, while repudiating the extreme teaching of Augustine, nevertheless held to many aspects of his doctrine. In particular, it despised heresy and brooked no interference with its ecclesiastical authority. It had no sympathy with freedom or tolerance and it regarded democracy as a delusion and a sham. Make your submission to the pope, it said to the reformers; go to mass, and maybe the Lord will be satisfied with sending you to purgatory. On the other hand, the Calvinists snapped their fingers at the pope and retorted, Who can lay anything to the charge of God's elect? Everlasting perdition they were sure awaited all who had not been chosen from eternity to salvation and it did not behoove one to be too squeamish about dealing gently in this world with those who were certain to be victims of unending conflagration in the life to come. Hence the Puritans believed in war, capital punishment, the torture of witches and anything else which the stern logic of their creed seemed to demand.

One of the most interesting features of the later development of Calvinism was its influence upon the rise of modern capitalistic enterprises. It is only during recent years that the relation of Calvinism to capitalism has been thoroughly pointed out. The German author, Max Weber, followed by R. H. Tawney in his *Religion and the Rise of Capitalism,* shows with conclusive logic that the doctrine of election was not only the primary factor in the rise of modern democracy but that it was also the chief influence in the development of our modern economic system. Weber points out that Calvinism was responsible for the development of capitalism in two distinct ways: first, it supplied a motive of moral obligation which was entirely lacking in the money-making of the Middle Ages, and second, it fostered a spirit of aceticism which the accumulation of wealth on a large scale absolutely demands of its votaries. With regard to the first of these considerations it should be said that throughout the Middle-Age period the making of money was looked down on. Usury, which in those days meant interest of any kind, was denounced by the church and not infrequently penalized by the state. Most of the money-making was done by the Jews, and they were hated and despised by all other classes. The nobles and the intelligentsia spurned the idea of accumulating wealth. In any event, no one thought of making money for the sake of making it or of even trying to secure it except for the purpose of spending it and obtaining something in return for it. The modern capitalist who feels impelled to make money and ever more money and to reinvest most of what he makes in his business was quite unknown during the period before the Reformation. Benjamin Franklin, as Weber shows, laid down the principle which governed the change of spirit in his *Advice to a Young Tradesman*:

Remember that time is money. He who could make ten shillings a day through his work, but goes walking half the day or idles in his room, even if he spends for his amusement only a sixpence, may not count this alone, but he has, in addition, given up five shillings, or rather thrown it away. Remember that credit is money. If anyone leaves money with me after it falls due, he makes me a present of the interest. This amounts to a considerable sum if a man has good credit and makes good use of it. Remember that money can beget money. Five shillings turned over become six . . . and so on till they are a hundred pounds sterling. He who kills a sow destroys its progeny till the thousandth generation. He who wastes five shillings murders all that might have been produced by it, whole columns of pounds sterling.

Here it is obvious that the accumulation of money is regarded as a distinct obligation, and with this introduction of the motive of duty capitalism assumes an entirely new form. That which had been looked down on at an earlier date now becomes the very goal of existence. The same stern doctrine which impelled the followers of Cromwell to cut off the head of Charles I led the successors of Oliver to bend all of their energies to the accumulation of wealth. The dignity of the capitalistic enterprise was born and with it came redoubled energy and power.

Not only in the change of the capitalistic spirit but also

in the inculcation of the ascetic method was Calvinism responsible for the development of modern industry. The real capitalist is always abstemious, frugal, self-denying and industrious. He is the monk of the Middle Ages turned wrong side out. He knows that it is impossible for him to succeed in the great game which claims his attention unless he conquers his appetites, repudiates ease, and is willing to sacrifice his physical comfort at every turn of the road. He denies himself as thoroughly as the ancient Benedictine or Capuchin but for an entirely different reason. That indefatigable energy and loyalty which Ignatius Loyola put into the service of the church in Protestantism passes into the avenues of business and trade. No wonder that the spirit of John Calvin stalks behind the ever-widening commerce of the world. Modern business owes more to the sallow and sickly apostle of Geneva than it does to any other man on earth.

V

The influence of Calvin upon the later history of theology was extensive and profound. The *Institutes* went everywhere and speedily outclassed every other book in the literature of the Reformation. In France Calvinism became the leading foe of the established church, and under Henry IV promised to dominate the nation. Had the King of Navarre been less of a politician and more of a statesman the religious history of his nation might have been different. No man who thinks that a crown is well worth a mass ever deserves to wear the crown. Following the Massacre of Saint Bartholomew and Henry's desertion came the utter destruction of Protestantism in France. The tenets of Calvin passed into Holland where they became embedded in the structure of the Dutch Reformed theology, crossed the channel into England where for a time they ruled the state and were crystallized in the immortal dogmas of the Westminster Confession; went on across the Tweed into Scotland where they achieved their greatest triumph in the complete dominance of the frugal natives of the land, and last of all traversed the high seas to the New World and laid the foundations of the greatest commercial empire to be recorded in the annals of time.

Calvin developed a new ecclesiastical polity which sought to combine the freedom of democracy with the strength of monarchy. How far he succeeded in his ambition may be left to the historians, religious and secular. His followers are wont to claim that the Constitution of the United States was modeled after the Presbyterian church, and there is some truth in their contention. Calvin gave considerable authority to the minister and had no patience with the idea that the layman had the same privileges in the church as the clergy. He went beyond Roman Catholicism itself in refusing to lay members of the church, the right to baptize under extreme circumstances. In Volume II, Chapter 15 of the *Institutes* he writes, "The custom which has been received and practised how many ages past, and almost from the primitive times of the church, for baptism to be performed by laymen, in cases where death was apprehended, and no minister was present in time, it appears to me impossible to defend by any good reason." In other respects he asserts the general Protestant doctrine of the essential priesthood of all believers, but there was more than a touch of the old clericalism in the sacramental prerogatives which he preserved for the minister. As for the government which he instituted at Geneva and which has spread so widely over the world, while possessing certain elements of freedom it has always had teeth in it. Essentially oligarchichal in character, it rests upon a basis of democracy and possesses much merit, especially where the citizenry is not ready for a greater measure of freedom. Here, too, the iron imprint of Calvin is written large in the history of the world.

The stern theology of Geneva became modified with the passing of the years. Nearly two centuries after Calvin it found its most brilliant interpreter in the greatest metaphysician of the New World, Jonathan Edwards, of Princeton. Edwards had a mind like a razor and in his faultless logic the somber tenets of predestination receive their most perfect embodiment. Determinism never had an abler advocate. If the mere logic of the intellect could settle the question Edwards would have it sewed up for all time. Through his theory of the strongest motive as the necessary determinant of choice he effectually pulverized the free-will advocates of his day. For the rest he was a typical Calvinist, somber, just, reverential, and with the smoke of the bottomless pit in his nostrils by day and night. Never before or after was there such preaching of hell-fire as one discovers in his sermons. No wonder that they are still cited as classics in this particular field. The amazing thing is that he could work himself up into such a fury of evangelism with the certainty of unchanging predestination forever in the background of his mind. Of course, there are both theological and psychological answers to the enigma, but this fact does not lessen its grotesque character. One reads his *Sinners in the Hands of an Angry God* and wonders how Edwards himself could have believed it. But he did. Of that fact there can be no doubt. And so did others. Small wonder that not a few of the weaker minded during these early days went mad under such strong preaching for fear that by some chance they might belong to the non-elect.

The modern descendants of Calvin take his teachings

quite mildly. The statement of the doctrine of election, for example, contained in the *Handbook of the Presbyterian Church in the United States of America* is moderate enough to include any one who even squints in the direction of Augustine. Certainly it is a far cry from the pitiless logic of the companion of Farel. Nevertheless, the world moves, and if it has after some centuries passed beyond Calvin, his triumphant shade can point to the future and cry aloud, "But for me you would not have been!"

CHAPTER XIV

ARMINIUS

THE Netherlands, it has been remarked, are distinguished for two things: to wit, windmills and the Arminian theology. Some facetious individuals may infer a connection between the two, but however this may be, Arminianism at least has achieved fame around the world. The Netherlands themselves gave rather cold comfort to the doctrine but it became naturalized on alien soil and speedily attained distinction. It seems probable that the majority of Protestants at the present time are advocates of the teaching of Arminius. Especially in the Anglo-Saxon world has the new philosophy made headway. Both in England and in America Arminians are in the majority and are likely to continue so. It may be well for us to inquire a little more particularly into the new way of thinking.

I

Jakob van Herman, or Arminius as his flat Dutch name became when it assumed its Latin form, was one of the leaders in the theological movement known as the Remonstrants which arose in Holland in the early part of the seventeenth century. About the time when Shakespeare was retiring from his active stage career to settle down in comfortable affluence at Stratford on the Avon, and while the King James translators were wrestling with Hebrew roots and Greek derivatives in the Jerusalem Chamber, a group of sturdy Dutchmen put forth a document which they called *The Remonstrance.* It contained five positive and an equal number of negative points, the one list being substantially the correlative of the other. There was much furor aroused when this document appeared, and great opposition to its principles was developed. The name of Arminius was associated with it along with those of Simon Episcopius, Jan Uyttenbogaert, and the most talented figure in the group, the great statesman and lawyer Hugo Grotius. The Spanish persecution and the urgent need for unity in the Protestant ranks did not prevent the Reformed theologians from violent contentions with one another. It was the general feeling that the ark was in danger, and the faithful rallied to its support. In 1619, nine years after the appearance of *The Remonstrance,* the Synod of Dort administered a crushing rebuke to its supporters. The party of Arminius, although defeated, did not give up its opposition. His friends continued the battle, and while they never gained the ascendency in their own country they succeeded in impressing their ideas upon a large section of the Protestant world.

What was it that constituted the doctrine which was so violently repudiated by the Synod of Dort? Perhaps the best answer to the question may be found through an interpretation of the platform which the Synod itself put forth. This document has become famous because it enunciated clearly the so-called Five Points of Calvinism. These points, in their correct order, are: (1) unconditional predestination; (2) limited atonement; (3) human inability; (4) irresistibility of grace; (5) final perseverance of the saints. Upon all of these features Arminius locked horns with his opponents. He attacked unconditional predestination, alleging that some place must be found for the human will in the scheme of salvation. He denied that the atonement was limited and asserted on the contrary that it was full and complete. Human inability he accepted only to the extent that man's will needs the cooperation of the divine spirit in order to achieve salvation. He denied the irresistibility of grace, although he affirmed its necessity; that is, that there could be no salvation without it, and he also appears to have asserted the possibility of falling from grace, but the last point is not made perfectly clear in *The Remonstrance.*

In the above outline of Arminianism we have perhaps gone somewhat beyond the actual thought of Arminius himself. He was much more of a Calvinist than were his spiritual descendants, and the ultimate tendencies of the movement which he originated were probably quite beyond his own imagination. The primary consideration involved in his position was his repudiation of the Calvinistic scheme of predestination. The fact that he tried to modify the doctrine without entirely eliminating it possesses little significance. As Calvin saw long before, the strength of predestination consists in its logical simplicity. Carried through unfalteringly it constitutes one of the most unassailable theological systems, but once there is the slightest deviation from the plain statement of the doctrine its whole logical effect is destroyed. It was Calvin's merit that he saw this clearly and never veered from it. He made his system a doctrine of iron, but along with the hardness and inflexibility of the teaching there went clarity, reason and power. The Arminians lost in logic what they gained in ethics, but the exchange no doubt appeared to them worth while. In any case, the rigid Calvinism of the old school was destined to disappear. The modern world, despite its scientific determinism, remains cold to the doctrine of election. Free will is in the ascendency, and Arminius, its prophet, is coming into his own. As we have already indicated, he was not much of an advocate of freedom from the present point of view. Nevertheless, if he could come back to earth he would doubtless rejoice in the success which has been achieved in his name.

Arminius was born at Oudewater-an-der-Yssel, October 10, 1560. His father belonged to the guild of the cutlers, and like Erasmus, the youthful Jakob was left an orphan at an early age. He appears to have drifted around considerably while a lad, living for a time at Utrecht and later at Marburg. When he was fifteen years of age he was entered for study at the newly founded University of Leyden, where he remained seven years. It was here, he tells us, that he imbibed a great distaste for Aristotle, whose name was still one to conjure with in the academic world. From Leyden Arminius passed on to Geneva, which Calvin had made the Mecca of the reformed churches. The distinguished scholar, Beza, was teaching in the Swiss city at this time, and the Dutch lad spent nearly six years under his tutelage. Once during the period indicated he visited Basel but remained for only a few months. It was here that at the request of his teacher, Grynæus, Arminius delivered several lectures on his own account. These productions were received with such applause that their author would have secured the degree of doctor had he not with unusual modesty declared himself too young to become the recipient of the distinction. After finishing his work in Geneva in the year 1587, while Philip II of Spain and Queen Elizabeth were preparing for the death-struggle which was to determine the destinies of Europe, Arminius, the Protestant theologian, quietly made a trip to Italy, visiting Padua and Rome quite unmolested and returning to Amsterdam in 1588.

Arminius was now twenty-eight years of age. His reputation had preceded him, and he was immediately called to become the pastor of a Reformed church at Amsterdam.

He preached with vigor and power and always with unswerving loyalty to the principles of John Calvin. During this time opponents of the orthodox faith arose, and it became the duty of the young minister to chastise them in public debate. As a result of his efforts in this direction Arminius found his own views slipping, and in the end he was substantially converted to the opposition. He always maintained that his ideas were not inconsistent with a proper interpretation of the doctrinal standards of his church, which assertion may be true enough if we accept the premise upon which it is based. In the year 1603 he was appointed a professor at the University of Leyden, which had become the great training school for ministers of the Reformed church. He was regarded as a liberal when he was appointed to his position and his views speedily aroused the opposition of his conservative colleagues, especially a certain professor named Gomarus. Arminius stood his ground and although the utmost pressure was brought upon the University officials to dismiss him they refused to interfere. Worn out by the ceaseless attacks of his enemies Arminius died at Leyden on October 19, 1609, a year before *The Remonstrance* appeared and ten years before the convocation of the Synod of Dort.

In his private life Arminius was courteous, unostentatious and just. He was a scholar as well as a preacher and was loyal above everything else to the truth as he saw it. He was not a genius of the first order, like Erasmus, but he was a straightforward, cultured and thoroughly conscientious student, and he deserves the fame which has come to him. There have been greater intellects in the history of theology, but there have been few if any more noble characters or more worthy ministers of the Word.

II

The greatest name associated with the rise of the Arminian movement in Holland was undoubtedly that of Hugo de Groot, or Grotius in its Latinized form. This distinguished theologian and publicist was born at Delft on April 10, 1583. His father was burgomaster of the city and at one time in his life had been Curator of the University of Leyden. Like Erasmus and Leibnitz, the other two in the trio of great scholars of the early modern era, Grotius was a precocious lad, and at the age of eleven years was matriculated as a student in the university with which his father was associated. At Leyden the boy came under the influence of the famous scholar and teacher, Joseph Scaliger. At the age of fifteen Hugo received his degree and in the following year he was associated with Barneveldt, the Grand Pensionary, on a diplomatic tour to France. It was upon this occasion that the attention of King Henry IV was directed to the lad, and had this monarch lived he would probably have retained Grotius in his service. The way things turned out the young scholar came back to his native land and began the practise of law, being admitted to the bar at the Hague in 1599, when he was little more than sixteen years of age. Eight years later he was appointed Fiscal General, and six years after this he became Council Pensionary at Rotterdam.

It was about this time that the dispute between the Remonstrants and their old-line Calvinistic opponents was at its height. Barneveldt, the patron and friend of Grotius, was a protector of the more liberal group. The lad naturally followed his employer and used both his tongue and pen in opposition to the principles set forth by the Synod of Dort. In these days to be a religious heretic was also equivalent to political treason. It was not long before both Barneveldt and Grotius were arrested, tried and condemned by the dominant party in the state at that time under the leadership of the famous Prince Maurice. Barneveldt was beheaded in 1619, and Grotius was sentenced to imprisonment for life in the castle of Loevenstein. Like David, the old King of Israel, and many another figure in the romance of history, Grotius succeeded in escaping from prison through the wit and cleverness of his wife. After leaving Holland he wandered about the Catholic sections of the Netherlands for some time in the most destitute circumstances. At last he escaped to France, where the Catholic King, Louis XIII, for some peculiar reason gave him a pension. Only a part of the amount stipulated was paid and the King later withdrew his contract. Some time afterward Grotius was invited to return to his native land, and he accepted the invitation. As a result of the opposition of his enemies he was again brought to trial and sentenced to perpetual exile. By this time his scholarship and literary works had made him known throughout the world.

When the news of his banishment went forth he received invitations with promises of friendly treatment from the Kings of Denmark, Poland and Spain, and from Queen Christina of Sweden. He decided to accept the last named proposal and in 1634 he entered the Swedish service. He was at once sent as ambassador to the French court, which position he held for ten years. Upon his return to Stockholm he was received with the greatest attention by the Queen and her court, but the atmosphere of the northern kingdom did not appeal to him and he determined to return to France. The Queen, finding it impossible to retain him, presented him with the sum of ten thousand crowns together with much costly plate, and in addition placed a ship at his disposal to convey him across the Baltic. It so chanced that a storm forced the vessel ashore on the coast of Pomerania. While journeying toward Lubeck Grotius fell sick and died at Rostock, August 28, 1645.

Grotius is famous in the history of theology by reason of four things: First, as the founder of international law and the author of the first treatise on the subject he laid the foundations of all modern peace movements. Second, he, along with Erasmus and Leibnitz, takes his place as one of the foremost advocates of Christian union at a time when religious schism was the order of the day. Third, in his treatise entitled *The Truth of the Christian Religion,* published in Leyden in 1627, he produced the first text-book in the field of Christian evidences, or apologetics, in the modern sense of that word. Fourth, he formulated a new theory of the atonement which speedily achieved a position of no slight importance in the realm of Reformed theology. Only the last of these points would seem to require any further elaboration at our hands.

During the Middle Ages the orthodox view of the cross was either the ransom theory of Gregory, which held that Jesus was put to death as a payment to Satan in order to deliver humanity from thraldom, or the satisfaction theory of Anselm, which taught that the ransom was not paid to Satan but rather to the Deity in order to satisfy the divine justice which had been offended by the sin of Adam. Both of these theories were built upon what is usually known as the retributive conception of punishment. From this point of view any sin is looked on as a debt which must be paid before the account can be squared. There can be no crime which does not involve a penalty, and justice is never done unless the penalty is exacted. Christ took the place of Adam by virtue of the Incarnation, and therefore paid the penalty and satisfied the demands of justice. This, as we have seen, always constituted the essential feature in the orthodox view of the atonement.

About the same time the acute and penetrating intellect of Abelard, building upon the more modern idea of punishment as reformatory, put forth the moral view of the atonement which has exercised such an influence upon later thought. This conception looks upon punishment as designed solely for the improvement and cure of the criminal and as serving no other rational end. From this point of view the famous definition of Mr. Henry Ward Beecher was derived. The atonement, he said, is nothing more than suffering love healing the sins of the world. Liberal theology of every type has always adhered to the moral theory and during recent years even conservative theologians have manifested a tendency in this direction.

The theory of Grotius, sometimes known as the legalistic view of the atonement, occupies a position between the standpoints of Abelard and Anselm. Jurists usually recognize three theories of punishment, the retributive, the reformatory and the deterrent. Anselm represents the first in the field of theology, Abelard the second and Grotius the third. According to the last-named view penalties are not exacted on the basis of abstract retribution or with the desire of reforming the criminal, but rather for the purpose of preventing other individuals from committing crime, in the interest of public welfare. The deterrent theory has always been popular with lawyers, and Grotius showed keen insight in his application of it to the realm of Christian theology. Christ died on the cross, according to this position, not in order to satisfy the demands of any abstract justice nor for the sole purpose of reforming humanity, but rather to manifest the heinousness of sin in order that men might be led to shrink from it. The cross, Grotius said, is the picture of what sin is and should forever remain as a deterrent force in the conflict between good and evil. This conception became a part of the so-called federal theology and was accepted by Jonathan Edwards and many other later theologians. Its purely legalistic character has prevented it from receiving wide-spread endorsement by the church at large. To-day it is probably less popular than it was a hundred years ago. Nevertheless, it unquestionably takes its place as one of the great contributions of the human intellect to the field of soteriology.

III

Arminianism found its most popular exponent in a certain itinerant preacher who came upon the scene some fifty years after the death of Grotius and whose life spanned almost the entire period of the eighteenth century. His name was John Wesley, and he was born in 1703 and died in 1791. His father was the rector of Epworth, a country town inhabited by some two thousand ignorant and vicious peasants. His mother was the twenty-fifth child of a distinguished scholar, and John himself was the fifteenth out of nineteen children. Obviously, these statistics indicate an age far removed from the modern attitude toward birth control. Susanna, shortly after the arrival of John, wrote concerning his future, "I do intend to be more particularly careful of the soul of this child that I may instill into his mind the principles of true religion and virtue." It must be admitted that later history furnishes a strong presumption that she successfully carried out her resolution.

Wesley's father received a very small salary and found nineteen hungry mouths rather more than he could manage to fill on his income. As a result he was imprisoned for debt, but managed to get out and to resume the labors of his parish. At the age of eleven John was sent to the Charterhouse School, where he achieved no great distinction. At seventeen he became a matriculate of Christ Church College, Oxford, on a scholarship of forty pounds a year. Wesley began his university life in rather conventional

fashion. He read the classics but was not particularly interested in religion. At the age of twenty-two through the
influence of two books, *The Imitation of Christ*, by Thomas
à Kempis, and Jeremy Taylor's *Holy Living and Holy Dying*, he experienced a species of conversion which led him to
resolve to set apart an hour or two a day for religious retirement, to commune every week and, to quote his own
language, "to watch against all sin whether in word or
deed." Two years later he was elected a Fellow of Lincoln
College. He stayed at Oxford until he was thirty-two
years of age.

In November, 1729, he organized the Holy Club, which
date on this account is sometimes marked out as the beginning of Methodism. This organization was made up
of a small group which met regularly three or four times
a week. Its members took communion every Sunday and
fasted twice every seven days. They divided their time
methodically and engaged to live by certain set rules.
Among other things, they agreed to persuade as far as they
could everybody with whom they came in contact to attend
public prayers, sermons and sacraments. The Holy Club
included in its membership John and Charles Wesley and
George Whitefield.

At the age of thirty-two Wesley was called by General
Oglethorpe, the founder of the new colony of Georgia, to
come to America in order to preach to the settlers and
Indians of the community. The young cleric went, more
with the idea of converting himself than anybody else. To
quote his own words, "My chief motive is the hope of saving my own soul. I hope to learn the true sense of the
gospel of Christianity by preaching it to the heathen." He
did not achieve his expectation, but upon his return from
Georgia on the evening of May 24, 1738, at a Moravian
meeting in Aldersgate Street, London, he tells us that he

felt his heart strangely warmed and from that moment he dated his real conversion.

The story of his life for the next half-century is an astonishing record of activity and physical and mental endurance. He averaged about four thousand five hundred miles a year on horseback, preaching from two to five sermons a day, or a total of over forty thousand discourses. Most of this preaching was done in the open air, and he appears never to have become hoarse or fatigued. At the age of seventy he spoke to over thirty thousand people in one open-air assemblage. Once in his journal he makes the entry, "wet from morning to night but I found it no matter of inconvenience." He never weighed over one hundred and twenty pounds, and in his early life he had suffered from hemorrhage. No marvel contained in the gospel which he preached was so great as the miracle of his own life. Strangest of all was the influence he had over his audiences. Read to-day, his discourses are dry, tedious and unimpressive, but when delivered to multitudes of illiterate coal miners or workers in the fields they produced an impression little short of magical. Sometimes hundreds of the hearers would fall down as if dead, and the most profound emotions were always aroused by this simple little man with his quiet, unimpassioned manner of speech. A typical illustration of his work as a preacher may be found in the entry in his diary for Monday, August 11, 1740.

Forty or fifty of those who were seeking salvation desired leave to spend the night together, at the society-room, in prayer and giving thanks. Before ten I left them, and lay down. But I could have no quiet rest, being quite uneasy in my sleep, as I found others were too, that were asleep in other parts of the house. Between two and three in the morning I was waked, and desired to come downstairs. I immediately heard such a confused noise, as if a number of

men were all putting to the sword. It increased when I
came into the room and began to pray. One whom I partic-
ularly observed to be roaring aloud for pain was J——
W——, who had been always, till then, very sure that
"none cried out but hypocrites" : so had Mrs. S——ms also.
But she too now cried to God with a loud and bitter cry.
It was not long before God heard from His holy place.
He spake, and all our souls were comforted. He bruised
Satan under our feet; and sorrow and sighing fled away.

Instances of this kind occur again and again. The up-
shot of the matter was that Wesley revolutionized the whole
lower-class population of England and influenced civilization to an extent perhaps greater than that exercised by any
other man of his century.

The theology of this new reformer was simplicity itself.
He rejected predestination, although he adhered to the idea
of original sin and to the orthodox dogmas in general.
Conversion was due to a mystical experience produced by
the Holy Spirit acting in conjunction with the will of the
sinner. The process involved was primarily emotional and
volitional, with little or no appeal to the intellect. It had
about it a universal quality which gave it wide-spread popularity. The prevailing deism of the age had degenerated
into a species of intellectual dry-rot, and Wesley's movement
came in the nature of a welcome reaction. The common
folk heard him gladly, and his gospel of free will brought
comfort to troubled hearts. The high Calvinism of the
older days had produced despair in many minds who were
fearful lest they were enrolled in the ranks of the non-elect.
Wesley's gospel gave them joy and peace and set their feet
upon a rock. Of course, his emotional type of conversion
did not appeal to all minds. The more educated classes
especially found it unattractive and impossible. Wesley
himself in his later life placed less emphasis upon the emo-

tional manifestations which in his earlier years had appeared so significant. Nevertheless, he never lost his faith in "experimental religion," as his followers were wont to style it.

In certain respects John Wesley was the greatest organizing genius of his day. His emotional conversion would have evaporated into thin air if it had not been for the marvelous manner in which he conserved the results of his preaching. Everywhere he organized his societies and classes, and while his methods, like his preaching, were simple and direct they were marvelously efficient. It was at this point that he exerted the greatest influence upon the course of history. Without his genius for organization the movement which he originated would inevitably have come to naught.

The private life of Wesley, while above reproach from the standpoints of honesty and traditional morality in general, possessed certain peculiarities which are difficult to explain. He believed devoutly that the earthquake at Lisbon was the direct judgment of heaven upon the inhabitants of the city because of their impiety and wickedness. Many of his theological conceptions were crude and reactionary in the extreme. His relations with women constitute an interesting part of his biography. During his residence in Georgia he fell in love with Miss Sophy Hopkey, who he tells us was "a beautiful, modest, and affectionate girl of eighteen." Some of his friends having represented to him that marriage with this young lady might prove a detriment to his religious work, he decided to cast lots in order to determine what he should do. When he drew out a slip of paper on which was written the word "think no more of it" he immediately accepted the decision as the voice of God and did not hesitate to obey it. When he came back to England he proceeded to fall in love with a certain Mrs.

Grace Murray, who had nursed him through a period of
sickness, but his brother Charles considered the match so
ill-advised that he resorted to vigorous action in order to
break it off. At last, when John reached the age of forty-
eight, he took things in his own hands and married the
widow of a London merchant, Mrs. Vazeille, who is described as an essentially vulgar woman with a tendency to
hysteria. Whatever may have been the cause there can be
no doubt that the marriage was an exceedingly unhappy one.
Robert Southey, in his Life of Wesley, says that the latter's
wife should be classed along with the spouses of Socrates
and Job as the three bad wives of history. Reading Wesley's own statements we are not always sure that the fault
belonged to his wife. Once upon a time he wrote to her,
"Of what importance is your character to mankind? If
you were buried just now, or if you had never lived, what
loss would it be to the cause of God?" Upon another occasion he issued a tract upon marriage in which he says
rather baldly that the duties of a wife may be reduced to
two: she should recognize herself as the inferior of her
husband and she should behave as such. These were before
the days of feminism, but it may be that Mrs. Wesley, like
her husband, was inclined to look ahead of her own age.

Wesley died on March 2, 1791. His last words were,
"The best of all is, God is with us." He had collected
thousands of dollars during his travels, but like Calvin no
money ever stuck to his fingers. He set in motion currents
which permanently altered the life of humanity. He was in
no sense of the word a theologian, but he helped to promote
an interpretation of religion which possesses unsurpassed
elements of popular appeal. He will remain a figure to be
reckoned with by the future historian.

IV

Arminianism achieved its greatest triumph when it converted John Wesley. It is fair to say, however, that Methodism represents only a small section of the free-will movement in Protestantism. In the Church of England, where Roman Catholic semi-Pelagianism did not control the thinking of the clergy, most of them deserted Calvin for his Dutch successor. A large proportion of the non-conformist bodies outside of the Wesleyan followed in the same pathway. Some Baptists and Congregationalists remained Calvinists but the vast majority became advocates of free will. More striking still was the effect of the movement upon the old-line views of election. Little by little the traditional doctrine became modified until it changed its meaning entirely. It is questionable whether any one of his followers to-day interprets predestination with precisely the same meaning which the reformer of Geneva attached to it. Arminius has in effect conquered the Protestant world.

Dutch theology did not come to an end with Arminius or Grotius. It flourished extensively for years, and Holland remained the theological center of the Reformed faith for more than a century. The so-called federal theology, or the doctrine of the Covenants, owed its origin or at least its most extensive exposition to a Dutch thinker by the name of Cocceius. This learned exegete taught that the Scriptures contain two covenants, one of works and the other of grace. The covenant of works lasted from the Creation to the Fall, and the covenant of grace has been in effect since that time. The result of this teaching was to suggest a progressive development in the process of revelation which distinctly foreshadowed later critical views. The tendencies of the position were not at first recognized but later became apparent. Cocceius himself was an old-line Calvinist and was long regarded as a staunch defender of the orthodox faith.

Upon one point he was somewhat rudely challenged by his contemporaries. He insisted on rejecting the idea that the Christian Sunday should be styled the Sabbath, and asserted on the contrary that only the seventh day, or Saturday, deserved this title. His intimate and accurate knowledge of the Hebrew language caused him to recognize the impropriety of the common usage. Modern scholarship has fully sustained him in this position, and the development of various movements advocating the seventh day as the true Christian Sabbath would probably have been avoided if his position had been more generally accepted. The early Christians who were Jews doubtless observed both the seventh day and the first. The Gentile followers of Jesus accepted only the latter. In any case, it seems perfectly clear that the Sabbath was always the seventh day and the Lord's Day the first of the week. Upon this new memorial occasion the disciples met for worship, including the breaking of bread, as the eucharist was styled in the early days. At these services there was preaching if an acceptable speaker could be had. Cocceius had a much more accurate conception of the meaning of the Scriptures than was true of most of his contemporaries. Like Grotius, Leibnitz and Erasmus, he was an advocate of Christian union and deplored the sectarian divisions which existed among Protestants. His influence was perpetuated in the thinking of the English and Scottish churches which adhered to the Presbyterian faith. He possessed a distinctly modern mind and his name deserves to be remembered with gratitude by intelligent Christians throughout the world.

It is sometimes difficult to separate the Arminian influence from the earlier free-will tenets of the Anabaptists and the humanists. Religious groups like the Friends, Mennonites, German Baptists, Congregationalists and others go back to the older sources for their inspiration. The regular Baptists undoubtedly have the same origin but later took on in different sections Calvinistic and Arminian tendencies. So diverse are the forces back of some of these later movements that it is often difficult to disentangle them. The Anglican theology, with its combination of Catholic and Protestant principles, illustrates this situation. The doctrine of High Church representatives and of Anglo-Catholicism in general differs in no essential respect from the thought of Thomas Aquinas as expressed in the decrees of the Council of Trent. Low Church and Broad Church movements, while characterized by a wealth of learning and intellectual acuteness, manifest a surprising lack of originality. At one time we are taken back to Origen, at another to Erasmus, and at others to Calvin or Arminius, but nearly always to somewhere or to somebody. There has never been a really independent Anglican theology. One thinks of Hooker when he writes these words, but with all his brilliancy Hooker makes no pretensions to originality of thought. Anglicanism may well be regarded as a synthesis of what it conceives to be the best thinking of all the schools, but it has so far failed to develop a supreme theologian of its own.

No great name appears in the history of theology from the time of Arminius until after Immanuel Kant laid the foundations of modern philosophical idealism at the close of the eighteenth century. The scepter which had passed from Switzerland to Holland was transferred to Berlin. Just what happened there must constitute the subject of the next chapter.

CHAPTER XV

SCHLEIERMACHER

AFTER Calvin the greatest name in the history of modern theology is that of Schleiermacher. Whatever attitude any one may take concerning his views he can not doubt their significance. Whenever a budding theologian emerges in these latter days it is the practise of exuberant friends to inscribe upon the jacket of his latest book that he bids fair to become the greatest theologian since Schleiermacher, or words to that effect. Usually such shots are wide of the mark, as witness the recent case of Karl Barth. It is true that Albrecht Ritschl has won a place of first-rate importance since the days of Schleiermacher, but he stands alone in having done so. Distinguished disciples he has had in plenty, but no one has challenged the supremacy of the master. Schleiermacher and Ritschl represent the last word in doctrinal discussion since the days of Arminius.

The founder of modern theology, as he is often styled, is not easy to read. Only in 1929 the first English translation of his monumental work, *The Christian Faith,* has appeared. Previously we had some excellent discussions of his thought from the pens of Professors Selbie and Cross, plentifully interlarded with quotations, and a volume of sermons, badly printed and accessible at the second-hand stores only. This situation continued for years, while theologians the world over were proclaiming Schleiermacher as the greatest religious thinker of the modern age. Obviously, it is not necessary for one's books to be read in order to be crowned a leader in the intellectual field. What a distinguished critic said of Wordsworth, to wit, that he was the poet whom it was fashionable to praise but not to read, applies likewise to the foremost figure in modern theology. There are indications, the new translation of *Der Christliche Glaube* being one, that people may actually begin to read Schleiermacher, at least in the English-speaking world. Let us hope that our anticipations may not be disappointed.

Reasons are not lacking for the comparative neglect of the great man. The average student who fumbles with Schleiermacher comes away with a vague sense of mystification and little else. He knows that he has been reading something which he is willing to consider important, but he is not quite sure as to what it is all about. The same interminable backing and filling, winding in and out, and general practising of all the approved arts of obfuscation which is so characteristic of Hegel, is likewise a feature of his contemporary's style. There are certain respects in which Schleiermacher's mystical tendencies make him more obscure even than Hegel. His views upon divers important questions are still matters of dispute and will probably never be determined with absolute accuracy. Indeed, it is possible that he had not so determined them himself. Beyond any question, the main outlines of his epoch-making thought are sufficiently easy to discover. As for the details, we need not concern ourselves overmuch about matters which are at best of only secondary consequence.

I

Friedrich Ernst Daniel Schleiermacher was born at Breslau on the twenty-first day of November, 1768. This was slightly less than eight years prior to the Declaration of Independence made by the thirteen American colonies.

Schleiermacher's father was a poor army chaplain who belonged to the Reformed faith. He appears to have been a man of rather exceptional piety, although not especially burdened with intellectual discernment. His mother was likewise a very pious woman and in addition would seem to have possessed at least certain glimpses of pedagogical insight. Fritz was their first son, and his father being away from home a great deal the burden of early education fell entirely upon his mother. The great man himself tells us later that when he was only five years of age his mother sent him to school where he soon distinguished himself by reason of his varied and encyclopedic knowledge. He admits that at this period he had a very exaggerated opinion of his own ability, a disease which he later outgrew.

When he was ten years of age Friedrich Ernst Daniel moved, along with his parents, from Breslau to Pless, and later to Anhalt, where his mother took him out of school for two years in order that he might regain his health. He was of delicate constitution, small in body and slightly deformed, but with a strangely cultured and classical type of countenance and with eyes which spoke more vividly than even the eloquent phrases which were wont in later years to flow from his lips. There were three children in the family, Fritz the oldest, Karl and Lotte. The last named remained the beloved and trusted friend of her brother until the day of her death in 1831.

From his tenth year or earlier Schleiermacher, like Luther, was bedeviled with thoughts of eschatology. The difference between them consisted in the fact that whereas the older reformer was desperately afraid of hell on his own account Schleiermacher lay awake at night because he was unable to come to a satisfactory conclusion "concerning the mutual relation between the sufferings of Christ and the punishment for which these sufferings were a substitute."

In other words, the ten-year-old student of Anselm was exercised because he could not solve a theoretical problem and not because he was afraid of the personal consequence which that problem might involve. Nothing could more clearly bring out the difference between the temper of the sixteenth century and that of the nineteenth than this apparently trivial incident. During the two years when Schleiermacher was out of school he came in contact with sundry youthful skeptics who disturbed him not a little with their doubts, but whose views he refused to adopt without further investigation. It may be that his father sensed the situation and decided to forestall the danger by placing his family where he felt sure they would be steeped in genuine religion. The only place he could think of in Germany which fulfilled the requirements at this time was the retreat of the Moravian brethren which Count Zinzendorf had founded some years before. The Moravians were essentially mystics and must be given credit for furnishing the point of departure of two great figures in the history of religion, John Wesley and Friedrich Schleiermacher.

When the lad took up his residence in Niesky at the Moravian school he was only fifteen years of age. He was glad to find a haven from the natural corruption of the world within the simple but pious fraternity of the Moravians. It is quite certain that the impressions of these early years were never entirely erased from his mind. His whole philosophy was colored by them down to the day of his death. Mystic he always was, although he made a more desperate and successful effort to rationalize his mysticism than any other thinker since the days of Plotinus. If it had not been for the Moravians Schleiermacher might have gone the way of Strauss, or at any rate of Semler. In spite of the fact that he became so well grounded in the religion of the brethren it was not long before he began to have in-

tellectual difficulties.   Like many another seminary, the
school at Niesky kept its orthodoxy uncontaminated by
the simple process of ignoring all views which disturbed the
placid purity of its faith.   Modern rationalism its directors
never mentioned, although Germany was seething with it
and all the popular newspapers and magazines carried expressions about it in their columns.   Schleiermacher became
uneasy when the facts filtered into his brain.   He could not
understand, he tells us, why his teachers declined to refute
views which were so widely expressed and which were so
damaging to the citadel of orthodoxy.   He concluded that
there must be more in the heretical theories than he had
hitherto supposed.   In his case the technique of the brethren
produced the opposite result from that which they desired.
Instead of preserving his faith entire the lad began to avow
heterodox interpretations of such sacred dogmas as the incarnation, the atonement, eternal damnation, and others
of equal solemnity and importance.   His father was very
much distressed when he discovered what was going on.   He
could see nothing in his son's attitude except pride, original
sin and a longing after the world and its honors.   The intellectual problems which young Friedrich was beginning to
grapple with never made a dent upon the turgid cerebral
equipment of his parent.   The old man threatened to
disown his unworthy offspring, but thought better of the
proposition and took him back.   Doubtless he regarded the
whole affair as a passing ebullition of youthful exuberance;
in time, he had no doubt that any one who had intelligence
enough to be a son of his would settle down and come to
his senses.

The brethren at Niesky were not so tolerant.   With sur-
prise, wrath and indignation they discovered that in spite
of their intellectual quarantine the very devil had taken up
his abode in their midst.   It was a foregone conclusion that

no such situation could exist for long if the ark was to be preserved. Short shrift was accordingly given to Freidrich Ernst Daniel with his upstart views concerning the dogmas of the Fathers. They extirpated him bag and baggage, and that in short order. He himself would fain have stayed on probation, but the faculty was anxious to disdain even the appearance of evil. Fortunately, he found an asylum with his Uncle Stubenrauch, his mother's brother, who was a professor of theology at Halle. This intelligent and devout teacher took his nephew into his home and brought him up under his own personal direction. He allowed him to read anything he pleased and did not appear disturbed by the idea that the faith needed to be hermetically sealed in order to be preserved. The result was that Schleiermacher, finding that no one discouraged his skepticism, speedily became more conservative on his own account. He read Plato and Spinoza and Kant, and was especially impressed by Spinoza. Stubenrauch permitted him to go on after his own fashion, occasionally dropping a word of comment or criticism but very wisely never attempting to set bounds to the intellectual range of his pupil. Theology owes much to this comparatively unknown preceptor of Halle.

In the summer of 1790 Schleiermacher passed his examinations as a licentiate of theology and soon afterward obtained a position as a private tutor in the family of a German count. He lost his job after three years of service because he was not permitted to carry out what he believed to be correct pedagogical methods, and he could not in good conscience adopt others. He went to Berlin for a few months and from thence to Landsburg, where he secured a position as assistant parson. This place he filled for two years, after which he received an appointment as preacher to the Charity House in Berlin, where he remained for the next six years.

II

It was while in Berlin that Schleiermacher made the first
of those semi-romantic friendships which constitute an interesting feature of his biography. The lady in question was
a Jewess, the wife of Doctor Marcus Hertz, a physician of
note in the city and a man whose home was patronized by
many of the leading people of the community. Henrietta
Hertz was beautiful and brilliant and a charming hostess.
She liked the intellectual penetration of Schleiermacher, and
remained his friend for years. So devoted did this companionship become that Lotte developed a touch of anxiety lest
her brother should be involved in scandal. She accordingly
wrote to him from her cloistered seclusion among the Moravians, where she remained practically all her life, warning
him against too close an association with handsome and
brilliant women who might happen to be the wives of other
people. Freidrich wrote back at once, stoutly protesting his
innocence of anything except the purest type of Platonic
devotion. Like Henry Ward Beecher, he asserted that high
and noble friendships of this kind were essential to the cul-
tivation of his mind and heart, and that he was therefore,
entitled to them. As a matter of fact, no scandal was ever
attached to his relations with Frau Hertz, although they
continued for many years.

It was during this Berlin period that Schleiermacher
made the acquaintance of Friedrich Schlegel, with whom he
shared his lodging for a time. Both of these men were
geniuses of the first order, the theologian being the
greater of the two. At first Schleiermacher looked on his
friend as infinitely superior to himself. It was probably the
stimulation of this sort of intellectual competition which led
to the production of the famous *Reden,* or *Discourses on
Religion,* the first work of outstanding importance from
the pen of its author. This book was published in 1799,

and we are told that it startled Germany as with the blast
of a trumpet. Neander was not the only important figure
who regarded the reading of it as the turning-point in his
career. The *Discourses* were speedily followed by the
Monologues, a volume which produced a profound impression on Amiel. This work in turn was followed by a collection of sermons, published at the urgent request of his
friends and dedicated to his good Uncle Stubenrauch.
Schleiermacher has left on record the statement that he was
opposed to the publication of any and all sermons, and of
his own in particular. If this sentiment is anything more
than mere politeness his friends deserve congratulation because of their successful importunity. These sermons are
among the classics in this kind of literature, ranking along
with those of Luther, Bossuet, Robertson and Phillips
Brooks.

Schleiermacher left Berlin because of a love-affair with
Eleanore Grunow, a cultured and gifted woman who was
unhappily married to a clergyman entirely unsuited to her.
The young theologian came to sympathize with her situation
very profoundly and held that it was her duty to dissolve a
union which had ceased to possess any inner significance.
How much of his argument proceeded from sound logical
premises and how much from his own personal attachment
it would be unfair to attempt to determine. The law of
Prussia at this time permitted divorce by mutual consent,
and there is no good reason for impeaching Schleiermacher's
motives in urging his inamorata to forsake her ogre of a
husband and marry her lover. Notwithstanding all of his
arguments Eleanore was never able to come to a decision.
It may be that some sort of subconscious Roman Catholicism
interfered with her romantic desires or she had, perhaps, a
lingering suspicion that she might not be happy if she cast
in her lot with another person. In any case, she kept

Schleiermacher so tortured by her fluctuating attitude that in sheer despair he left Berlin in the spring of 1802, and accepted an appointment as Court Preacher at Stolpe, in Pomerania, thus condemning himself, as it were, to voluntary banishment.

At Stolpe in the autumn of 1803 he published his *Critical Enquiry into the Existing Systems of Ethics,* in which he criticized Kant and Fichte rather viciously and gave high praise to Plato and Spinoza. Some years earlier, in collaboration with Schlegel, he had begun a translation of the works of Plato into German. Schlegel soon became weary of the task and gave up his part of it, but Schleiermacher, with true German doggedness, kept on until the work was completed. It was a contribution of immense importance to German literature as well as to the theologian's personal development. Schleiermacher was always a good deal of a Platonist, and aside from Spinoza, he was influenced more by the great Athenian than by any other thinker. In May, 1804, he was appointed preacher to the University of Halle and Professor Extraordinarius of Theology. About this time he paid a short visit to his friend Willich, who was just on the point of marrying Henriette von Muhlenfels, a charming and beautiful girl of sixteen, who at that time was living in the house of her married sister, Charlotte von Katten. Schleiermacher immediately adopted the young girl as his daughter and corresponded with her when he went back to Halle on these terms. In October, 1805, occurred what he styles the great tragedy of his life. Oppressed by his absence Eleanore wrote to him that she had decided on the great step and that she had gone to the house of her brother who had undertaken all the details of the divorce and her husband had given his full consent. Schleiermacher was overjoyed at the news and wrote to Henriette that he hoped to visit her soon and bring with him the best loved of all his treasures, his excellent Eleanore. What happened afterward is not exactly clear. All that we know is that his lady-love suddenly reversed her decision, went back to her husband and cut off all communication with the founder of modern theology. Schleiermacher was crushed. He never entirely recovered from the blow but, like many another man, pulled himself together and went on with his work.

In October, 1806, the battle of Jena prostrated Prussia completely under the iron soldiery of Napoleon. The university was closed, the students dispersed, and Schleiermacher was deprived of his occupation. In addition, he tells us that the French soldiers took nearly all of his personal possessions, including all of his shirts except five and all of his silver spoons except two. The following spring, in 1807, during the siege of Stralsund, the husband of Henriette contracted a fever which raged in the city at the time and after a short illness passed away. The young widow, who was only nineteen, appealed to Schleiermacher for consolation and did not appeal in vain. From a purely fatherly affection his feeling deepened into a more ardent emotion. Early in 1809 he was appointed pastor of Trinity Church in Berlin, and shortly afterward was married to Henriette. He was nearly twenty years her senior but they were well adapted to each other, and his home life was all that he could have desired. In 1810 the University of Berlin was reorganized with Fichte as rector. Schleiermacher was called to the Chair of Theology, which he filled until the day of his death. From this time on his life was a perpetual triumph. As a preacher he was perhaps the leading voice in the nation. As a professor his lectures attracted wide attention and were received with universal admiration.

During much of his early career at Berlin he was interrupted by the vicissitudes of the war with Napoleon. Like

Fichte, who was an ardent patriot, Schleiermacher encouraged the people to rise against their invaders and to take part in the war for freedom.   It is a peculiar commentary upon the altruistic impulses of these noble philosophers that the free Germany for which they fought speedily became the most despotically governed empire on the face of the earth with the sole exception of the land of the Muscovites to the East.   In 1820 Schleiermacher's only son was born, and he rejoiced exceedingly over this event. His joy was turned to mourning a few years later when the boy very unexpectedly died.   He had two daughters of his own and two stepdaughters whom Henriette had previously borne to Willich, her first husband.   Some time during his residence in Berlin his sister Charlotte, who had spent practically her entire life among the Moravians, came to live with her distinguished brother and found the atmosphere of Berlin so attractive that she stayed there permanently.

In the year 1821 Schleiermacher published his *magnum opus, The Christian Faith,* a treatise on systematic theology. Critics are pretty generally agreed that this is the most important book in its field which has appeared since the days of Calvin's *Institutes*.   It was received with much criticism, and its author was openly accused of heresy.   Previous to this time he had led the movement for the union of the Reformed and Lutheran churches which was finally consummated in the organization of the Evangelical or State Church of Prussia.   He had aroused a great deal of bitterness at this time on the part of the more orthodox groups, and these people were disposed to look with disfavor on everything he did.   Nevertheless, the public at large hailed him more and more as the leading theologian of his day. He visited England in 1828, the year before the death of his son, Nathaniel.   In 1831 the King of Prussia conferred upon him the order of the Red Eagle.   In the summer of

1833 he started on a tour through Sweden, Norway and Denmark, which was somewhat in the way of a triumphal procession inasmuch as he was received with the utmost enthusiasm wherever he went. He returned to Berlin and made preparations for celebrating his silver wedding in May. He did not live to realize his anticipation. The slight cold of which he complains in his last letter developed into pneumonia and in a week he passed away. He had just partaken of the holy communion when the end came. His final words were a declaration of faith in the atonement. Strikingly enough, he breathed his last on the anniversary of Abraham Lincoln, February 12, 1834. He was given a great funeral. The King and the Crown Prince led the procession which was composed of hundreds of carriages. The streets and the cemetery were thronged with thousands of people. His body was borne to the grave by thirty-six of his students. Best of all, his reputation did not die with him. After the lapse of nearly a century his position remains secure. As Halleck said of Marco Bozzaris, "He is one of the few, the immortal names, that were not born to die."

III

The theological system of Schleiermacher is comprehended in its entirety in the second edition of *Der Christliche Glaube,* which appeared with his own introduction in April, 1830, four years before his death. This voluminous treatise occupies over seven hundred and fifty pages in the English translation and requires two ponderous German tomes in the original. It is organized with true Germanic thoroughness and revels in introductions, appendices, and all kinds of divisions and subdivisions. Schleiermacher imitates Spinoza in introducing theorems into his work, thus giving it a species of mathematical coloring. He deals with practically all the material of dogmatics in the course of his interpretation. Like the *Critique of Pure Reason,* the book is one which obstinately stands in the way of all who pretend to any knowledge of the subject with which it deals, and shouts aloud, "Read me before you dare to express an opinion." It is not easy reading but will amply repay extended study. In any case, a knowledge of it is essential to a thorough understanding of Schleiermacher.

The central theme which runs through the book is its definition of religion. To the author religious feeling is in its last analysis a sense of dependence upon the Absolute. He rejected the Hegelian idea that this discipline is essentially a matter of thought or of reason and equally opposed the position of Kant and Fichte, that religion and morality are identical and that both are primarily products of the will. Instead of these theories, Schleiermacher fell back on a certain basic and fundamental feeling which he asserted is the tap-root of all religious experience. This God-consciousness, as he styled it, is inherent in every individual. The business of the church and of religious worship is to cultivate and strengthen it. The skeptic and the irreligious man crush and stifle it but are never quite able to eliminate it entirely. On the other hand, the process of redemption is very simple. It means primarily the fostering and development of the God-consciousness in the human soul. The supreme characteristic of Jesus Christ was that He perfectly embodied the God-consciousness in the form of humanity. Through this perfect embodiment he becomes equivalent to Deity, and Schleiermacher lays great stress upon this cardinal dogma of the older faith. Sin, on the basis of his theory, becomes essentially a refusal to develop the divine within us, a substitution of the purely individual and selfish nature for the Deity who might be ours. Throughout the system one can not avoid catching an echo of Spinoza again and again. The problem of evil, as is the case with all absolutists, is largely ignored or minimized. While it is never reduced to unreality it occupies no very large place in his thinking.

Schleiermacher has been styled a mystic, and with excellent reason. It is obvious that his early Moravian training is essentially responsible for the form of his theology. It is a mystical consciousness which is, after all, the fundamental fact in religion rather than an appeal to reason or a standard of right living. Not, indeed, that Schleiermacher repudiated either the philosophical or the ethical approach to his subject. He did not cast them away, but he subordinated them to the claims of mysticism and gave feeling the place of honor in his system.

Nothing can be clearer than the fact that this point of view must prove of immense service to Evangelical Protestantism. Founded, as it was, upon Luther's mystical interpretation of the dogma of justification by faith, the reformed religion was in sore need of some such philosophical buttressing. It was only natural that in spite of certain rather glaring heresies the German thinker should be hailed with approval by those who stood in need of his support. Schleiermacher's carefully wrought out interpretation was especially valuable to Protestants who had broken away from the older Calvinistic theology. Hence it was received with special eagerness by the followers of Wesley and by the Arminians in general. It is interesting in this connection to note that Karl Barth and his disciples, who take the slogan "Back to Calvin" as their watchword, expressly repudiate Schleiermacher and all his works.

It does not require any very acute penetration to see that the constant effort throughout *Der Christliche Glaube* is to interfuse Christian dogma with the pantheism of Spinoza. It is a very difficult task and we can not say that the issue is altogether successful. Certain it is that the Latin theology, the transcendent monism of Augustine and Calvin, has given place to the more distinctly immanistic point of view of the old Greek theologians and of Spinoza. It is this emphasis upon the divine immanence which shifted modern theological thinking from Augustine to Origen. Ever since the days of Schleiermacher Latin theology has been on the decline among Protestants. There are occasional reactionary flurries, like the present-day Barthian movement, but they do not appear to possess the element of permanence. Schleiermacher has apparently exorcised Augustine for good and all in Western Protestantism.

At certain points it must be acknowledged that the Berlin theologian skates upon very thin ice. For example, his teaching concerning the Divine Personality is vague and evasive. Likewise, in discussing the question of personal immortality he seems more or less uncertain and hazy in his thinking. As for hell and the devil, he eliminated both of them with no attempt at disguising his attitude. The devil, he admits, is mentioned rather frequently in the New Testament, but he contends that Christ adds no new doctrine concerning him and that he is not, therefore, a necessary factor in Christian dogmatics. Hell, in the old sense of the word, he regards as quite impossible from the Christian point of view. He has no difficulty in showing the contradictions involved in the orthodox teaching, apparently forgetting that it was of the very essence of the older orthodoxy that it should be self-contradictory. On most of the ancient doctrinal positions Schleiermacher is conservative, laboring manfully to fashion them in such a way that they will accommodate the new point of view. Like Calvin's, there is a marvelous unity and logical consistency in his thought. He formulates a real system and fits it together piece by piece with careful nicety. Sin, grace, redemption, justification and all the other dogmas find a place in his interpretation. Starting from a single and universal standpoint he explains everything in the light of his position, and it must be admitted that he succeeds remarkably well. He set theology going once more in Germany and indeed throughout the world. The older Calvinism had lost its appeal to an age which was demanding increasing freedom and which refused to think in monarchical terms either here or hereafter. Arminianism possessed no real systematic insight and could scarcely be called an independent theology. Schleiermacher's prominence arose from the fact that there was a real need for his work. The theology of feeling, as it was styled, was not long in establishing its dominance in most of the circles of Protestantism. Of course, the Roman Catholics held aloof from it and the more radical rationalists were displeased with its mysticism, but the vast majority of evangelicals pounced upon it with eagerness. The immediate consciousness of dependence upon God and of direct relationship to Him constituted a splendid philosophical basis for the mystical type of evangelism which was becoming popular throughout the Western World.

Schleiermacher was not entirely a mystic. He lays large stress upon the sacraments, especially baptism, and he attached very considerable importance to the church. He was in advance of his age in urging with especial emphasis the desirability of Christian union. The invisible church he held was already one, and he thought that the visible church ought to strive toward that unity. Like Erasmus and Locke, he was irenic, tolerant and always willing to give consideration to the arguments of others.

IV

It is easy enough to find flaws in the theology of Schleiermacher. His thinly disguised pantheism is, of course, his weakest point. Moreover, his effort to adjust his philosophical position to the orthodox creed is at times exceedingly strained and artificial. His conception of personality, either human or divine, lacks clearness and force. He obviously fumbles and gropes about in his efforts to explain the nature of evil and the fact of personal immortality. It seems reasonably clear that he believed in the latter, but he has left no convincing apologetic in its favor. His predisposition to Spinozistic determinism left him weak in the matter of human freedom, and he is not always consistent in his expressions upon this question. Like Luther, he occasionally breaks through his own dogmatism in his sermons. Many of these are filled not only with sincere religious feeling but also with extraordinary flashes of insight.

It is his tendency to make mysticism central in religion which led to the modern revolt against his views with which we shall have to deal in the next chapter. Important as feeling is, and significant as the mystical element has always been in the history of religion, the fact remains that reason, in the last analysis, must be given the highest place in every form of human experience. This does not mean that it possesses exclusive claims or that it is to be deified at the expense of other faculties. It does mean that feeling of any kind is blind and vague and indefinite without the guidance of reason. Religion concerns the whole man, emotional and active as well as intellectual, but the place of leadership must always be given to that "right reason" which is the highest attribute of humanity. It was inevitable that Schleiermacher should be followed by Ritschl. Nevertheless, there is a place, and a great place, for feeling in religion, and whatever may happen in the future the fame of the older theologian is settled and secure.

CHAPTER XVI

RITSCHL

MODERN theology concludes with Ritschl. It may be that some other great master will arise to take his place, but at the present time of writing there appears to be no such figure on the horizon. The suggestion of Karl Barth is a mere flash in the pan. Barth, as we have already indicated, is neither original nor significant. Wherever he is consistent and clear in his thinking he simply revives the old-line Calvinism, and when Germany gets over the morbid pessimism caused by the war she will have no further use for outworn dogmas. Barth's prominence is of significance in connection with the psychology of military defeat, but it would seem to possess little value otherwise. Barth's teacher, Hermann, was a Ritschlian and a much greater theologian than his disciple. The other competing thinkers who possess any prominence, such as Harnack and Kaftan, are or were Ritschlians. Of course, there are a few exceptions and side-currents, but these only serve to prove the rule. Just as certainly as Ritschl was the only great theologian from the period of Schleiermacher to his own, just so certainly no figure comparable with him has arisen since his day. There are various currents in English and American thought which may grow into something significant, but up to the present time they have achieved no results of outstanding importance.

I

Albrecht Ritschl was born in Berlin in 1822. He was the son of a Bishop in the Lutheran church. His father

gave him a good classical education at the University of
Bonn and later at Tübingen, where he came under the influence of Baur. The latter was pleased with him, so the
story goes, and perhaps thought of him as his successor.
When thirty-one years of age Ritschl became professor extraordinarius at Bonn, and in 1860 professor ordinarius.
According to the German system it is much more significant
and honorable to be an ordinary professor than it is to be
an extraordinary one. Four years later, when the fortunes
of the Civil War were being determined in America, Ritschl
moved to Göttingen, where he remained until his death in
1889. It was through his influence chiefly that the university where he taught for practically a generation became the
Mecca of aspiring theological students from all parts of the
world. He achieved a position of prominence in the established Hanoverian church and for a time was popular
with conservatives and radicals alike. Ultimately the tide
receded somewhat, but he retained his position as the leading figure among the theologians of his day until the close
of his life. Since his death he has not lost in reputation.
It is perhaps a little early to prognosticate, but as far as one
can foresee at present his fame seems as secure as that of
Schleiermacher. Ritschl was a great deal of a humorist and
could wield a sarcastic tongue upon occasion. His students
recall his animated mannerisms and certain peculiarities
which gave distinction to his personality. He had a warm
heart, for all his theological prepossessions and his antag-
onism to religious emotionalism. Harnack carried on his
tradition, somewhat in his own spirit but without adding
anything especially new to his thought. In England even
critics as severe as Garvie acknowledge their indebtedness
to the master. In sober truth, since his time the students
of theology have been either Ritschlian or anti-Ritschlian;
his system of thought has been their point of departure.

We have referred to Schleiermacher as preeminently the theologian of feeling. Ritschl reacted from this point of view in giving first place to reason in his system. At the same time, he also reacted from the Hegelian deification of the intellect which tended to make religion in all its aspects identical with theological speculation. Hence, while he was strenuously opposed to mysticism he was almost equally antagonistic to metaphysics. There are certain respects in which he was more indebted to Kant than to Schleiermacher or to Hegel. The philosopher of Koenigsburg had practically identified ethics with religion and had made the good will the essential fact in the whole concept of theology. In this he had been followed by Fichte, to whom Ritschl was also indebted for certain suggestions. Perhaps to Lotze more than to any one else Ritschl turned for his immediate starting-point in his thinking. The conception of judgments of value, which is so essential with Ritschl, is primarily Lotzian, and there are other points of contact. The truth is that Ritschl was a great deal of an eclectic, picking up ideas here, there and everywhere, always restless and always changeable, and yet retaining a thoroughly consistent thread of thought throughout his career.

II

The simplest way in which to grasp the central features of Ritschl's system is through his own figure of the ellipse. Even elementary students of mathematics will recall that the ellipse looks like a somewhat elongated circle with two centers instead of one. These two centers are known in geometrical parlance as foci and are of equal significance in the practical construction of the ellipse. Ritschl, seeing the pitfalls which had beset the extreme forms of both the individualistic and the socialistic interpretations of Christianity, sought to avoid these perils by saying that the Christian religion is an ellipse with two foci, the one being individual redemption and the other the Kingdom of God. Christianity thus becomes neither a gospel of individual salvation alone nor a mere fantastic dream of a social millennium. In actual practise the church has veered from one to the other and the German thinker was unquestionably right in seeking to avoid both of them. As a starting-point for Christian ethics it will be difficult to get beyond the ellipse of Ritschl.

His emphasis upon the practical and ethical side of Christianity led the Göttingen thinker into sharp conflict with Schleiermacher. If feeling is central in religion, ethics must inevitably take a minor place. The advocate of such a position appeared to Ritschl to be following a will-o'-the-wisp. Feeling in itself is blind, individualistic, and the ultimate recourse of all lovers of superstition and magic. Ritschl did not intend to rule the emotions entirely out of court, but he did mean to make them everywhere and always subordinate to reason. For historical mysticism he had little use. Like Professor Leuba in our own day, he looked on most of it as moonshine and as an indication of mental aberration. He did not go as far as Leuba, but he certainly leaned in that direction.

Speculative and metaphysical conceptions of theology were dismissed quite as vigorously as was mysticism. Ritschl saw the futility of making doctrinal theology central in religion and leveled some of his most vigorous shafts of sarcasm against it. The significant thing is to accept Christ as Lord and to follow His way of life rather than to fuss and fume over the Trinity or any of the other antiquated theological dogmas. Religion thus becomes a practical matter above everything else, and here too the German theologian was in exact accord with the spirit of the new age. Nevertheless, it was at this point that he met his most vigorous opposition. Not since the days of Athanasius, when the Alexandrians disputed all night long concerning the inner nature of the Godhead, has there arisen such a theologically enamored and dogmatically besotted system of Christianity as Lutheranism in Germany after the time of Melanchthon. Even the medieval scholastics took no such delight in split-ting hairs and in making the split fragments essential re-quirements for salvation. Under these circumstances it was no wonder that the sermons of the orthodox speedily lost all value except as soporifics and that churchgoing tended to become the exclusive prerogative of women and children. The women endured the avalanche of hortatory dogmatics because of their rather remarkable combination of piety and patience, and the children endured it because under the German system they had to do so. When Hans or Friedrich grew up he went to the university and, as Count von Bernstorff once remarked, he read Strauss and quit going to church. Ritschl sought to stop this leak. The scholastics died hard, but the tide was against them. The Barthian movement shows that dogmatism is difficult to kill. The orthodox stormed at Göttingen and asserted that Ritschl's teaching was rank infidelity. Without saving faith, they argued, there could be no escape from destruc-tion, and the essentials of faith are incorporated in the sacred articles of the creed. They raised the old cry against Ritschl which has been urged with more truthfulness against Kant, that he had reduced religion to a system of ethics and had thus identified it with its moral content alone.

Ritschl met the dogmatists with his great book on justi-fication, in which he asserted the preeminent importance of the concept of redemption and the essential place of Christ the Redeemer in his system. There was a shrewd touch of irony in his selecting the very citadel of dogmatism, the old Lutheran watchword of justification by faith, as the title for his pragmatic pronouncements. In fact, he extracted the meat from the cocoanut of the old dogma and left the husks for his theological antagonists to quarrel over.

III

Professor Garvie, in his discussion of Ritschl, says that his thought may be summed up under four heads, to wit: (1) religious pragmatism, (2) philosophical agnosticism, (3) historical positivism, and (4) moral collectivism. This somewhat adroit analysis reminds us inevitably of Robert Browning's *Soliloquy of the Spanish Cloister:*

> There's a great text in Galatians
> Once you trip on it entails
> Twenty-nine distinct damnations
> One sure if another fails.

There are at least three separate damnations in this outline from the standpoint of ordinary orthodoxy. To call a man a pragmatist, an agnostic and a positivist all in the same sentence ought to be enough to eliminate him without further argument. Even the word "collectivist" since the rise of bolshevism has come to have a bad odor in the West. Of course, Doctor Garvie does not mean to use these terms in their popular significance. From a purely technical standpoint there is little to deprecate in his statement except that most readers are not technical critics. Many a man has been plucked from his high estate by the power of objurgatory epithets. Even the illustrious Volstead, who it is true owed his fame far more to fortuitous circumstances than to the possession of native genius, was forced to bow before the Idols of the Market-place. Confronted on the hustings by the accusation of atheism from his opponent, an orthodox man of God, the doughty Andrew bit the dust, although restored to his position through a fortunate legal quibble.

The history of politics, like the history of religion, is filled with this sort of thing. The simplest and cheapest way to eliminate an antagonist is to call him by some dire name like "atheist" or "bolshevist," or in America "socialist" or "communist." Nine out of ten people will condemn a man without argument if the epithets can be made to stick. This is probably because, as the army test disclosed, the majority of people are slightly above the eighth grade level of intelligence, and it is the majority that is moved by this species of attack.

Ritschl has survived the barrage of Doctor Garvie, doubtless because the question has not been left to the masses to determine. The simple fact is that Ritschlianism in its essential features is the only theology which does justice to present-day scientific needs and which therefore makes a real appeal to the modern mind. In his opposition to mystical superstition Ritschl agrees with the scientific temper which can no longer endure the childishness of medieval dogmatism. In his rejection of any authoritative metaphysic as an essential characteristic of religion he is again in harmony with the modern tendency to repudiate the old absolutisms in the interest of the open field in philosophy. Certainly he is here in harmony with the position of Jesus Himself, as we read the record of His life in the Synoptics. Ritschl did not disparage theological or metaphysical speculation, but he refused to crystallize any of it into dogma. This practical elimination of the older theological creeds was a distinct step forward in the religious field. Even in orthodox circles most adherents of the older creedal symbols interpret them in a Ritschlian sense. They are looked upon as ancient and venerable features of the church ritual but as possessing little other significance. The Athanasian Creed, for example, is one of the three ecumenicals and therefore ought to be adored by Catholics and Protestants alike. As a matter of fact, the American Episcopal Church does not even include it in the prayer-book, and the other communions honor it more in the breach than in the observance so far as any practical acquaintance is concerned. Ritschl's pragmatism has largely superseded the older attitude toward the creeds. Future theology is not likely to reverse its steps in this particular.

IV

It is on the side of what Garvie calls his "moral collectivism" that Ritschl has made his most significant contribution to modern thought. Protestantism, after running wild in a mad riot of individualistic anarchy, has at last come to see that Jesus was primarily a collectivist in His thinking. The chief burden of His teaching as He went about through Galilee and Judea was the story of the coming of the Kingdom. This note in His message was almost forgotten in the days of Luther and Calvin, and its revival is one of the most striking features of the twentieth century. The social gospel, as it is styled, is all the rage nowadays, and it is largely Ritschl who is responsible for the movement. Of course, there is a tendency to swing to extremes again and to minimize individual salvation entirely, as some of our Christian Positivists are doing to-day, but the great theologian himself was too wise to make this mistake. Garvie thinks, and perhaps rightly, that Ritschl was more interested in the social focus of his ellipse than in the other, but this was only because it needed more emphasis in order to secure a place in the thinking of his contemporaries. Individualism has dominated Protestantism for so many centuries that it required overemphasis on the collectivistic side to restore the balance.

The social gospel of Ritschl must more and more take

its place as a leading feature of modern religion. The tremendous advances in scientific transportation and communication, the fact that nothing can happen in the world
without its being known almost immediately in the remotest
corners of the globe, the rapid rise of cooperative methods
in business as manifested in the efficient administration of
great corporations, the tendency toward international com-
ity and the judicial settlement of international disputes,—all
of these things conspire to make Ritschl's emphasis on the
Kingdom one of the appealing categories of present-day
religion.

It is here that Ritschl cut the ground from under the
atheistical socialism of Karl Marx and his successors. The
latter repudiated individual redemption and the idea of immortality. As a consequence their goal was a short-sighted
materialism which could never bring peace to its adherents
but only the dust and ashes of sensual satiety. Ritschl had
no difficulty in showing that the very heart of Christ's
teaching was His doctrine of eternal life. Deliverance from
sin means primarily the overcoming of individual selfishness
and adherence to the glorious brotherhood of the Kingdom.
This society of the redeemed on earth is likewise the earnest
of eternal redemption. The sting of death which Marx
could neither gloss over nor conquer is taken away, and the
pale shadow of the Material is illumined by the undying
radiance of the Eternal. Ritschl's doctrine of the Kingdom
has only begun to exercise its influence on Christianity.
The future belongs to it and will have much to say about
it. It is the one gospel which can save our madly moving,
scientific civilization. If the church clings to outworn
dogmas formulated when men possessed not a single discovery of our modern civilization humanity will pass up its
pronouncements as only the musty mummering of antiquated
dialectics. Without that religion which the church alone can

give the spirit of destructive science, as Henry Churchill King once said, will speedily send the world to the devil. The gospel of the Kingdom, as Jesus taught it originally and as Ritschl has uncovered it, is the one and only power which can save humanity from suicide.

It is, of course, possible that Ritschl went too far in his attacks upon every form of mystical religion. Doubtless Schleiermacher will always have a word for the world, although in our judgment not the final word. Scientific research during the last twenty years has done much toward the revival of mysticism. Rutherford and Einstein have led us to where reason fades into a sort of mystical faith in something which we can appreciate rather than understand. There will always be a place for the mystics and there is no good reason why there should not be. Schleiermacher and Plotinus prove that there is such a thing as rational mysticism which is incompatible with neither science nor religion. The danger in the situation, as Ritschl clearly saw, is its tendency to pass beyond rational control into those extravagant vagaries which have given such variegated coloring to the pages of religious history.

Ritschl tended to substitute the social for the mystic note in religion, and in this attitude he has had many followers. His critics have made much of the fact that he knew nothing of the pyschology of religion or of the modern interest in the study of other religious systems aside from Christianity. They have also attacked his acceptance of the New Testament as a revelation of God and especially his constant emphasis upon the historical Jesus. Most of this criticism is one-sided and unfair. It is true that Ritschl knew nothing of the psychology of religion as a distinct science, but there is little of importance in the technique of this latest department of knowledge which he did not foreshadow and anticipate. The only exception to this state-

ment is the fact that he might have been a little more charitable toward mysticism if he could have lived forty years
longer.

As for his exclusive interest in Christianity, the accusation may be admitted without serious detriment to his fame.
As Albert Schweitzer has shown recently in such convincing
fashion, there is no other world religion that possesses the
breadth of appeal which the teaching of Jesus, stripped of its
theological excrescences, commands. Had Ritschl possessed
the time, opportunity and apparatus to examine critically
all other religious systems it is not probable that it would
have affected his theological attitude to any appreciable
degree. Nor has the criticism of the New Testament in-
validated his emphasis upon the authority of the historical
Christ. All that we certainly know about Jesus is still
contained within the pages of the Gospels. Any other
sources are so insignificant as to possess no distinctive value.
If the Jesus made known to us through the New Testament
Scriptures is not accurately revealed then the foundations
of Christianity are destroyed. There is no question of
verbal infallibility involved here, but there is a question of
accurate history. Either the Gospels reveal Jesus to us, or
else we know nothing about him. To rely on later mystical
revelation is to surrender the very essence of Christianity.
Ritschl was right in clinging unflinchingly to the traditional
Protestant emphasis upon the Scriptures.

V

The average student is apt to become confused when
he is asked to explain what he understands by judgments of
value. Ritschl popularized both the term and its meaning.
The idea involved goes back to Kant, with his distinction
between the scientific field, as interpreted in the *Critique of*

Pure Reason, and the ethical or religious field as expressed in the *Critique of Practical Reason.* The ordinary natural or descriptive sciences are concerned with facts in their various relations, while ethics and religion have to do with values, or what ought to be rather than what is. The objects of the religious consciousness are essentially values, and affirmations about them constitute what Ritschl meant by value judgments. Such conceptions belong to the realm of faith as distinguished from the realm of exact scientific knowledge.

It is not to be inferred that the German theologian meant to draw too absolute a line between the two distinct classes of judgments. Obviously enough, facts and values are interwoven in actual experience and can not be separated entirely. This simply means that our universe necessarily hangs together after some fashion, whether it possesses systematic unity or not. For purposes of clear thinking the Ritschlian distinction between judgments of fact and judgments of value is decidedly worth while. In this connection it may be remarked that the field covered by judgments of value is not that of philosophy or metaphysics. From Ritschl's point of view knowledge may be thought of as having three separate provinces: first, the domain of the natural or descriptive sciences, made up of judgments of fact; second, the field of the normative sciences, like ethics, esthetics and logic, built upon judgments of value; and third, metaphysics, which includes all speculations about the nature of ultimate reality. Religion, as we have seen, was grouped under number two, along with ethics and esthetics. By following this classification, Ritschl escaped the necessity for treating religious phenomena after the fashion of ordinary scientific data and also avoided the pitfalls lurking beneath an identification of religious faith with any particular metaphysical theory.

The disciples of Ritschl have branched off from certain features of his system at various points, but have not seriously deviated from his central position. Some of the more radical of them have developed the positivistic side of his thought to the exclusion of other features and have formulated a radical social gospel which has eliminated the supernatural entirely. This one-sided view-point was not agreeable to the thought of the master himself and is not likely to possess permanent significance. These ultra-modernists have had much to do with the emergence of the opposite or Barthian extreme in later-day German thought. Ultimately the adherents of both positions will turn back to Ritschl. Not that the Göttingen teacher has said the final word in theology, and he himself would have been the last to claim any such prerogative, but simply that his thinking presents the highest level which has thus far been achieved in his field, and any worth-while forward steps must take their point of departure from him.

The romance of theology is the romance of life on its highest level of intellectual achievement. When men cease to possess or use "those thoughts that wander through eternity" they will cease to be men. Bundles of reflexes, mechanical machines, fortuitous concourses of atoms may dispense with theology and philosophy, but human beings will always desire to voyage through strange seas of thought in search of the Divine.

THE END

BIBLIOGRAPHY.

BIBLIOGRAPHY

General Works:

Workman, H. B.   *Christian Thought to the Reformation.* Scribner's, New York, 1920.

McGiffert, A. C.   *Protestant Thought before Kant.* Scribner's, New York, 1920.

Moore, E. C.   *Outline of the History of Christian Thought since Kant.* Scribner's, New York, 1920.

Harnack, A.   *History of Dogma.* English Translation. Little, Brown & Co., Boston, 1903.

Hagenbach, K. R.   *A Text Book of the History of Doctrines.* English Translation. Sheldon & Co., New York, 1867.

Shedd, W. G. T.   *History of Christian Doctrine.* Scribner's, New York, 1863.

Fisher, G. P.   *History of Christian Doctrine.* Scribner's, New York, 1897.

Allen, A. V. G.   *Continuity of Christian Thought.* Houghton, Mifflin & Co., Boston, 1884.

Consult also the general reference books, especially the Catholic *Encyclopedia,* Hastings' *Encyclopedia of Religion and Ethics,* the Schaff-Herzog *Encyclopedia,* the new *Britannica,* and *International Encyclopedias.* For the works of the theologians themselves consult *The Ante-Nicene Fathers* (Edinburg. T. & T. Clark, 1868——, edited by A. Roberts and J. Donaldson) and *Post-Nicene Fathers* (New York. The Christian Literature Co., 1886——, edited by P. Schaff).

351

Books on the Special Theologians:

Kennedy, H. A. A. *Philo's Contribution to Religion.* Hodder & Stoughton, London, 1919.

Drummond, J. *Philo Judæus.* Williams & Norgate, London, 1888.

Plutarch *Lives.* DeWolfe, Fiske & Co., Boston.

Aytoun, R. A. *City Centers of Early Christianity.* Hodder & Stoughton, London, 1915.

Conybeare, W. J., & Howson, J. S. *Life and Epistles of St. Paul.* T. Y. Crowell & Co., New York, 1908.

Glover T. R. *Conflict of Religions in the Early Roman Empire.* Scribner's, New York, 1909.

Holmes, A. *The Mind of St. Paul.* Macmillan, New York, 1929.

Stevens, G. B. *The Pauline Theology.* Scribner's, New York, 1892.

Kennedy, H. A. A. *The Theology of the Epistles.* Scribner's, New York, 1920.

Bigg, C. *Christian Platonists of Alexandria* (Bampton Lectures), Oxford, 1914.

Inge, W. R. *The Philosophy of Plotinus.* Longmans, Green, & Co., London, 1919.

Gwatkin, H. M. *Studies of Arianism.* 1900. Pickering, London.

Newman, J. H. *The Arians of the Fourth Century.* Basil, Montagu, Pickering, London, 1876.

McGiffert, A. C.   *The God of the Early Christians.* Scribner's, New York, 1924.

McGiffert, A. C.   *The Apostles' Creed.* Scribner's, New York, 1902.

Briggs, C. A.   *The Fundamental Christian Faith.* Scribner's, New York, 1913.

Benson, E. W.   *Life and Times of Cyprian.* 1898.

Cunningham, W.   *St. Austin and His Place in the History of Christian Thought.* 1886.

Schaff, P.   *Life and Labors of St. Augustine.* 1851.

Clarke, W. R.   *Saint Augustine.* Society for Promoting Christian Knowledge. London.

Augustine   *The City of God.* Temple Edition, J. M. Dent & Co., London, 1903.

Augustine   *The Confessions.* Andrew Melrose, London, 1904.

Dudden, F. H.   *Gregory the Great,* His Place in History and Thought. Longmans, 1905.

Rigg, J. M.   *Anselm of Canterbury.* 1896.

Anselm   *Works,* translated by S. N. Deane. Open Court Pub. Co., Chicago, 1910.

Storrs, R. S.   *Bernard of Clairvaux.* Scribner's, New York, 1912.

Abelard, P.   *The Love Letters of Abelard and Heloise.* Ariel booklets, G. P. Putnam's Sons, New York, 1905.

McCabe, J.   *Life of Peter Abelard.* Putnam's, New York, 1901.

Dante   *The Divine Comedy.* Translated by H. F. Cary. Frederick Warne & Co., London.

Ruskin, J.   *Mornings in Florence.* Dana Estes & Co., Boston.

Froude, J. A.   *Life and Letters of Erasmus.* Scribner's, New York, 1912.

Rein, W.   *Life of Martin Luther.* Translated by G. F. Bebinger. Funk & Wagnalls, New York, 1888.

Lindsay, T. M.   *History of the Reformation.* Scribner's, New York, 1917.

McGiffert, A. C. *Martin Luther, The Man and His Work.* Century, 1911.

Jackson, S. M.,   "Huldreich Zwingli," in *Heroes of the Reformation,* New York and London, 1901.

Richard, J. W.   *Philip Melancthon.* Putnam's, New York, 1898.

Walker, W.   "John Calvin, the Organiser of Reformed Protestantism," in *Heroes of the Reformation,* 1906.

Vedder, H. C.   *Balthasar Hubmaier, the Leader of the Anabaptists.* Putnam's, New York, 1905.

Eddy, S., &   *Makers of Freedom.* Doran, New
  Page, K.   York, 1926.

Wesley, J.   *Journal.* Abridged Edition. Jennings & Graham, Cincinnati, 1903.

Fox, G.   *Journal.* Edited by N. Penney. Cambridge, 1911.

Southey, R.   *Life of Wesley.* London, 1846.

Allen, A. V. G.   *Jonathan Edwards.* Houghton, Mifflin, & Co., Boston, 1889.

Selbie, W. B.   *Schleiermacher.* Chapman & Hall, London, 1913.

Cross, G.   *The Theology of Schleiermacher.* Univ. of Chicago Press, Chicago, 1911.

Schleiermacher, F. E. D.   *The Christian Faith.* English Translation. T. & T. Clark, Edinburg, 1928.

Schleiermacher, F. E. D.   *Sermons.* Translated by Mary F. Wilson, Edited by W. Robertson Nicoll. Funk & Wagnalls, New York.

Barth, K.   *The Word of God and the Word of Man.* English Translation. The Pilgrim Press, Boston, 1928.

Garvie, A. E.   *The Ritschlian Theology.* Edinburg, 1894.

Harnack, A.   *What is Christianity?* Translated by T. B. Saunders. Putnam's, New York, 1902.

Kaftan, J.   *The Truth of the Christian Religion.* Edinburg, 1894.

Swing, A. T.   *The Theology of Albrecht Ritschl.* New York, 1901.

Edghill, E. A.   *Faith and Fact, a Study of Ritschlianism.* Macmillan, 1910.

Mackintosh, R.   *Albrecht Ritschl and His School.* London, 1913.

INDEX

INDEX

Abelard, 97, 113, 227, 238, 239
  compelled to burn books, 208, 217
  conceptualism in theology of, 198
  controversy with Bernard of Clair-
    vaux, 218-220
  jealousy against, 215
  letters of
    to Heloise, 213, 214
    to Philintus, 202
  life story of, 202*ff.*
  moral interpretation of atonement,
    216, 308, 309
  rationalization of doctrine of
    Trinity, 216
  scholarship of, 202-203, 204, 206
  Sic et Non, 217
Abraham, 19, 24, 57
Abyssinia, 140
Acts, book of, 44, 77
Acts of Paul and Thecla, The, 43-44,
  52
Acts of Philip, 78
Acts of Thomas, 78
Adam, 30, 57, 63, 101, 157, 171, 175,
  176, 180, 191, 193, 195, 308
Adeodatus, 158, 162, 166
Adrian VI, 249, 250
Albertus Magnus, 221
Alexander, Bishop of Alexandria,
  116, 117, 119
Alexander the Great, 20, 136
Alexander VI, 194
Alexandria, 30, 38, 70, 97, 108, 109,
  136, 137, 153
  church at, 90-91
  Cleopatra typical of, 26, 27
  commerce of, 23
  compared with Antioch, 137
  compared with Athens, 23

Alexandria—*Cont.*
  culture of, 25, 30
  founding of, 20
  importance of, 20
  library of, 21-22, 29, 32
  Neo-Platonism developed in, 26-27
  people of, 23-25
  Philo a native of, 19, 20
  public buildings of, 22
Allen, A. V. G.
  Continuity of Christian Thought,
    XV-XVI
Amalek, 81
Ambrose, Saint, 161, 162
Amiel, 326
Amsterdam, 243, 304
Anabaptists, 254, 256*ff.*, 278, 281, 293,
  317
Anhalt, 321
Anselm, 113, 132, 149, 236, 239, 322
  ontological argument of, 188-190,
    225
  popularized Roman Church in
    England, 187
  present-day influence of, 200-201
  realism of, 196, 199-200
  satisfactory theory of atonement,
    188, 191-192, 193-195, 200,
    215-216, 218, 308, 309
  Trinity, doctrine of, 198-199
  works of
    Cur Deus Homo, 188, 190, 194,
      200
    quoted, 192-193, 195-196
    Monologium, 188, 198
    Proslogium, 188
Anselm of Laon, 203, 206
anthropology, 143, 144
Antioch, 70, 109, 115, 116, 136*ff.*, 251

359

Antony, Mark, 26, 27, 203
Aosta, 187
Apollo, 37, 114
Apollonaris, 141-142
Apostles, 19, 20, 78, 85, 97, 289
Apostles' Creed, 81, 83, 85
Aquinas, Thomas, 49, 99, 113, 125, 198, 200, 235, 239, 240, 241, 251, 318
  Aristotle's influence on, 222
  Dante's interpretation of, 227-230
  Dominicans and, 238
  inclusiveness and organization of, 222-224
  influence of
    on art, 233ff.
    on literature
      see Aquinas, Dante's interpretation of,
    on science, 225-226
  interpreter of religion, 237
  life story of, 221, 233
  reason and revelation, 224-225
  Roman Church's attitude toward, 221, 223, 227
  Summa Theologiæ, 222, 223, 224, 225, 227, 230, 237
Arabia, 45
Areius, 27
Arezzo, 228, 229
Arians of the Fourth Century
  Newman, 16
Aristotle, 22, 25, 49, 106, 115, 135, 139, 160, 185, 190, 199, 200, 222, 223, 225, 237, 252, 304
  nominalism of, 197
  traducianism, doctrine of, 62
Arius, 119, 120, 121, 126, 129-130, 137, 138, 140, 217
  Trinity in conception of
    see Nicæa, Council of
Arminius, 113, 304, 316, 318, 319
  character of, 305
  education of, 304
  liberalism of, 305

Arminius—Con't.
  predestination repudiated by, 303
  professor at University of Leyden, 305
Arno, 229
Artemis, 114
Asia Minor, 116, 118
Athanasian Creed, 84, 121, 123, 342
  quotations from, 122
Athanasius, 35, 99, 100, 104, 108, 112, 119, 120, 122, 124, 126, 127, 128, 129, 131, 134, 137, 153, 340
  see Nicene Creed
Athens, 20, 23, 25, 136
atonement
  deterrent theory of, 308, 309-310
  moral theory of, 216, 308, 309
  ransom theory of, 191, 131-132, 218, 308
  satisfactory theory of, 188, 191-192, 193-195, 200, 215-216, 218, 308, 309
Augustine, 43, 49, 57, 62, 63, 64, 66, 84, 86, 88, 99, 100, 104, 106, 113, 135, 146, 147, 149, 200, 223, 236, 251, 268, 333
  at Carthage, 158, 159, 160, 165
  at Tagaste, 165, 166
  belief in eternal damnation, 180-182
  Bishop of Hippo, 165-166
  combat with Pelagius, 166-168, 178
  communal colony of, 165
  concubines of, 158, 162, 163
  contrasts in, 174, 175
  conversion to Christianity, 163-164
  death of, 170-171
  Donatists, conflict with, 166, 167-168
  education of, 157-158
  evil, doctrine of, 175-176
  honored by Rome, 178-179
  imperialism of, 171ff.
    reasons for, 173-174

Augustine—*Cont.*
life story of, 155*ff.*
Manicheans
as one, 159, 161-162, 175
conflict with, 166-167
morbidity of, 158-159, 161
parents of, 155-156
position of, 155
predestination in, 143-144, 168, 177,
283-284, 292-295, 300
Reformation, effect on, 293
see Luther, Augustinianism of
Saint Jerome, conflict with, 169-170
Saint Ambrose, teacher of, 161
sensuality of, 158
source for torturing in Middle
Ages, 182
teacher at Rome, 161
total depravity, doctrine of, 175
works of
City of God, The, 166
quoted, 179-181
Confessions, 161, 166, 171, 173,
252
quoted, 156, 158, 163-164, 172
Aurelius, 293
Averroes, 235
Avicenna, 235

Bacon, Roger, 237
Opus Majus, 228
Bagoas, 97
Baptists, 260, 316, 318
Barnabas, 47
Barnabas, Epistle of, 80
Barneveldt, 306, 307
Barth, Karl, 319, 332, 335
Basel, 245, 249, 289, 304
Basil, 131
Basilides, 70, 79
Baur, 337
Beatrice, 203
Beecher, Henry Ward, 216, 309, 325

Belloc, Hilaire, 238
Benjamin, 45
Berengar, 186
Berenger, 205
Berlin, 318, 324, 326, 327, 328, 329,
330, 336
Bernard of Clairvaux, 40, 191, 218-
220
Bernstorff, Count von, 340
Bethlehem, 169, 170
Beza, 62, 304
Biel, Gabriel, 240
Boccaccio, 229, 234
Bockhold, John, 258
Boethius, 236
Boleyn, Anne, 245
Bologna, University of, 228
Bonaventura, 125, 232, 238
Boniface, 151
Bonn, University of, 337
Bora, Catherine von, 274
Boso, 192
Bossuet, 326
Bozzaris, Marco, 330
Brahman, 31, 114
Brennan, Reverend Richard, 261
Breslau, 320
Brooks, Phillips, 326
Browning, Robert
quoted, 341
Bruges, 243
Brussels, 243
Brutus, 231
Bucer, 290
Buddha, 32
Bundy, 77
Bure, Idelette de, 292
Burma, 140
Businger, Reverend Father
*Church History for the Use of
Catholic Schools*
quoted, 261
Butler, 190

Cæsar, Julius, 26, 27, 28
Cæsarea, 116
Calas, Jean, 89
Caligula, 83
Calvary, 72
Calvin, John, 43, 57, 61, 62, 144, 155,
    174, 179, 247, 248, 258, 278, 305,
    316, 318, 319, 333
    at Geneva, 289-290
    Augustinianism of, 283-284, 289,
        292, 294
    compared with Luther, 283, 284
    death of, 290
    ecclesiastical polity of, 298
    education of, 287-288
    Jonathan Edwards and, 299
    flees from France, 289
    influence on history, 297-298
    Institutes of, 98, 258, 289, 297
        quoted, 298
    life story of, 287ff.
    marriage of, 292
    predestination of, 276, 277, 283,
        292-295, 303
    rise of capitalism affected by, 295-
        297
    Servetus burned by, 216, 290-292
Campaldino, 228
Campeggio, Cardinal, 253
Canticles, 40
Cappadocian school, 131
Caprona, 228
Carlyle, Thomas
    quoted on Luther, 263
Carthage, 20, 165
Cassius, 231
Caxton, William, 243
Celsus, 99
Chalcedon, Council of, 168, 251
Channing, William Ellery, 256
Charles I, 296
Charles V, 273
Charles the Bald, 186
Charles the Bold, 243

Charmion, 28
Chaucer, 229
Chillingworth, William
    Religion of Protestants, a Safe Way
        to Salvation, The
        quoted, 276
China, 140
Chesterton, G. K., 238
Christina, Queen, 307
Christian Faith, The
    Schleiermacher, 319, 320, 329, 330,
        332
Christian Thought to the Reforma-
    tion
    Workman, xv
Christian Thought since Kant
    Moore, xv
Chronicles, 146
Chrysostom, John, 137, 139, 147-148
Church History for the Use of
    Catholic Schools
    Businger, 261
Cicero, 158, 237, 244
Cilicia, 44
City of God, The
    Augustine, 166, 179-181, 183
Civil War, 337
Clement of Alexandria, 30, 87, 88,
    90, 91-95, 110, 112, 137, 286
    Instructor, The
        quoted, 91, 92, 93, 94
    life of, 97
    theology of, 95-96
Clement IV, 228
Clement V, 236
Clement, Epistle of, 80
Cleopatra, 26, 27-28, 203
Cocceius, 316-317
Colossians, Epistle to, 56
Columbus, 240, 243, 266
Comprehensive System of Theology
    see Summa Theologiæ
conceptualism, 198

Congregationalists, 260, 316, 317
Constantine the Great, 68, 117, 118, 119, 120, 121
Constantinople, 109, 119, 127, 130, 140, 240, 251
Councils of, 130, 133, 147
Contarini, 260
Continuity of Christian Thought
Allen, 15-16
Cop, Nicholas, 288
Copernicus, 25
Corbeil, 204
Corinth, 64, 77
Corinthians I, 55, 64, 77, 78
Cotta, Conrad, 266
Cotta, Ursula, 266
Council of Trent
see Trent, Council of
Covenants, doctrine of, 316
Critical Enquiry into the Existing System of Ethics
Schleiermacher, 327
Critique of Pure Reason
Kant, 188-190, 331, 346-347
Cromwell, Oliver, 278, 293, 296
Cross, Professor, 319
Crusades, 218, 220
Crypto-Calvinism, 282
Cur Deus Homo
Anselm, 188, 190, 192-193, 194, 195-196, 200
Cyril, Bishop of Alexandria, 24, 109, 112, 137, 153, 140
Cyril of Jerusalem, 130

Damascus, 45, 50, 59, 152
Dante, 102, 104, 203, 227, 238
eschatology of, 230*ff.*
life of, 227-229
works of
Divine Comedy, 227-229
Vita Nuova, 228
Darwin, Charles, 135
Origin of Species, 190

David, 235, 307
DeGroot, A. T., xvi
Deismann, 77
Delft, 306
Delphi, 37
Demas, 52, 53
Demiurge, 70, 72
Denmark, 307, 330
De Principiis
Origen, 98
Der Chrisliche Glaube
see *Christian Faith, The*
Descartes, 106
Desiderius, 184
Dietz, John, 276
Diodorus, 137, 138, 145, 148
Dionysius the Areopagite, 148, 186, 236
Disciples, 260
Discourses on Religion
Schleiermacher, 326
Divine Comedy
Dante, 227, 229, 230, 231, 232
Division of Nature, The
John the Scot, 186
Domenichino
Last Communion of Saint Jerome, 170
Dominic, 232
Donatism, 167-168
Dort, Synod of, 302, 305, 306
Dougall, Lily
Lord of Thought, The, 102
Duns Scotus, 198, 222, 229, 238-239

Eastern World, 68, 109, 116
Eddy, Mary Baker, 162, 176
Eddy, S., and Page, K.
Makers of Freedom, xvi
Edessa, 148
Edward IV, 243
Edwards, Jonathan, 144, 299, 309
Sinners in the Hands of an Angry God, 299

Egypt, 19, 20, 21, 23, 24, 25, 29, 114, 116

Einstein, 345

Eisenach, 262, 266

Eisleben, 264

Elijah, 57

Elizabeth, Queen, 304

England, 187, 243, 245, 246, 256, 259, 298, 301, 313, 329, 337

Enoch, book of, 102

Ephesus, 77

Epicurus, 102

Epiphanius, 75, 150

Episcopius, Simon, 302

Epworth, 310

Erasmus, 215, 217, 279, 286, 305, 306, 308, 318, 334
   Christian union, attitude toward, 317
   free will, attitude toward, 247-248
   humanism of, 254-255
   influence of
      Anabaptists
      see Anabaptists
      Socinians
      see Socinians
   lack of bias in, 248-252
   letter to Adrian VI
      quoted, 249-250
   life of, 242-245
   popes' attitude toward, 246-247, 253-254
   Praise of Folly, 244, 247
   schism, attitude toward, 247

Erfurt, 267
   University of, 266

Esther, 146

Ethiopia, 140

Euclid, 237

Eusebius, Bishop of Cæsarea, 116, 119, 120

Eusebius, Bishop of Nicomedia, 116, 119, 120

Eutyches, 111, 140, 141, 142

Eve, 171

Exodus, 31

Ezra, 146

Fall, the, 57

Farel, 289, 290, 300

Farnell, Professor, 152

Farrar, Canon, 104

Faustus, 161

Felix, 44

Ferrero, 26

Fichte, 327, 328, 329, 331

Fisher, 15

Five Points of Calvinism, 302

Florence, 229, 237, 240

Fourth Gospel
   see John, Gospel of

Fourth Lateran Council, 186

France, 228, 289, 297, 306, 307

Francesca, 203, 231

Francis, Saint, 83, 232, 233

Francis I, 246, 289

Franklin, Benjamin
   Advice to a Young Tradesman
      quoted, 296

Frederick II, 231

free will, 168, 178, 240, 248, 256, 286, 303, 304, 316

Freiburg, 245

Friends, 260, 317

Froude
   Life and Letters of Erasmus, XVI, 245

Fullerton, Professor, 86
   Prophecy and Authority, 86-87

Gamaliel, 45, 49

Galatians, Epistle to, 46, 169

Galen, 291

Galileo, 25, 237

Garden of Eden, 30, 101, 177

Garvie, Professor, 337, 341, 342, 343

Genesis, 30, 39

Geneva, 104, 289, 290, 291, 297, 298, 299, 304, 316
Genseric, 170
Georgia, 311
Germany, 257, 264, 268, 272, 281, 282, 323, 326, 334, 336, 340
Gethsemane, 177
Ghent, 243
Gibbon, 99, 119, 130
Gibbons, Cardinal, 261
Gideon, 81
Giotto, 228
Gnosticism, 66, 69-73, 114
  dualism of, 71
God of the Early Christians, The
  McGiffert, 60, 82, 115
Gomarus, 305
Gospel of the Egyptians, 78
Gospel of the Hebrews, 78
Göttingen, 337, 340
Gottschalk, 293
Greece, 26, 37, 45, 114, 183
Gregory (the Great), 132, 147, 184
  letter to Desiderius
    quoted, 184
  ransom theory of, 308
Gregory Nazianzus, 131
Gregory of Nyssa, 131, 191
Grotius, Hugo, 302, 316
  apologetics, first text-book in, 308
  Christian union, attitude toward, 308, 317
  deterrent theory of atonement, 308, 309-310
  life story of, 306-307
  international law, founder of, 308
Grunow, Eleanore, 326, 327-328
Grynæus, 304
Gwatkin, H. M., 127

Hagenbach, xv
Hague, 306
Halle, 324, 327
  University of, 327

Halleck, 330
Hamlet, 214
Handbook of the Presbyterian Church
  in the United States of America, 300
Harnack, A., 336, 337
  definition of theological science
    quoted, 223
  History of Dogma, xv
Harvey, 291
Hebrews, Epistle to, 19, 42, 77, 80
Hegel, G. W. F., 107, 197, 239, 320, 338
Heine, H.
  quoted on Luther, 262
Helen, 203
Hellespont, 119
Heloise, 203
  letters to Abelard, 213-214
Henry IV, 297, 306
Henry VIII, 244, 245
Hermann, 336
Hermogenes, 52
Hero, 203
Herodotus, 22
Hertz, Henrietta, 325
Hertz, Doctor Marcus, 325
Hildebrand, 151
Hippo, 170, 183
Hippolytus, 70
History of Dogma
  Harnack, xv
Holland, 297, 301, 306, 316, 318
Holy Living and Holy Dying
  Taylor, 311
Holy Sepulchre, 220
Homer, 39, 157
Honorius III, 187
Hopkey, Sophy, 314
Horus, 114
Hosius, 117-118, 120, 129
Hubmaier, Balthasar, 258
Hume, David, 99, 197, 240
Hunchback of Notre Dame, The, 243

Huss, John, 89, 247, 273, 293
Hypatia, 24, 109, 110
Hypatia
  Charles Kingsley, 97

Iamblichus, 107
Iconium, 52
"iconoclast," 150
images, 150-151
Imitation of Christ
  Thomas à Kempis, 311
immanence, divine, 30-33, 34, 35, 41,
  56, 59, 99, 286, 333
India, 114, 140
indulgences, 193, 271
Inge, Dean, 73, 105
  Gifford Lectures, 105-106
Ingersoll, Robert, 99
Inquisition, 88, 103
Institutes
  Calvin, 98
Instructor, The
  Clement of Alexandria, 91
Ireland, 186
Irenæus, 70, 76, 82, 87
Isaiah, 235
Isis, 114
Israel, 37, 60, 113, 307
Italy, 221, 228, 246, 291

James, 77, 80
  Epistle of, 146
Japan, 140
Jehovah, 23, 25, 30, 38, 56, 57, 59,
  79, 113, 114, 115, 116
Jena, 328
Jeremiah, book of, 58
Jerome, 62, 146, 169-170
Jerusalem, 25, 45, 165, 251, 259
Jesus, 19, 32, 35, 43, 50, 51, 59, 65,
  71, 72, 73, 77, 79, 81, 82, 84, 89,
  103, 113, 114, 126, 127, 128, 138,
  141, 142, 155, 193, 195, 246, 266,
  282, 303, 317, 331, 342, 343, 345,
  346

Job, 146, 315
John, 66, 68, 77, 233, 235
  Gospel of, 19, 33, 35, 42, 77, 96,
  106
John II, 146
John III, 146
John of Damascus, 148, 152-153, 236
John the Scot, 149-150, 186-187, 200
  Division of Nature, The, 186
Judaism, 32, 72, 127
Judas Iscariot, 116, 117, 130, 231
Jude, 80, 146
Juliet, 203
Justinian, 236

Kant, Immanuel, 144, 225, 318, 324,
  331, 327, 336, 338, 340
  Critique of Practical Religion, 347
  Critique of Pure Reason, 188-190,
  331, 346-347
Katten, Charlotte von, 327
Kennedy, H. A. A., 19
King, Henry Churchill, 345
Kingsley, Charles, 24
  Hypatia, 97, 108
  quoted, 109-110
Koenigsburg, 338
Koran, 22
Krauth
  quoted on Luther, 263

Lælius, 255
Landsburg, 324
Lanfranc, 200
Last Communion of Saint Jerome
  Domenichino, 170
Laura, 203
Leander, 203
Leibnitz, 306, 308, 317
Leipsic, 270
Leo X, 246, 270, 272
Leo the Syrian, 150
Leonidas, 98
Letters of a Portuguese Nun, 215

Leuba, Professor, 339
  Psychology of Religious Mysticism,
    111
Leyden, University of, 304, 305, 306
Life and Letters of Erasmus
  Froude, 16, 245
Lisbon, 314
Locke, John, 334
Loevenstein, castle of, 307
Logos, doctrine of, 33-36, 41, 56, 96,
  111, 115, 198, 199
Lombard, Peter, 236
London, 23, 311
Lord of Thought, The
  Lily Dougall, 102
Lord's Prayer, 178
Lot, 39
Lotze, 338
Louis IX, 228
Louis XI, 243
Louis XIII, 307
Lourdes, 152
Louvain, 253
Loyola, Ignatius, 260, 297
Lubeck, 307
Lucian, 115, 116, 137, 138
Lucinius, 117
Luke, 44, 47, 49, 76, 77, 130, 149, 235
  Gospel of, 80, 85
Luther, Martin, 43, 61, 62, 80-81, 104,
  146, 155, 157, 163, 243, 247, 248,
  250, 251, 253, 255, 256, 257, 258,
  293, 321, 326, 335
  and indulgences, 272
  argues with Zwingli, 285-286
  at Diet of Worms, 273
  Augustinianism of, 247, 248,
    268ff., 277, 279-280
  becomes a monk, 267-268
  Bible only authority, 275-276
  burns papal bull of excommunica-
    tion, 273
  Businger's opinion of, 261
  Carlyle's opinion of, 263

Luther Martin—*Cont.*
  compared with Calvin, 284
  education of, 265-266
  eschatology of, 279-280
  family of, 264-265
  Heine's opinion of, 262-263
  justification by faith, 275, 276-277,
    279, 286, 332
  Krauth's opinion of, 263
  marries Catherine von Bora, 274
  nails theses to Wittenberg church,
    272
  predestination, belief in, 268, 283,
    284, 285, 288
  private judgment, advocates, 275,
    277-278
  quoted on interview with devil,
    273-274
  Rein's opinion of, 262
  sacraments, conception of, 280-281
    transubstantiation, 285
  state churches fostered by, 278-
    279, 281
Lycaonia, 47
Lyons, 290

Macedonius, 131
Macfadden, Bernarr
  Physical Culture Magazine, 93
Madaura, 157, 158
Madonna of San Antonio, 47
Magdeburg, 266
Maimonides, 235
Majorism, 282
Makers of Freedom
  Eddy and Page, XVI
Manes, 159
Manicheans, 159, 161-162, 166-167,
  175
Mansfeld, 264, 265
Marburg, 281, 285, 286, 304
Marcion, 60, 113
  ethical idealism, 88-89
  faults, 87

Marcion—*Cont.*
   formation of New Testament
      canon, 76, 79-80, 85
   Gnosticism of, 70, 79-80, 82, 87
   life of, 73-74
   matter-of-fact interpretation of
      Scriptures, 88-89
   responsible for Old Roman Sym-
      bol, 81, 83, 85
Marco Polo, 228
Marcus Aurelius, 68
Mark, 77, 85, 90-91, 235
Mars Hill, 49, 149
Martyr, Justin, 82
Marx, Karl, 344
Mather, Cotton
   letter to John Higginson
      quoted, 283
Matthew, 77, 85, 235
   Gospel of, 97
Maurice, Prince, 307
Mayflower, 293
McCloskey, John Cardinal, 261
McGiffert, Professor, 81-82
   God of the Early Christians, The,
      60, 82, 115
   Protestant Thought before Kant,
      15
Mecca, 304
Melanchthon, 245, 254, 260, 340
Melun, 204
Mennonites, 260, 317
Mesrour, 97
Methodism, 311, 316
Milan, 161
Milton, John
   Paradise Lost, 149
Mohammed II, 127, 240
Mohra, 264
Monologues
   Schleiermacher, 326
Monologium
   Anselm, 188, 198

Moore
   Christian Thought since Kant, xv
Monica, 156, 159, 161, 162, 163, 164-
      165
Monophysitism, 111, 140-141, 142
Monothelites, 142
More, Sir Thomas
   Utopia, 245
Morgan, J. Pierpont, 47
Moses, 31, 57, 235
Mount Horeb, 57
Muhlenfels, Henriette von, 327, 328,
      329
Murray, Grace, 314-315

Napoleon, 328
Narces, 97
Navarre, 290
Navigius, 156
Nazarenes, 45
Neander, 326
Nehemiah, 146
Neo-Platonism, 26, 31, 73, 106-107
Nero, 45, 67, 68, 83, 244
Nestorius, 139-140, 141, 142
Newman, John Henry, 270
   Arians of the Fourth Century, xvi
New Testament, 19, 34, 38, 43, 44, 69,
      76, 77, 78, 80, 81, 84, 85, 86, 101,
      102, 136, 146, 148, 246, 247, 251,
      254, 255, 260, 333, 345, 346
Nicæa, 35, 83, 84, 105, 114, 118, 119,
      121, 133, 141, 251
   Councils of, 115, 118, 126, 129, 150
Nicene Creed, 121, 130, 132, 134, 138,
      153
Nicene-Constantinopolitan Creed
   see Nicene Creed
Nicomedia, 118
Niesky, 322, 323
Nile, 140
Nominalism, 196, 197
Norway, 330

Noyon, 287
Numidia, 155

Old Testament, 29, 30, 31, 35, 36, 38, 39, 40, 71, 72, 76, 78, 79, 80, 81, 83, 85, 101, 102, 145, 220
Octavius, 26, 27
Ode to Proserpine
    Swinburne, 108
Oglethorpe, General, 311
Old Roman Symbol, 76, 81-83
Omar, 22
Onesiphorus, 52, 54
Origen, 30, 42, 62, 84, 109, 110, 112, 137, 146, 153, 169, 227, 286, 318, 333
    allegorical method of interpretation, 40, 101*ff*., 145
    Celsus and, 99
    Christology of, 100
    De Principiis, 98
    founder of systematic theology, 90
    free will doctrine of, 168
    "heresy" of, 103, 104
    Marcion and, 102
    moral superiority of, 101-102
    pupil of Clement, 96, 97, 100
    restitution, doctrine of, 103-104
    stigmatized by Third Council of Constantinople, 147
    theism of, 99-100
    Theodore of Mopsuestia and, 144, 145
Origin of Species
    Darwin, 190
Orléans, University of, 287, 288
Orontes River, 136
Osiandrianism, 282
Osiris, 114
Ostia, 46
Outline of History
    H. G. Wells, 20
Oxford, 310, 311

Padua, 304
    University of, 228
Page, K.
    see Eddy, S., and Page, K.
Paine, 99
Palestine, 24, 28, 169
Paley, 190
Pantænus, 91
Paolo, 203, 231
Paradise Lost
    John Milton, 149
Paris (son of Priam), 203
Paris, 186, 203, 204, 205, 221, 245, 287, 288
    Council of, 187
    University of, 290
Parker, 256
Paul III, 254
Paul of Samosata, 115, 138
Paul of Tarsus, 83, 94, 114, 116, 155, 162, 169, 235, 288
    Acts of Paul and Thecla, 43-44
    compared with Philo, 19-20, 29, 42, 43, 55
    correspondence in New Testament, 77-79, 80, 85
    descent from Abraham, 19
    family of, 29, 43, 44-45
    God in belief of, 55-57, 59
    immortality, doctrine of, 55, 64-66
    influence on Western World, 43, 66
    intellectual and spiritual background of
        conversion and mystical influence, 48, 50
        Greek influence, 48-49
        Jewish ancestry, 48
        Roman influence, 48, 49-50
    life story of, 44-46, 67
    man and soul, nature of, 55, 61-64
    Mars Hill, 149
    person of Christ, 55, 59-61
    personal appearance and characteristics, 46-47, 52

Paul of Tarsus—*Cont.*
  predestination of, 57-58
  premillenarianism of, 50, 51
  state, duty of subjection to, 50, 51
  women and ascetic life, 50, 51-52,
    55
Pelagius, 140, 166, 168, 217
  free will doctrine of, 178
  present-day influence, 178
Pentateuch, 31, 146, 235
Père La-Chaise, 213
Peter, 47, 60, 66, 77, 90, 115, 151, 169,
    184, 194, 232, 233
Peter II, 80, 146
Petrarch, 203, 229
Pharos, 22-23
Philintus, 202
Philip II, 304
Philo, 19, 56, 79
  allegorical method of interpreting
    Scriptures, 39-41, 85, 100-101
  and Clement, 95-96
  as a scholar, 29
  compared with Paul of Tarsus,
    19-20, 29, 42, 43, 55
  emphasis on divine immanence, 30-
    33, 41, 59, 95
  family of, 29
  Logos, doctrine of, 33-36, 96
  nexus with early Christian think-
    ing, 42
  purpose of, 30
  religiousness of, 29-30
  verbal inspiration, 36-38, 41
Pirna, 270
Pisa, 228
Pitti Gallery, 234
Plato, 22, 25, 32, 49, 137, 162, 185,
    199, 200, 222, 252, 285, 324, 327
  pantheism of, 31
  preexistence of soul, 62
  realism of, 197
Pless, 321

Plotinus, 27, 30, 322, 345
  Augustine and, 106
  emanations of, 73
  influence of to-day, 107
  pantheism of, 99, 105-106
Plutarch
  quoted on Cleopatra, 27-28
Poland, 256, 307
Pontus, 73, 75, 80, 83
Pope, Alexander, 215
Porphyry, 107
  Isagoge, 197
Praise of Folly
  Erasmus, 244
predestination, 57-58, 86, 143-144,
    177, 247, 276, 284, 286, 292, 299,
    302, 303, 313
Priscian, 237
Proclus, 107
Prophecy and Authority
  Fullerton, 86-87
Proserpine, 108
Proslogium
  Anselm, 188
Protestant Thought before Kant
  McGiffert, xv
Proverbs, 35, 146
Prussia, 329
Psalms, 31, 146
Psychology of Religious Mysticism
  Leuba, 111
Ptolemy Philadelphus, 21, 22
Pythagoras, 25, 31, 237

Radbert, Paschasius
  *Sacrament of the Body and Blood
    of Christ, The,* 185
  transubstantiation doctrine of, 185-
    186
Rape of the Lock, The
  Alexander Pope, 215
Raphael
  Madonna of San Antonio, 47
Ratram, 186

Ravenna, 229
Reden
  see Discourses on Religion
Reformation, 62, 81, 113, 146, 154,
  186, 191-192, 230, 240, 246, 247,
  252, 257, 272, 274, 278, 282, 283,
  285, 293, 296, 297
Regensburg, 260
Rein, Doctor William
  quoted on Luther, 262
relics, 151
Religion of Protestants a Safe Way
  to Salvation, The
  Chillingworth, 276
Remonstrance, The, 302, 303, 305
Remonstrants, 301, 306
Restitution of Christianity
  Servetus, 291
Revelation, book of, 41, 69, 77, 80,
  103, 146
Richard the Lion-Hearted, 127
Ritschl, Albert, 319, 335, 348
  judgments of value, 346-347
  mysticism, opposed to, 339, 342, 346
  pragmatism of, 339
  reason given first place by, 338
  social gospel of, 343-345
Rizpah, 101
Robertson, 326
Romans, Epistle to, 51, 58, 162, 269
Rome, 20, 21, 27, 29, 37, 45, 70, 73,
  79, 83, 117, 118, 125, 161, 167,
  168, 169, 173, 178, 183, 221, 231,
  245, 249, 278, 304
Romeo, 203
Rostock, 307
Rotterdam, 243, 306
Rousseau, Jean Jacques, 159
Ruskin, John
  Mornings in Florence, 233
Russell, Bertrand, 265
Rutherford, 345

Sabellius, 125-126

Sacrament of the Body and Blood
  of Christ, The
  Paschasius Radbert, 185
St. Paul's-without-the-Walls, 45
Saint Peter's Cathedral, 270
Samuel, 37
Santa Maria Novella, church of, 234
Sappho, 22
Saragossa, 290
Saturninus, 70, 79
Savonarola, 240
Saxony, 270
Scaliger, Joseph, 306
Schlegel, Friedrich, 325
Schleiermacher, Friedrich, 16, 337,
  338, 339, 345
  and Napoleon, 328-329
  death of, 330
  eschatology of, 321-322
  flaws in theology of, 335
  God-consciousness of, 331
  in Berlin, 324-325, 326
  marriage of, 328
  mysticism of, 322, 332, 334, 335
  other concepts of, 333
  pantheism of Spinoza, 332, 334-335
  professor of theology, University
    of Berlin, 328
  Schlegel associated with, 325ff.
  with Moravians, 322-324
  women in life of
    Eieanore Grunow, 326, 327-328
    Henrietta Hertz, 325
    Henriette von Muhlenfels, 327,
      328, 329
  works of
    Christian Faith, The, 319, 320,
      329, 330, 332
    Critical Enquiry into the Exist-
      ing System of Ethics, 327
    Monologues, 326
Schleiermacher, Karl, 321
Schleiermacher, Lotte, 321, 325, 329
Schleiermacher, Nathaniel, 329

Schopenhauer, 230, 239
Schweitzer, Albert, 346
Scotland, 298
Selbie, Professor, 16, 319
Seleucus, 136
Semler, 322
Seneca, 95
Septuagint, 21, 78
Sermon on the Mount, 72, 79, 81, 84
Servetus, Michael, 89, 216, 247
    life of, 290-291
    Restitution of Christianity, 291
Shakespeare, William, 26, 227, 301
    Hamlet, 214
Shanghai, 195
Shaw, George Bernard, 258
Shedd, xv
Shepherd of Hermas, The, 52, 80
Sibyl, 37
Sic et Non
    Abelard, 217
Simpson, Professor, 65
Sinners in the Hands of an Angry
    God
    Edwards, 299
Sinope, 75
Siva, 114
Society of Jesus, 260
Socinianism, 255-256
Socinus, Faustus, 255, 256
Socrates, 62, 285, 315
Solomon, 232, 235
Song of Solomon, 40, 145, 219
Sonnets from the Portuguese, 215
Soubrise visions, 152
Southey, Robert, 315
Spain, 117, 240, 246, 307
Spinoza, 324, 327, 330. 331-332, 333
Stephen, 103
Stevens, G. B., 65
Stoics, 31, 32, 35, 49
Stolpe, 327
Stralsund, 328
Strauss, 322, 340

Stubenrauch, 324, 326
Suetonius, 68
Summa Theologiæ, 222, 223, 224, 225,
    227, 230, 237
Sweden, 307, 330
Swinburne
    Ode to Proserpine, 108
Switzerland, 258, 285, 289, 318
Syria, 136

Tacitus, 68
Tagaste, 155, 157, 160, 165, 166
Taine, 246
Tarsus, 44
Tawney, R. H.
    Religion and the Rise of Capital-
        ism, 295
Taylor, Jeremy
    Holy Living and Holy Dying, 311
Tertullian, 52, 62, 68, 70, 71, 76, 87,
    88, 126
    quoted on Marcion, 74-75
Tetzel, 270-272
Thais, 108
Thecla, 52-55
Theodore of Mopsuestia, 87, 137,
    148, 153, 215, 227
    anathematized by Third Council
        of Constantinople, 147
    Biblical interpretation of, 145
    eschatology of, 144-145
    free will of, 143, 144, 168
    person of Christ in theology of,
        139, 147
    prophetic power of, 135-136
Theodoret, 139, 147, 148
Theodosius, 130
Theophilus, 76
Thirty Years' War, 282
Thomas à Kempis
    Imitation of Christ, 311
Tibet, 140
Timothy, 94
Timothy II, 79

Torquemada, 89
Toulouse, 290
Tours, 186
transcendence, 30, 32-33, 56, 58-59, 286, 333
transubstantiation, doctrine of, 185-186, 218-219, 223, 225, 281
Trent, Council of, 186, 254, 260, 281, 318
Trinity, doctrine of, 35, 114, 121*ff.*, 128, 130, 186, 218, 225, 256, 259, 290, 339
Tubal-Cain, 237
Tübingen, University of, 337
Tudela, 290
Tully, 95, 244
Tyre, 20

Uyttenbogaert, Jan, 302
Unitarianism, 255
Upanishads, 32
Utopia
    Sir Thomas More, 245
Utrecht, 304

Valentinus, 70, 79
Vandals, 170, 183
Vazeille, Mrs., 315
Venice, 90, 228, 243
Verona, 203
Vinland, 243
Virgil, 157, 227
Virgin Mary, 111, 138, 141, 152, 258, 267
Vishnu, 114
Volstead, 341
Voltaire, 99, 248

Wallace, William, 229
Washington, George, 278
Weber, Max, 295, 296

Wells, H. G., 117, 119
    Outline of History, 20
Wesley, Charles, 311, 315
Wesley, John, 16, 322, 332
    conversion of, 312
    emotionalism of theology of, 313-314
    death of, 315
    diary quoted, 312-313
    education of, 310-311
    family of, 310
    free will of, 316
    Holy Club of, 311
    letter to wife quoted, 315
    marriage of, 315
    organizing genius of, 314
    preaching of, 312
    quoted on going to Georgia, 311
Western World, 61, 66, 154, 183, 255, 256
Westminster Confession, 298
Whitefield, George
William of Champeaux, 203, 204, 205
William of Occam, 228, 239
Willich, 327, 328, 329
Wilson, Reverend William, 95
Wittenberg, 248, 287
Workman, H. B., 182, 197
    Christian Thought to the Reformation, 15
Worms, Diet of, 273
Wyclif, 293

Zeus, 108, 114
Zinzendorf, Count, 322
Zoroaster, 237
Zurich, 285
Zwingli, 247, 258, 278, 281, 287
    argues with Luther, 285-286
    humanism of, 286
    predestination of, 276
    rationalistic interpretation of sacraments, 286